Music

IN THE LIFE OF

Albert Schweitzer

Music

IN THE LIFE OF

Albert Schweitzer

WITH SELECTIONS FROM HIS WRITINGS

BY Charles R. Joy

With a Preface by Charles Munch

BEACON PRESS   *Beacon Hill*   Boston

64-4952

Contents

v

A Tribute to Albert Schweitzer

FROM THE DIRECTOR OF THE BOSTON SYMPHONY ORCHESTRA

THE name of Albert Schweitzer is linked with my childhood. It brings back recollections of wonderful evenings, when I heard him passionately discussing with my father every little detail in a score by Bach, after they had worked together performing it. At that time Albert Schweitzer played the organ for the concerts my father conducted at the church of St. William in Strassburg. He had studied previously with my uncle Eugène Munch.

Schweitzer had also studied with the great French organist, Charles Marie Widor. At that time Widor was very much perplexed by some of the Bach movements, and Schweitzer, who knew the texts of the old German chorales by heart, showed Widor how the words explained the music. Then they played through the chorale preludes one after the other, and a new Bach, that Widor had never known before, was revealed to him. At Widor's suggestion Schweitzer undertook to write a book on Bach. The book, which was begun in 1899, took him six years to complete, and brought forth a new interpretation of Bach's music, and of art in general.

Schweitzer's capacity for work is incredible. I have often seen him, after a full and strenuous day of activity, sit down with students and take time to correct their work and to guide them through new problems.

His talents and abilities are manifold. Through his great professional knowledge he has made an enormous contribution to the art of organ construction in France. His simple philosophy of reverence for life is the expression of a great man's faith in God and of his own humility. His work is an example of self-sacrifice and dedication to humanity.

There is another link that has brought us nearer together. In the Strassburg days my sister married Albert's brother.

As for me, his example and his advice have been present all through my life of work and strife. During the disaster of the last war and the

German occupation, it was his book, *Out of My Life and Thought*, which gave me courage and patience to endure the trial. It was this book which kept alive my hope, my belief in victory. It inspired my work and helped me to fulfill my duty. By a secret channel this same book was sent to our common nephew, Pierre Paul Schweitzer, who was arrested and imprisoned by the Germans at Fresnes, Paris, and then afterwards deported to the horror camp of Buchenwald. When he was released the precious book was lost.

On December 8, 1949, Albert Schweitzer wrote me from Lambarene:

"How curious is destiny! Who could have foreseen, when I used to take you out for a walk along the River Ill, near the Garnison church, you a small boy, that one day you would be helping me, working for me in the United States? Who could have told us that a day would come when we should both be known in America?

"I have been profoundly moved by what you and the Boston Orchestra have done for my work and myself. When I came back here on November 18th I was obliged to face a series of unavoidable expenses which I had not expected. I was depressed, overwhelmed by the prospect. And behold, you in Boston, a few days before, without my knowing it, had already relieved me of many material cares. Nobody knows what a burden of responsibility this hospital, grown so big, represents to me. It is terrible not to belong to oneself. But you have helped me to carry this responsibility at one of the critical moments of my life, at a time when I was really wandering in a dark valley.

"I wish I could have heard the orchestra, the organ, the compositions included in the program. The composition that would have interested me most was the *Concerto for Organ and Orchestra* by Poulenc. I try to imagine the Haydn *Concerto*, but without success, since the art of organ playing was not far advanced in Austria at this epoch.

"I am much moved by what you tell me of the place I occupy in your life. I have not forgotten that day after the first war in Strassburg, when you told me about that, and said, 'I have kept it all in my heart.'

"I have the great privilege of seeing my thought winning hearts in the world, a thing I should never have hoped for. I knew it had an importance, because it is elementary, and the result of reflection; it goes to the bottom of things, and establishes immovable values. But I never thought to see it already on the march. I accept it as a grace given me, as I accept the sympathy you have for me."

This, then, is Albert Schweitzer, a man who has devoted his life to music and his fellow men, a man near to my family and dear to my heart.

It is with deep emotion that I bid godspeed to this book.

CHARLES MUNCH

Boston, Massachusetts
January, 1951

Charles R. Joy is widely known as the friend, translator, and interpreter of Albert Schweitzer. He has visited Schweitzer three times in Africa and a number of times in the Alsatian village of Gunsbach. Of his eight books about Schweitzer, one, THE AFRICA OF ALBERT SCHWEITZER (with Melvin Arnold), was chosen among the fifty best books of 1948, and another, ALBERT SCHWEITZER: AN ANTHOLOGY, among the fifty best religious books of 1947.

In his own right, Dr. Joy is an eminent author, minister, and relief administrator. He was graduated from Harvard College in 1908 with distinction in English. He also holds S.T.B. degrees from both Harvard Divinity School and Andover Theological Seminary and an honorary S.T.D. from the Pacific Unitarian School for the Ministry. He has held pastorates in Maine, Massachusetts, and the Midwest. A former Administrative Vice President of the American Unitarian Association and Executive Director of the Unitarian Service Committee, he has also been an executive of the Save the Children Federation, and the chief of CARE's missions in Korea and Africa. He has been decorated five times by foreign governments, has received the French Palme Academique, and is an Officer of the French Academy. In 1940, he compiled and edited Harper's TOPICAL CONCORDANCE of the Bible, a standard work in its field and the first of twenty books he has published.

Concerned with what he terms "human geography," Dr. Joy has just completed his seventh book about Africa, devoting the rest of his time to lecturing and traveling. One of his most recent books, AFRICA—A HANDBOOK FOR TRAVELERS, has been cited as among the best reference books of 1958.

Foreword

THERE are no sidewalks in the little Alsatian town of Gunsbach. Some of the houses are set back from the road, but not the house of Albert Schweitzer. Behind the house broad meadows stretch down to the banks of the little river Fecht. There is no physical reason for it, but the house of Albert Schweitzer crowds on to the street. The man himself is not there often, but when he is there he wants to be as close as possible to his people. He wants to be able to look out through the ivy-edged window and see the passers-by, wave a friendly greeting and call out in his loved Alsatian dialect "Boshour." And if a visitor sets his feet directly from the running board of his car onto the steps that lead to his front door, Monsieur Albert can be there in a trice to meet him, for of all the rooms of the house his study-bedroom is closest to the main entrance, only a few feet away.

He sometimes calls this house the house that Goethe built, and in a sense this is literally true, for it was built with the money Schweitzer received from the City of Frankfort when he delivered at its invitation the Goethe Prize Address in 1928. To one of his friends who came to see him he told the story, and then said, standing on the threshold, "Tu vois, celui qui te reçoit ici véritablement, c'est M. Goethe!" There was no pride in his heart, and there was a twinkle in his eye when he said this, but there was a truth in the words, which Schweitzer himself would quickly and humbly disclaim, but which all his friends know to be so. There is no great man in this modern day whose life more closely resembles that of Johann Wolfgang von Goethe than Albert Schweitzer. Dr. Schweitzer himself once said to me: "Goethe is the personality with which I have been most deeply concerned." [1]

If, however, Goethe greets you from the house he built beside the road, it is Bach that greets you when this same man sits down on the

[1] For the striking parallelism between the lives of Goethe and Schweitzer, and for Schweitzer's acknowledged indebtedness to Goethe, see my introduction to *Goethe. Four Studies*, by Albert Schweitzer. Boston: The Beacon Press, 1949. C. R. J.

bench of the lovely little organ in the village church. The church is set back from the square on a knoll above the town, a bit remote from the community, as the beauty and the majesty of God must needs be from our human striving, but when Albert Schweitzer sits at that organ in the high balcony at the rear of the church, he becomes a mediator between God and man, and the words of mediation are usually found in the cantatas and choral preludes and Passions of Bach. Here is Bach reborn for our day.

Goethe had no close personal meaning for Schweitzer during the first half of his life. It was not until that Good Friday afternoon of 1913, when the bells were sweetly ringing from beneath the slender spire of the church, and the little train came clattering down from Munster trailing in the late sunlight its bright pennant of smoke, and Albert Schweitzer climbed up the steep steps into the third-class carriage on his way to Africa, that Goethe began to have a very intimate significance for him. But from that moment a clear-eyed sibyl might have seen the two lives going on into the future side by side like the converging tracks of the valley railway leading down to the plains of the Rhine.

Bach, however, took possession of him from his boyhood on. To Eugène Munch, his music teacher at Mulhouse, the Well-Tempered Clavichord had been in childhood a kind of daily food, and the flame of his ardor spread to his impressionable pupil, who felt in Bach that deep, religious fervor which was his own inheritance. He recognized the Leipzig cantor as a symbol of something very deep within his own soul, something that was perhaps more spiritual than musical. So Bach became to him "the Master," and he became from that time on a Minister of Music, trying to interpret to the world the religious significance of the cantatas and the Passions, himself more and more an embodiment of the man whose works he reproduced.

The life of Albert Schweitzer has been strung on a continuous, golden chain of music, which will not be broken until his fingers are silenced beneath the waving, sun-drenched palms of the hilltop cemetery at Lambarene, or within the lot beside the wall of the Friedhof at Gunsbach, where his mother and father and little sister already lie.

Albert Schweitzer has become one of the greatest living interpreters of the music of Bach; but the reverse is also true—that the music of

Bach is the only adequate interpretation of the life of Schweitzer. So one of his recent biographers states, "The St. Matthew Passion is alone adequate to cover the African venture, the joy of the journey and the disappointments, the magnificence of the aim, the apparent failure and eventual triumph." [1] The same writer in a later passage likens Schweitzer's life to another of Bach's magnificent writings, the B minor Mass. In that Mass the Kyrie Eleison would be his early theological controversy, strife and victory; the Gratias Agimus his musical triumphs, cheerfulness, and tranquillity; the Et Incarnatus his work in Africa, sacrifice and redemption; the Crucifixus his war experience." [2]

The purpose of the present book is twofold: first, to recount in simple human terms the story of this man as a minister of music, a story too little known outside of Europe; and second, to bring to the English-speaking world all of Albert Schweitzer's writings on music which have been hitherto unavailable in English. These writings, biographical and autobiographical, historical and critical and technical, have an importance which will be quickly recognized. Most of them are as timely today as when they were first written, and the few that are not have a value in tracing the development of music in the past half-century which should not be underestimated. For Albert Schweitzer is in large part responsible for the finer ideals in modern organ building and for our new understanding of the immortal Bach.

I am greatly indebted to William King Covell, of Newport, Rhode Island, for suggestions concerning the translation of technical terms in organ construction; to Harold Schwab of Los Angeles, formerly of the New England Conservatory of Music, who has given invaluable counsel; and to Archibald Thompson Davison, Professor Emeritus of the Department of Music in Harvard University, who has gone over the entire manuscript to my great profit. Without the generous aid of these friends this book would have been impossible. To them I extend my heartfelt thanks.

Acknowledgments are due to the following publishers and authors

---

[1] Albert Schweitzer: Life and Message, by Magnus Ratter. Boston: The Beacon Press, 1950, p. 43.
[2] Ibid., p. 54 f.

for permission to translate and include in this book copyrighted material controlled by them:

A. & C. Black, Ltd., London, and Harper & Brothers, New York, for quotations from *Albert Schweitzer, the Man and His Mind*, by George Seaver.

Breitkopf & Härtel, Leipzig, Germany, for several chapters from *J. S. Bach, Musicien-Poète; Deutsche und französische Orgelbaukunst und Orgelkunst*; and "Die Reform unseres Orgelbaues auf Grund einer allgemeinen Umfrage bei Orgelspielern und Orgelbauern in deutschen und romanischen Ländern," in *III Kongress der Internationalen Musikgesellschaft*, 1909.

The Deutscher Musikliteratur-Verlag, Berlin-Halensee, for "Warum es so schwer ist in Paris einen guten Chor zusammenzubringen," which appeared as an article in *Die Musik*, volume IX, no. 19.

The Dial Press, New York, for the quotation from *That Day Alone*, by Pierre van Paassen.

Editions F.-X. Le Roux & Cie, Strassburg, France, for the chapter "Souvenirs et Appreciations," by Albert Schweitzer, from *Un Grand Musicien Francais: Marie-Joseph Erb*.

P. H. Heitz, Strassburg, France, for "Souvenirs d'Ernest Munch" and "Zur Geschichte des Kirchenchors zu St. Wilhelm" from *Le Choeur de St. Guillaume de Strasbourg, un Chapitre de l'Histoire de la Musique en Alsace*, compiled by Erik Jung.

Imprimerie J. Brinkmann, Mulhouse, France, for *Eugene Munch, 1857-1898*.

L'Alsace Francaise, Strassburg, France, for the article "Mes Souvenirs sur Cosima Wagner" which appeared in volume XXV, no. 7, February 12, 1933.

Les Dernieres Nouvelles d'Alsace, Strassburg, France, and the author, Mr. Louis-Edouard Schaeffer, Strassburg, for "Das verschwiegene Bachkonzert für die weite Welt," which appeared on November 7, 1936.

The Macmillan Company, New York, for a brief passage from *The Prophet in the Wilderness*, copyright, 1947, by Hermann Hagedorn.

Musikzeitung, Zürich, Switzerland, for "Der runde Violinbogen," no. 6, 1933.

Mr. A. A. Roback, of Cambridge, Massachusetts, for quotations from *The Albert Schweitzer Jubilee Book*, Sci-Art Publishers.

Vandenhoeck & Ruprecht, of Göttingen, Germany, for "Zur Reform des Orgelbaues," in *Monatschrift für Gottesdienst und kirchliche Kunst*, volume XXXII, no. 6, June, 1927.

To all of these for their gracious co-operation my most sincere gratitude.

CHARLES R. JOY

Music
IN THE LIFE OF
Albert Schweitzer

PUBLISHER'S NOTE

The text of this book is set in Electra type. The introductory and explanatory material by Charles R. Joy is set in *italic*. The writing of Albert Schweitzer is set in roman.

I

Early Raptures

*T*HE old presbytery at Gunsbach was built in 1771. It was over a hundred years old when Louis Schweitzer, the new pastor, arrived there, bringing with him a frail little baby who had been born in another valley to the northeast, and it had all the friendly charm of an Alsatian home. Between the tiny stream, which the Alsatians called the Bachle, or little river, and the vine-clad Rebberg, which rose above the town, it stood in the midst of the village, not crowded among the other houses yet intimate with them. In this pleasant home the sickly baby grew well and strong in the health-giving air of the lovely Munster Valley, and there his earliest recollections were filled with music.

Perhaps time has made the notes more sweet, perhaps memory has filled the music with the faint, exquisite beauty of a dream, but Albert Schweitzer recalls the late afternoons of those earliest years, when he sat quietly in a big chair and listened to his father improvise on the piano, keeping time with hands and feet, while his little heart beat for joy. But even before the recollections begin, this music was molding the young life.

The square piano, on which his father played with no great technical skill, but with a gift for improvising, had come down the Munster Valley from Mühlbach, where Grandfather J. J. Schillinger, his mother's father, had been the pastor. The first World War left only a single house standing of all the buildings of Mühlbach—the Schillinger parsonage and the church went with the rest of the town; but the grave of Pastor Schillinger, behind the new church, is still a place of pilgrimage to Albert Schweitzer, and to others for whom the old truth-loving pastor is still a vibrant memory. He had a passion for organs, and was a brilliant musical rhapsodist. He used to travel about for the sole purpose of visiting new organs, particularly while they were being constructed, for then he could talk with the builder, and be one of the first to make the new pipes speak.

Perhaps it was from him, as Dr. Schweitzer states, that the passion for the organ was inherited, along with the square piano; but surely not from him alone. For his paternal grandfather was also an organist, as well as this grandfather's two brothers, and music had blossomed on many other branches of the family tree. It was a tradition in Germany and Alsace that the schoolmaster should study music, and usually he played two instruments, the organ (piano) and the violin. The long line of Schweitzer ancestors is full of schoolmasters and organists. It was as natural for Albert Schweitzer to become an organist as it was for Bach, with his ancestry, to become an organist.

Of course that was not Schweitzer's idea at first. When he was asked as a child what he wanted to be when he grew up, he replied that he wanted to be a swineherd. And anyone who has seen a swineherd in the smiling valleys of the Vosges, or has wandered with the cowherd in the lonely solitudes of the high alps, will understand the poetic appeal of that kind of occupation. But the family had other ideas. At five years old he was practising his scales on the old piano under his father's tutelage; at six he was overwhelmed by the voluptuous beauty of some duets which by chance he heard the big boys of the singing class give; a little later the harmony of brass instruments filled him with such rapturous ecstasy that the strings of his heart almost snapped within him; at seven he was showing his singing teacher, who played with one finger, how a hymn tune should be properly harmonized; at nine he was playing at times for the regular organist in the service, and playing also in Pastor Schillinger's old church at Mühlbach, where his grandfather had had a fine organ built under the direction of the organ builder Stier.

His father was not a very systematic teacher, and from the point of view of a thorough musician the boy's training was rather sketchy. He paid very little attention to notes. He liked to harmonize the familiar hymn tunes, but was in no way a promising youngster.

During the vacation periods he used to visit his godmother in Colmar, Madame Julie Fellner–Barth, and every day while he was there her daughter used to give him a piano lesson, so that he would not get out of practice and forget what he had already learned. His teacher, who is still living in Colmar, reports that in these brief ten-minute lessons he held his fingers rather awkwardly, and showed no particular aptitude for music. He was a rather placid, dreamy boy. Not many years afterwards he played the organ at his teacher's wedding, but by that time the awkward fingers had become supple and gifted, and the boy who showed no particular aptitude had become a brilliant organist.

In the seventh century the Benedictine monks had established themselves in the Munster Valley, for what reason no one knows, and there four kilometers above Gunsbach they had built a monastery in honor of their patron saint Gregory. From this Monasterium Sancti Gregorii the name Munster was derived, and Munster became in the course of the next twelve hundred years a considerable community dominating the valley. To Munster the boy Albert was sent, when he was nine, for a year at the Realschule,[1] and it was characteristic of the "placid, dreamy boy" that he preferred to walk to and fro between Gunsbach and Munster, not in the company of the other boys, but alone, that he might enjoy the changing seasons in the valley and indulge his own fantasies. It was for him the Happy Valley; and when next year the family judgment was passed down that he should go to Mulhouse to study, he was heartbroken. He was only ten, and going to Mulhouse (Mühlhausen in German) meant leaving his home.

The bridge is short that leads from joy to sorrow, the German proverb says. But the bridge is just as short in the other direction. It was a fortunate fate that brought Albert Schweitzer to Mulhouse, for there he met Eugène Munch, and through Eugène Munch he met Bach, and through Bach he became the musician that he was. Mulhouse made a great organist out of Albert Schweitzer.

He probably knew little about Bach when he went to Mulhouse (Mülhausen in German). His father did not care for Bach. Perhaps the boy did not even know that almost two hundred years before Johann Sebastian Bach had received an appointment to the organ of another Mülhausen, nearer to Weimar, and had agreed to

[1] The *Realschule* was the nonclassical secondary school in German education. C. R. J.

take in payment 85 gulden, 3 coombs of corn, 2 cords of wood, 6 trusses of brushwood, and 3 pounds of fish per annum. Bach had not been happy there, and had stayed for only a year. Two weeks before he came, a large part of the town had been destroyed by fire, the pietists and the orthodox were quarreling in the church, and music had been frightfully neglected. So Bach became discouraged, and a year later resigned to go to Weimar with his young wife. In his petition for dismissal he wrote: "My work has been done not without difficulty and opposition, and there is no apparent likelihood that things will be altered." His connection with Mülhausen had been very brief.

It is interesting that it was in the Alsatian Mülhausen that Albert Schweitzer first became acquainted with Bach, almost immediately after his arrival there.

Albert Schweitzer found himself at ten years transplanted from a little country town to an industrial city, whose cotton thread was known to the ends of the earth, even in the heart of the jungle to which he was later to go. Except for the magnificent Hotel de Ville, however, there was very little of beauty in the city. The old church of St. Stephen, erected in the twelfth century, with choir and steeple of the fourteenth century, had been demolished in 1858, and a huge building of doubtful artistic taste had taken its place.

It was also an austere and rather gloomy home to which the impressionable lad went, under the kindly but rigid discipline of Uncle Louis and Aunt Sophie. As elementary school director for the city, Louis Schweitzer, the half-brother of Albert's paternal grandfather, had an official apartment in the École Centrale, and there for eight years the boy lived while attending the Gymnasium.[1] He was a poor scholar at first, but the good teaching he received gradually aroused him. He had no great enthusiasm for the piano either, but Aunt Sophie insisted upon regular practising after the noonday meal, and, when the home lessons were completed, after school at night.

Then, one day, something memorable happened. Uncle Louis and Aunt Sophie took him to a concert, the first he had ever attended. The concert was by a young Alsatian musician, Marie–Joseph Erb, who had been born at Strassburg in 1858, had studied in Paris at the Niedermeyer School of Classical and Religious Music, and then,

[1] The Gymnasium was the classical secondary school in German education. C. R. J.

refusing an appointment to the school as professor, had returned to his native land. He began to give brilliant piano recitals and to publish his first compositions. In 1883 he accepted a post as organist at St. George's in Selestat, and had private pupils there and in Strassburg. He remained at Selestat until 1890, when he moved to Strassburg. The years from 1884 to 1890 were fertile years, when his musical genius found expression in highly personal works of rare loveliness and pure style. It was during this period that he came to Mulhouse to give the concert attended by Albert Schweitzer, the boy of eleven or twelve, to whom the piano was still drudgery. Sixty years later the memory of that concert was still so vivid that every impression was fresh in his mind.

This is his account of it.

❧

MY FIRST CONCERT [1]

MY first memory of Marie–Joseph Erb is all mixed up with my memory of the first concert I attended. It must have been about 1887; I was then eleven or twelve years old.

The concert was held in the hall of the stock exchange in Mulhouse, where I had been living since 1885 with my great-uncle, Louis Schweitzer, the director of the Écoles Communales, who had taken me in to permit me to go to school in that city. My uncle and aunt took me to this concert. I was astonished to see all the people in evening clothes, and I wondered what kind of figure I was cutting in my Sunday suit, which had become too small. The women were sucking bonbons. And now suddenly the hubbub which had been reigning subsided. A gentleman who seemed to me to be very tall and thin, in an evening suit, went onto the platform, and was immediately greeted by applause.

This, then, was Mr. Erb, who had recently come from Paris, after having had a brilliant success in his musical studies. He sat down at the piano, played a prelude until there was complete silence, and then

---

[1] From *Un Grand Musicien Français: Marie–Joseph Erb*. Strassburg–Paris: Editions F.-X. Le Roux & Cie, pp. 83 f.

attacked with spirit the first number on the program. I then realized what a *virtuoso* was. I was stunned to see his hands whirling around on the keyboard. And all by heart, without hesitation, without a mistake! I was lost in astonishment. With my modest knowledge of piano-playing, I tried to figure out how he went to work to launch those cascades of arpeggios and those bursts of shooting stars, to make the melody come out so clearly, to achieve those *pianissimi* in which, nonetheless, not a single note was lost. . . .

After the first piano pieces, which had kept me in a state of rapture, the artist rose, bowed as the entire assembly applauded, disappeared behind a door, came back when the applause did not die down, disappeared again, came back, disappeared. Finally there was silence. People studied the rest of the program. The women offered each other bonbons. I could not understand why all these people, after having applauded so heartily, did not remain like me, under the spell of what they had heard, and how they could resume their chatter.

But here was Mr. Erb back again, smiling, and mounting the platform beside the singer. The latter had curls like those that young girls wore for their first communion, and carried long white gloves. She put a big bouquet of flowers on a chair, made a curtsy, opened her sheet of music, which trembled a bit in her hands, coughed lightly, looked at the pianist and made a slight sign with her head, to which he replied by beginning immediately the first measures of the accompaniment. I was very much aware of the beauty of the singing, but still my attention was especially attracted to the accompanist, who followed the singer so well when she accelerated or decreased the tempo, when she passed from *pianissimo* to *fortissimo* or returned from *fortissimo* to *pianissimo*. Never could I have imagined such flexibility. The display of virtuosity at the end took my breath away. It was for me a sudden revelation of the possibilities of the piano. On the way home I walked as in a dream.

The following days I worked on my scales and finger exercises and struggled with the Czerny studies with an unprecedented ardor, even when they were starred with sharps and double sharps, which I had so detested theretofore.

Afterwards I heard the most celebrated piano *virtuosi*. But none of them ever agitated me and stirred me as Erb did, when as a little student in the collège I heard him for the first time.

❦

BESIDE the church of St. Stephen stands a plain three-story stucco house, on the second floor of which the organist of the church used to live. There, from the age of ten on, Albert had been going regularly to take piano lessons from Eugène Munch. It was not a pleasant experience for either master or pupil. For the master, Albert was the worst of all pupils, his "thorn in the flesh." His playing was expressionless and faulty. No wonder, for Albert preferred to harmonize, to improvise, to play at sight; and he disliked the drudgery involved in the thorough mastery of the pieces given him by his teacher. Even the wholesome effect of that first concert wore away; and when he played for his teacher there were few signs of either technical excellence or personal appreciation. Again and again his teacher fumed and scolded, but to no effect. Then one day something he said stung the boy to the quick; and when he came back a week later he played the Mendelssohn Lied ohne Worte which had been assigned to him in such a way that the teacher felt at last that the boy had been won. A few weeks later Albert began on Bach, which was this teacher's perfect tribute of praise.[1]

Albert Schweitzer never fully approved of the great new church of St. Stephen, because it had no chancel. A chancel, he thought, was a necessary part of the perfect church—an aid to devotion, a spur to the imagination. But he did approve of the organ, one of the several lovely instruments which it was his good fortune to know as a youth. It was a Walcker organ of sixty-two stops and three manuals, built when that concern was constructing wonderful organs in the sixties and seventies; and when, on Palm Sunday, 1890, Eugène Munch played as a processional the stirring "Lift up your heads, O ye gates!" from Händel's Messiah, and Albert marched in with the other

[1] For a delightful account of Albert Schweitzer's early life, see Memoirs of Childhood and Youth, by Albert Schweitzer. New York: The Macmillan Company, 1949. C. R. J.

boys to be confirmed, his own heart was lifted up like the everlasting portals through which the King of Glory passed. Two things moved him deeply: one was the holiness of the spiritual experience, an experience he felt much more profoundly than old Pastor Wennagel, who thought him indifferent, had ever suspected; and the other was the promise of his music teacher that after his confirmation he himself would be permitted to have lessons on that marvelous instrument pouring out its heavenly harmonics from the gallery above his head.

He was already familiar with the organ. For Dr. Munch had been in the habit of taking him every Saturday evening to listen in the organ loft, while he practised for the Sunday service. There at ten years of age he had first become acquainted with the chorales of Bach, and there he had been strangely stirred as he listened to the mysterious sounds losing themselves in the dark nave of the great church. And now he himself was to learn to make music from the manuals and pedal keyboard, from the levers and stops and soaring pipes of this magnificent instrument.

He had played an organ before, for Daddy Iltis, the organist at Gunsbach, and in Grandfather Schillinger's church at Mühlbach; but this was a great organ, and he was to study under a great organist. Now at last music became to him a serious business, and into it he poured all the resources of his gifted mind, all the riches of his sensitive soul. In another year he was occasionally taking the place of his teacher at the organ console, and soon after he was playing the organ accompaniment of Brahms' Requiem, while Eugène Munch conducted the choir and orchestra.

Another stirring incident from these days of plastic adolescence occurred when for the first time, at the age of sixteen, he was permitted to attend the theatre, and heard the overpowering music of Richard Wagner's Tannhäuser. For days afterwards he went about in a trance, reliving the rapture of that evening, unable to attend to his work at school.

So the Mulhouse years came to an end. Much of what was musically significant there are only memories to Albert Schweitzer now. On September 4, 1898, Eugène Munch died prematurely, forty-one years old, and about the same time the wonderful Walcker organ was "modernized," by the same firm that built it, and its lovely tone disappeared. "How are the mighty fallen!"

Immediately after the death of his beloved teacher, Albert Schweitzer wrote a little brochure in French, for the family and friends of Eugène Munch. This tribute to the great teacher who gave direction to his musical life was Schweitzer's first published writing. In the Avant-Propos of his J. S. Bach. Le Musicien-Poète, unfortunately omitted from the later English version, he says:

"When I undertook to write the chapter on the chorales, memories of these first, profound, artistic emotions came flooding back to me. Certain phrases came to the point of my pen all formed, and then I realized that I was only repeating the words and using once more the imagery by which my first organ teacher had opened my understanding for the music of Bach." [1]

❦

MY FIRST ORGAN TEACHER [2]

> Blessed are the dead which die in the Lord from henceforth:
> Yea, saith the Spirit, that they may rest from their labors; and
> their works do follow them.
>
> REVELATION 14: 13

EUGÈNE Munch was born on April 3, 1857, at Dorlisheim, where his father held the posts of teacher and organist.

The year after his birth his parents moved to Niederbronn. It was in this pretty little village of our Alsace that Eugène Munch spent the years of his youth. After the loss of an elder sister, who was taken from her loving parents in her ninth year, death for a long period spared this household, where six children were growing up under the strict guidance of a father esteemed by all who knew him. Very early Eugène Munch showed a great talent for music. The father

[1] J. S. Bach. Le Musicien–Poète, by Albert Schweitzer. Paris: Costallat, 1905, p. v.
[2] Eugène Munch, 1857–1898, by Albert Schweitzer. Mulhouse: J. Brinkmann, Publisher, 1898.

himself directed the musical education of his children, and he laid the foundation for the musical career of his oldest son by introducing him to the works of Bach. Eugène Munch delighted later in saying that Bach's *Well-Tempered Clavichord* had been from infancy his daily bread. On Sundays, when his father played the organ for the church service, he stood at his side. Soon he was in a position to substitute for him. When he was sixteen he entered the normal school at Strassburg. After having passed the final examinations he remained for seven years at Niederbronn, as assistant and colleague for his father. In 1883 a dream came true: he went to Berlin with his brother Ernest to study music there. Mr. Haupt, the teacher of organ in the *Musikhochschule*, became greatly interested in the two young Alsatians, whom he numbered among his best pupils, and never did he fail to ask for them after he had lost sight of them.

Upon his return to Niederbronn, Eugène Munch resumed his work as teacher, and established a church choir, which continued for only a few months after his departure.

In 1885 he was called as organist to the Protestant Temple at Mulhouse, and it was in this city that he was thenceforth to pursue his artistic career and establish his home. In February, 1886, he married Miss Bockenhaupt of Wissembourg. The young household was plunged into profound grief by the death of their first child, a little daughter. With the birth of their son, Ernest, happiness again brightened their home. Six children were born in succession, and filled the house with gaiety. In 1889, Eugène Munch suffered the great sorrow of losing his father. A heart ailment proved fatal before he was able to see his son reach the highest steps in that artistic career whose beginnings had filled him with happiness.

When Eugène Munch came to Mulhouse he was primarily an organist. His talent was revealed to the public at the outset through the fine instrument that was entrusted to him. At that time he was not yet the great organist which we knew in his last years. He was just leaving the Conservatory; he was still a pupil. At Mulhouse he found the one organ of all the imaginable organs which best suited his personality. We can say that this instrument completed his education as an organist, and led him to heights where we marvelled at him. The remarkable sonorousness, the delicacy of tone, in this organ invited those refinements in registration in which he excelled. The faulty mechanism of the instrument made clear and precise playing difficult, and imposed upon him that tranquillity which gave his playing an imposing and majestic quality. The instrument demanded delicacy and serenity, and his nature responded to it. However, this harmony between the character of the instrument and the personality of the organist would not of itself alone have produced the great artist, if Eugène Munch had not had the perseverence and the indefatigable energy that are the essential conditions of all artistic achievement. More than any other instrument the organ exacts these qualities of those who come to it as slaves, before recognizing them later as masters and rendering obedience to them.

By ceaseless toil Eugène Munch had developed himself into a remarkable mechanism. His hands and his feet obeyed him admirably. At the same time he had a touch that many better known organists might have envied. This touch had an extraordinary suppleness; it was quite inimitable. The quality of his playing impressed all the organists who heard him, and gave a strange stamp to his interpretations. One day he insisted laughingly that a good organist playing *fortissimo* ought to be able to create in the listener by his touch alone the illusion of *crescendi* and *diminuendi*. These words made clear the great importance he attached to touch in organ playing. This, however, escaped the novice. Another thing fascinated them more because the ear caught it more easily, namely the registration. Through constant experimentation he had come to know all the sonorous combinations of his rich instrument. For some time he kept at his organ a piece of paper on which he noted all the combinations to try, from the simplest to the most exotic. Audacities which at first thought seemed impossible succeeded admirably with him, thanks to his experience. For every theme in the Bach fugues he sought tirelessly the sonorous quality which it required. He was not content, however, to seek the sonorities suitable for the portions; what he wanted most of all was harmony among the sonorities, so that the piece would produce the impression of unity. This effect never ended for him: he corrected, noted, eliminated, only to begin again. One can get some idea of this work by casting an eye on his notebooks. Often one finds five or six registrations indicated for a single piece, and each registration is the result of long reflection and many trials. For years he worked on the registration of Bach's *Toccata*.[1] Twice he played this majestic work in organ concerts, as well as the *Passacaglia in C minor*. In private auditions he sometimes played the same thing ten times in succession, always working it over, forever changing and correcting, only to take it up another time afresh. The effects of registration he produced while accompanying solo instruments (I am thinking of the organ concerts given with Adolph Stiehle as soloist) were amazing. One day at one of these auditions, when Stiehle's marvelous violin blended with Monsieur Munch's exquisite playing, one of those present could not refrain from saying: "What a happy marriage!" How true! But in spite of these gifts of touch and registration, Eugène Munch would not have been this marvelous organist had he not added to his performance a taste for simple and exact phrasing, which was the connecting link between the two qualities we have just emphasized. In phrasing he was infallible. The component parts of it were simplicity, truth, and good taste. These things he never sacrificed to get registration effects. First of all he tried to bring out the great lines, which he called "the plastic art of organ playing." He delighted in comparing this effort with that of the artist who brings to birth from a block of marble the harmonious forms of human beauty. This quality made him majestic as an organ player, and, added to his talent as an accompanist, produced surprising effects. The last time he played at Strassburg—he took his place at the organ to play Bach's great *Mass*—his manner of bringing out the plastic structure of the first chorus surprised everyone who was able to appreciate this artistic feat at its true worth. It was like a revelation. His playing was fine and simple, or, rather, it was fine because it was simple. All effects which could prevent the unfolding of the beautiful forms in a work were odious to him, all those sonorities which obscured it were proscribed. "One must be a miser with organ *fortissimi*," he said one day. "The audience ought to feel the *fortissimo* before it comes; it should await it, watch for it, even hear it, before it is overwhelmed by it."

What delicacy, and at the same time what emotional veracity!

[1] Schweitzer does not indicate to which *Toccata* he is referring. C. R. J.

Refinement and simplicity, art and nature were happily wedded in this gifted organist, and gave to all his performances the classic beauty which everyone admired in his playing. He knew how to take advantage of everything, and detested nothing but pedantry; but that he detested profoundly. These were the characteristics which this organ *virtuoso* displayed in his playing; he was the equal of all his confrères, many of them he surpassed.

I have often asked myself why Munch did not travel, why he did not try by giving organ concerts in the great cities to make a name for himself which would have reverberated far beyond the frontiers of our Alsace. If anyone had asked him that question he would have certainly replied: I do not want to be a *virtuoso*, I want to be an organist. Those who heard him only in concerts never knew the real organist Munch, but those who heard him every Sunday in the church service understood him. The organ in a concert hall left him cold, the organ in a church concert interested him; the organ played for the service—that was his life and his happiness. It was then that he poured out his soul, bestowing all that was best within him as man and as artist. With exquisite feeling he knew how to select the pieces that best suited the nature of each service. He never permitted himself to be carried away into playing something that had no place within the frame of Protestant organ music. Nevertheless he was not narrow. I have heard him play in the service some of Beethoven's sonata adagios and some of the *courantes* [1] from Bach's clavier suites. With the organ, however, the deep emotions of Beethoven's adagios took on through his interpretation of them a severe and religious character, and the gaiety of Bach's *courantes* took on a majestic dignity. In preparation for his part in the service he used to play the chorale preludes from Bach's fifth volume.[2] He liked to use them in the service, and many people whose musical understanding did not at first appreciate the reverent beauty of these pieces learned to love them through hearing them over and over again in a receptive mood, and, thanks to the interpretation which Munch gave to them,

[1] The *courante* was one of the four traditional movements of the *suite*. C. R. J.
[2] Bach did not collect his organ works in numbered volumes. The final collection of choral preludes in the famous Bach *Gesellschaft* edition appeared in 1890, and was numbered Volume Four. C. R. J.

came to comprehend the spirit which the great Leipzig master had embodied in them. "When I am tired of all kinds of music," he said one day, "I turn to these chorale preludes and recover the inspiration of the art which I was vainly seeking." The inspiration of religious art: he knew how to transmit it to those who listened to it receptively. The consciousness of contributing to the beauty of the religious service, of translating religious ideas into music, of "preaching with the organ," as he used to say, was a more genuine satisfaction for the organist than long newspaper articles and the applause of concert goers would have been for the *virtuoso*. By virtue of his being an organist he was indeed a *virtuoso*, worthy of that title. The concert public forgets quickly; but a congregation edified by its organist cherishes an ineffaceable remembrance of him—it is as if the spirit of his life clung to the instrument and ennobled it.

If one may say that the Mulhouse organs educated the organist, it is not less true to say that the *Chant Sacré* molded the musician, the director. Between him and the *Chant Sacré* existed a relationship that was mutually instructive. Without this society he would never have had the opportunity to direct Bach's *St. Matthew Passion* or the *Requiem* of Berlioz. He would have continued to be a remarkable organist, but he would not have become the universal musician that he was. Without him the music lovers of Mulhouse would not have had this artistic center, where the beauty of religious music, both classical and modern, was revealed to a public which was accustomed to look elsewhere for entertainment of this kind. This development was the result of serious application over a period of many years, on the part of the director and on the part of members of the society. What a difference between the day when Monsieur Munch had a modest choir located in the corner to the left of the organ sing Bach's chorale *"Jesu meine Freude"* [Jesus, my joy], and the moment when, filled with noble pride, he nervously gave the signal for the attack upon the *Requiem* of Berlioz to a choir which was entirely equal to its high and difficult task.

It would be false to say that Eugène Munch had any special talent as director or orchestra leader. On the contrary, he had more difficulties to overcome than many another. This type of musical performance was completely unknown to him when he went to Mulhouse.

If he became the able director that our listening to the Bach's *St. Matthew Passion* or Berlioz' *Requiem* revealed to us, he reached this goal only by an enormous amount of work. He knew by heart the score he was to direct. Even during his last illness, when the *St. Matthew Passion* and the *Requiem* of Berlioz occupied his mind, his memory never played him false in regard to an *entrée* or a *recitatif*. He had moreover two qualities which were of great help to him in his development as a director, his modesty and his patience. He did not ask too much of the choir, and did not suddenly set before them tasks that were too difficult. He let them go on slowly and progressively to arrive the more surely at the ideal end he had planned: the rendition of the masterpieces of religious music. How many times before he felt it possible to put on the *St. Matthew Passion* did he not go over this admirable score by himself at the piano; how many times did he not beat out, as in a dream, the generous measure of the first chorus—then he closed the book: not yet, too soon. Concerning another of Bach's monumental works that he dreamed of doing one day, the great *Mass*, we say sadly: too late, alas. The performance of the *St. Matthew Passion* was one of the most beautiful days of his life. The evening following the rendition we were with him; his face shone like the face of a happy child. Then, suddenly, turning to his brother, he said: "If only my father were still with us to share my joy!" Certainly his father was the only one who could have completely understood his rapture.

One moment for rest, for rejoicing, then on again. It was often hard and sad, that onward march. The hall for rehearsals was not always a happy place for him. The elements of which the choir was composed often arrived before him untrained. He had to clothe himself with patience, begin again the work that he thought was already done. The false notes, the bad tones—his ear suffered from them after the weariness of the day. His remarks often had a nervous accent, a note of entreaty which betrayed his suffering, especially during the last winter, when he had fallen into a state of prostration that was realized only by his intimates. By patient endeavor he succeeded in giving cohesion to this choir with all its different elements. Its members did not come for the *Chant Sacré*; they supped in haste, they braved the bad weather—for Monsieur Munch. He knew it and was grateful, though his words did not interpret his feelings as he wished. He was not an orator, especially not one before the singers. His discourses at the first rehearsal of the season or after a concert were recitatifs punctuated by chords struck on the harmonium. Though not an orator, he had a very special gift for making himself understood in a few words, of painting the idea as it lived in him. "Ladies, weep!" he said one day at a rehearsal of Mozart's Requiem, when the choir did not get the intonation of the "Lacrimosa" as he wanted it. This was said with so much earnestness that they were impressed by it. The ironic imitations he often used were not always flattering, but he was excused for them because the final result pleased everyone.

The concerts given by the Chant Sacré were all successful, for nothing was neglected, and everything thoroughly prepared. Each concert showed progress. In these performances, as in his organ playing, the delicacy of his intonation and the brilliancy of his phrasing gave a special charm to the works he was directing. One felt that the personality of the director had entered into the choir. There was an interesting unity which gave an original stamp to the performance. The "Hallellujah Chorus" of the Messiah had more of nobility than of crushing grandeur. These constantly repeated successes formed a bond between the choir and its director which grew closer from day to day. The society saw in him not only its director, but also the artist whose needs it knew and understood. It knew that one cannot always produce without having from time to time some stimulation from without to give new ideas and to enlarge the horizon. They arranged for him to have this joy of seeing and hearing something new, of escaping from the isolation of his artistic life at Mulhouse, by sending him to Bayreuth.

The society certainly believed that they were giving him a great pleasure; but it was impossible for them to imagine the exuberant joy with which this journey filled him, for he was not the kind of man to reveal his intimate feeling in public. This journey to Bayreuth was the luminous point of his closing years. He went there already knowing by heart the scores; and there he lived through moments sublime. The orchestra, the singers, Parsifal, the Twilight of the Gods—he used to dream of them and speak of them often. It is impossible to see the Bayreuth letters without being moved by the happiness they breathe forth. I saw him a little while afterwards in the Munster Valley. We were sitting at the edge of the road; it was a beautiful day in September; the mists which softened the lines of the mountains announced already the coming of autumn. In our conversation we were exchanging our memories of Bayreuth. "Oh! those last pages in the *Twilight of the Gods* when all the themes of the trilogy are massed together and engulfed, when the world falls into ruins!" he said. "And *Parsifal*—such music, such chimes; they thrill you, they exalt you, they lead you upward, ever higher; you are no longer conscious of the earth, it disappears. . . . I must go back, I must see it again, I must hear it again." A year later, on that very day the solemn tolling of the bells of Niederbronn were announcing that the soul of an artist was rising ever higher and higher . . . and had left the earth. . . .

The journey to Bayreuth marked the beginning of a new epoch in the artistic life of Eugène Munch; he came back resolved to devote his talents not only to the masterpieces of religious music, but also to the great works of secular music. At Bayreuth he became aware of the close kinship between them. He felt keenly how much of religious character the masterpieces of tragic music had in themselves by virtue of their beauty. He foresaw already the possibility of giving the *Ninth Symphony* of Beethoven some day at Mulhouse. It was not by chance that during his last winter he was primarily occupied with Beethoven and Berlioz, the two representatives of secular music who have grafted the style of this music on religious music, one in his *Requiem* and the other in the *Missa Solemnis*. The forms and effects are borrowed from secular music; the subject and the sublime character make them religious. The speech that Monsieur Munch made at the first rehearsal of the *Chant Sacré* after his return from Bayreuth clearly reveals the new direction which from that moment his activity was to take. Then it was that he resumed the direction of the *Sainte–Cécile*, the members of which assisted him greatly in the performance of the *Requiem* of Berlioz. In his mind this change, or rather this development, had been in preparation for a long time, from the day when he began to study the esthetics of art. It was Lessing who first attracted him. He studied him with pleasure and often returned to him. The study of this great theoretician of the arts had a lasting and enormous influence upon his development. Here he caught a glimpse of the close bond between the law of beauty and the law of truth, which bring together the most widely diverse arts. Later, in his last years, the theoretical works of the French school particularly interested him. He read many of them, and his delight in them reconciled him to the modern art of France, with the recent musical compositions of which he had very little sympathy. The study of the works of Wagner before his journey to Bayreuth led him still farther into this kind of work. He took great satisfaction in studying the purely musical questions, and in setting them against a vaster background—that of art in general. There again he came into touch with Beethoven, who had tried to include the total literary and intellectual movement of his time in his musical interpretation. The score of the *Missa Solemnis* thrilled him, followed him—he did not study this work, he lived it. His last wish to direct it in its entirety with an orchestra, even if only at a rehearsal, was realized. This was pure delight for him. He did not hear the work as the choir and the orchestra gave it, he paid no attention in this rehearsal to faults—he heard Beethoven's Mass in its perfection. As he closed the score after the last rehearsal he said with great happiness: "It is not completely beautiful, but I have heard the work; now I know it." This was his last moment of artistic delight.

If he did not exercise upon the totality of the artistic life of Mulhouse the influence of which he had dreamed, if he departed too soon, not only for his own people but also for the task which was left for him to do in Mulhouse, it still remains true that what he created in this sphere cannot be lost, what he planted will bear its fruit some day. It is strange! On the last page of the score of Beethoven's *Missa Solemnis* he wrote in pencil the following quotation: "It is enough that the wave should drive the wave, and that the result should remain nameless." [1]

This was the public side of his artistic activity. It was happy. The great vexations, the sense of working without seeing results, were spared him. Alongside this ideal part of his artistic activity, he had to cultivate, like most of his colleagues, the prosaic side of the musi-

---

[1] *Genug, wenn Welle Welle trieb, und ohne Namen Wirkung blieb.*

cian's life. He gave lessons. He gave them all day long. His pedagogical talent, developed in the Strassburg normal school, assured
him of an incontestable superiority in teaching music. He used to
say laughingly that in order to give good lessons in music one had to
be first of all called to the profession of schoolmaster. The calm and
friendly manner in which he made his remarks quickly dissipated the
embarrassment and the timidity of his pupils, and tempered the
irony with which he was accustomed to season his criticism. His judgment was severe, but a word of praise from his mouth had all the
more value because of it. His lessons were always interesting. He was
in the habit of playing himself the pieces he gave pupils to study,
adding his appreciation and his historic and artistic comments. All
this made comprehension easier and invited reflection. In this way
the piece became familiar before one had studied it. Sometimes he
told what impression such and such compositions—especially the
preludes of the *Well–Tempered Clavichord*—had made on him
when he played them for the first time. His teaching bore the stamp
of his personality. His ambition was not to form violoncellists or
pianists; he wanted to make of his pupils musicians capable of loving, comprehending, and interpreting with good taste all kinds of
beautiful musical works. But he did not neglect to teach them musical structure. Each lesson began with a quarter of an hour of exercises; but the intellectual and artistic development outdistanced the
progress in technique. He often gave his pupil pieces to play that
exceeded his capacity, and then permitted him to leave them before
all the details had been perfectly mastered. "You will take them up
again later." It was a comfort to the pupil. In this way he avoided
excessive toil and weariness, and gave with every new piece new
courage. The end of the lesson was devoted to pleasant things. They
played at sight, four hands, a symphony. They turned the pages of a
score. What lovely memories! Sometimes during the closing period
—though very seldom—he would take his violoncello and have his
pupils accompany him, to initiate them in the art of accompaniment,
which he himself possessed in a remarkable degree. His pupils left
him regretfully. During the last years he was so overburdened with
care that the musical education of his own children became difficult.

He was compelled to select the early morning hours to give them their lessons. He witnessed only their first efforts. His children will not even have the memory of the charm which characterized the musical instruction of their father, they will not have enjoyed the quarter hours of delightful talk on the seat of his pedal piano, which the more advanced of his pupils will forever remember.

In spite of the unconstraint he sometimes displayed, he never became intimate with his pupils. This was one of the most striking traits in his character. He knew no true intimacy beyond the circle of his family, at least he never sought it. He had many friends at Mulhouse, but no comrades. The members of the *Sainte-Cécile*, which he directed at the beginning and at the end of his career, appreciated him, and on his side he greatly valued the sympathy and regard for him shown by the members of the society; but the frank comradeship between the director and the singers one finds in other societies did not exist. The nature of Monsieur Munch did not at all lend itself to this. In conversation he permitted himself to go up to a certain point, and then it was as if something prevented him from unveiling his ideas and his private opinions, as if he were afraid to reveal himself as he was. Certainly he did not lack interest in the questions discussed. One could talk with him about anything except politics. But he never knew the joy of debating with friends the topics of the hour. Only when he met again his former classmates did he let himself go completely. In his last years he narrowed even more the circle of his close friends. Except for the pupils he had known when they were young, he never used the intimate form of address.

This characteristic, this impossibility of giving himself, of letting himself be intimately known, was regrettable. Our friend missed that interchange of ideas of which he often felt the need. He was plunged into an isolation that led him to judge badly those who were outside the group of his intimates, and among whom he ran the risk of not being well understood. Must one attribute to this isolation the gloomy ideas that sometimes obsessed him, especially during the last winter, ideas that seemed to presage his untimely end?

To understand the reason for this we must return to the period of his childhood. He had caught a cold which resulted in a permanent ear trouble. Every illness, even every disturbance, was felt in this weak spot in his constitution. The moral suffering which came with the physical suffering weighed even more heavily upon him. In vain he sought the treatment of a specialist. Each year the pains returned, always with greater intensity. The thought of becoming deaf, of no longer hearing his organ, of no longer being able to direct his society, tortured him. During his last winter the pains became particularly alarming. His lugubrious premonitions attracted him to Beethoven: in the accents of Beethoven's music he found again his own anguish. Might he also have shared the fate of the great composer, might he have had to lay down with tearful eyes the director's baton, if premature death had not snatched it away from him? This idea may be a feeble consolation for those who lament him.

He said little about his apprehensions. The allusions he made during the rehearsals of Beethoven's *Mass* were incomprehensible to those who did not know what it was all about. He sought and often found forgetfulness in his work and in the life of his family. In the midst of his loved ones, with his children on his knee, he was happy. His home breathed calm, and a gracious simplicity idealized by music. It reminded one of the home of J. S. Bach, his ideal. In 1891, at Christmas, the *Chant Sacré* gave him as a gift the fine picture "Family Worship in the Home of Bach." He used to show it to everyone who came to visit him, and evinced his pleasure; which arose not simply from the artistic conception of the picture, but also from the remarkable resemblance between his own family ideal and the scene pictured by the artist.

In Mulhouse his seriousness and his work gave a kind of austere character to his family life. But what a happy moment was the departure for the vacations! They talked of it the whole summer. Finally the day arrived when the train transported the happy family to Wissembourg, and later to Niederbronn. The vacation had a special charm. The days usually passed gaily in perfect relaxation—the severe father remained behind at Mulhouse.

During these vacations he became the joyous companion of his children in their pleasures and excursions. Thanks to his camera, he has preserved some of these charming scenes: the children on the grass, or harnessed to the baby carriage, and many others. His children will look at them some day, and with the memory of a happiness not yet understood will mingle a feeling of regret. The second half of his vacation was passed at Niederbronn; in the beautiful forests there he regained his strength. In the midst of his brothers and sisters, surrounded by memories of his youth, he gave himself over to the gaiety that one hardly ever saw at Mulhouse. This summer as well, we hoped that he would come back restored to health, but he did not himself have that confidence. He was very tired when he left Mulhouse. The last time he touched his organ, on a Sunday afternoon, he was so exhausted he could hardly finish the service. At Wissembourg he seemed to recover. He even recovered his gaiety on a Sunday he spent with his brother at Strassburg.

Upon his return to Wissembourg, the terrible illness which was to be fatal became slowly evident in an inexplicable weariness. As usual, he left Wissembourg at the end of August to pass the second half of his vacation in his mother's home. He arrived there on Saturday evening, the twentieth of August. Even his brother's children noticed the change in his features, and spoke about it to their father. The following Sunday he tried to take a walk with one of his sisters. He carried his little sister in his arm, but the burden became too heavy for him and he had to return. It was the last time that he saw the mountains of Niederbronn. In the evening they called the doctor; it was too late. He went to bed, never to get up again; to die surrounded by his own family in his dear Niederbronn. The sickness developed rapidly; fever seized him. He remained gentle and patient. The smallest service done for him touched him. The physician soon saw the dangerous turn which the sickness took, and which he diagnosed as typhoid. He ordered that his wife and his children, who had caught the same illness, should be separated from him. A moving exchange of words and news took place from one chamber to another.

He was resigned. Only his eyes betrayed his suffering and his anxiety. The Wednesday before his death he had a completely lucid evening. Seeing the end draw near, he requested his younger brother, the vicar at Strassburg, to administer holy communion to him. He asked that his family gather around his bed. He looked about to see if everyone was present. One of his sisters was missing; they had to look for her. Then he raised himself a little in his bed and began to speak to them—as if it were a dream, in short phrases, interrupted by long silences.

"My life has been short, but lovely through the art which I have cultivated. It will be more beautiful in heaven." These words set the mood for this touching meeting. He said farewell to each member of his family in turn, and for each he found an affectionate word. But he could not see his wife and his children. "I commend my wife and my children to you," he said. "Bring the children up simply; let a place be found for each of them suitable to his ability." The *Chant Sacré* was much on his mind, this choir he had created, and to which he had given the best of his strength. "You will be able to bring up my children," he said to those who surrounded him, "but it is the *Chant Sacré* that I leave with the greatest regret. Say farewell to them for me. There is no one at Mulhouse who will be able to continue my work in accordance with my ideas."

Then he passed into a state of delirium. Art glorified his last moments. Secular music did not enter the shadow of oblivion; he no longer knew anything but religious music. Even the Beethoven *Mass* did not have a place in his delirium. He directed the Berlioz *Requiem* and the *St. Matthew Passion*. The recitatifs, which he sang until his dry throat could no longer utter a sound, were present with him note by note. He wished to hear the chorales. "Find the children for me," he said, "so that they can sing the chorale." His sister and brother had to begin singing "When some day I must part." [1] This calmed him. And always he kept thinking of his choir. In his delirium he sat up suddenly and said, thinking that he was addressing the society: "I bid you farewell. Be happy. I can do no more." One morning when the regimental band, which was on manoeuvres at Niederbronn, was passing, he listened attentively. "How beautiful it was," he said, "when the chords lost themselves in the distance." When he heard the retreat, he remarked, "That is the signal for me to prepare." He spoke a great deal about his organ. "What will be-

[1] *Wenn ich einmal soll scheiden.*

come of my organ?" This question recurred ceaselessly. He consoled himself with the words: "I shall be an organist in heaven."

On Sunday, the fourth of September, about two o'clock in the afternoon, while the church bells were sounding, he gave up the spirit.

II

Widor's Pupil

ON June 18, 1893, Albert passed his final examinations at the Gymnasium and prepared to enter the University. He had already made up his mind that he would study philosophy, theology, and music. But before he went up to the University it was decided that he should spend a few weeks in Paris with Uncle Charles, his father's brother, and Aunt Mathilde. It was hoped that he might take a few lessons from the great organist of St. Sulpice, for whom Eugène Munch thought he was now ready. So this handsome young man, with the small moustache, the well-trimmed eyebrows, and the luxuriant dark hair set off for the great metropolis to visit Uncle Charles and to see Charles Marie Widor.

Widor had been born in Lyon in 1845, and at the age of twenty-five had been called to succeed César Franck as professor at the Conservatory of Music and to play at the great Church of St. Sulpice with its wonderful organs, which had been completely rebuilt and enlarged by Aristide Cavaillé–Coll. Widor was then at the height of his fame, known everywhere as a great composer. But he thought of himself first of all as an organist. Organ music was to him "a special kind of music, the music of the eternal, awakening thoughts of immortality." To play the organ, he said, was "to manifest a will filled with the view of eternity." That meant, therefore, to play Bach, for Bach had this mystic sense of the eternal. When Widor was not improvising or playing his own compositions he played Bach almost exclusively. He could not imagine any organ playing as sacred which was not somehow hallowed by certain preludes and fugues of Bach.

Armed with an introduction from Aunt Mathilde, Albert went at once to the great seventeenth-century church on the left bank of the

Seine, almost as large as the cathedral on the Ile de la Cité, in which the architects sought to replace the traditional Gothic elegance by a Greco–Roman majesty. Seeking out Widor, he asked if he might play for him. "Play what?" Widor asked. "Bach, of course," was the young Alsatian's reply. And suddenly Albert found himself sitting before the five manuals and the hundred speaking stops of what was universally regarded as the greatest organ in Europe, and probably the most beautiful in the whole world, the masterpiece of Europe's greatest organ builder.

It is needless to ask how well he played, for Widor, who seldom took any pupils outside the organ class of the Conservatory, not only consented to give him instruction, but to give it without charge.

By the end of October, Schweitzer was in Strassburg to begin his work at the University, where his student days continued until 1899. Strassburg was the administrative, military, and intellectual capital of Alsace. It was a fascinating place, with its old quais on the River Ill, its quaint bridges and square towers, its old palaces and timbered houses, its ancient fishermen's quarter called "la petite France." And above it all towered the glorious spire of the cathedral, when built the tallest structure erected by man since the time of the great pyramid. At once gigantic and delicate, fantastic and exquisite, the whole fabric was one magnificent upthrust of man's aspiration. And at sunset the rosy gray of the stone took on new and startling colors, so that it seemed like "petrified fireworks."

The University, with its faculties of medicine, law, letters, and Protestant theology was recognized on both sides of the Rhine as a great institution of learning, and students flocked to it from every land. It had a little of what has sometimes been considered the profound but confused thinking of German scholarship, illustrated by the remark of a Württemberg metaphysician to an Alsatian critic, "Now that you are no longer analyzing my books, I no longer know exactly what I think." Nonetheless it was a truly great university.

These student years were devoted to theological and philosophical studies, but with one exception all the interludes were musical. The exception was his year as a soldier in the army. He studied piano under Gustav Jacobsthal, professor of music at Strassburg, who had been a pupil of the musical theorist and composer Bellerman of

Berlin. Jacobsthal, Schweitzer said, "refused to acknowledge as art any music later than Beethoven's," but to him Schweitzer was indebted for excellent instruction in counterpoint.

His acquaintance with Wagner had begun with that memorable performance of Tannhäuser at Mulhouse, but at Strassburg all the operas except Parsifal were given under the direction of Otto Lohse; and as he witnessed them one by one his admiration for Wagner grew apace, until he began to venerate him as he did Bach. His knowledge of the operas was completed with a visit to Bayreuth in 1896, made possible by tickets presented to him by friends in Paris, and by his own self-abnegation. To make ends meet he ate but one meal a day.

It was worth it. Richard Wagner's great tetralogy, Der Ring der Nibelungen, with his last and crowning work, Parsifal, had been performed for the first time in 1876 in a building specially erected for the purpose. And then for a score of years it was not repeated. When in 1896 it was once more performed at Bayreuth, Wagner was dead, but Hans Richter, who had conducted the 1876 orchestra, was still there, and Heinrich Vogl, who had played Loki, and Lilli Lehmann, who had been one of the Rhine daughters, but who now played Brunnhilda. And Cosima Wagner was there—the daughter of Liszt and Wagner's second wife, whom he had married in 1870— imperiously directing the performances. Schweitzer was deeply moved by the opera, and particularly by the singing and acting of Loki, the god of fire, restlessly swinging his red cloak from one shoulder to the other, symbol perhaps of the flaming destruction of Valhalla, when the gods who have broken the moral law pass and give way to a new era of truth and love.[1]

On his way back from Bayreuth in the fall of 1896, Schweitzer stopped at Stuttgart to see the new organ which had been installed in the Liederhalle of the city. The instrument had been much praised; but when the organist of the Stiftskirche played a Bach fugue on it, and Schweitzer could not follow the separate voices, he was filled

---

[1] See Out of My Life and Thought, by Albert Schweitzer. New York: Henry Holt and Company, 1949, pp. 11 f. This book is Schweitzer's own account of his life up to 1929, and is supplemented by a postscript by Everett Skillings, which brings the story down to 1949. C. R. J.

with dismay about the modern organ. This he called his "Damascus at Stuttgart," and his experience led him to a careful study of organs and organ building, which bore fruit at the end of the following decade.

On May 6, 1898, Schweitzer passed his first theological examination, set by the government, and then spent the summer in the study of philosophy. In October he returned to Paris, to continue his philosophical studies at the Sorbonne, to write a thesis on the religious philosophy of Kant, and to study organ again under Widor.

At the same time he continued with his piano, studying under two teachers, J. Philipp, afterwards of the Conservatory, and Marie Jaëll–Trautmann, a fellow Alsatian and a pupil of Franz Liszt. The former was a capable but conventional teacher; the latter was developing her theory of touch, working from a physiological foundation, and educating the hand to feel and know. As teachers they did not think highly of each other but Schweitzer gained much from both.

With Widor, however, a collaboration soon began which far transcended the usual teacher-pupil relationship. It all came from a chance conversation. This is the way Widor reports it: "As Schweitzer knew very well the old Lutheran texts, I explained to him my uncertainty in the presence of certain works of Bach, my inability to comprehend certain chorales which passed abruptly from one order of ideas to another, from the chromatic to the diatonic scale, from slow movements to rapid ones, without any apparent logical reason. What can the composer's thought be, what did he want to say? If he breaks the thread of his discourse in this way, he must have another purpose than that of pure music, he must want to emphasize some literary idea . . . but how are we to know this idea?

" 'Simply by the words of the hymn,' replied Schweitzer, and then he recited the words of the chorale in question, which completely justified the musician, and showed the flexibility of his descriptive powers when dealing with the text, word by word; it had been impossible to appreciate the composition without understanding the significance of the assumed words.

"And so we began to run through the three collections to get at the exact meaning of things. Everything was explained and clarified, not only the great lines of the composition but even the slightest detail. Music and poetry were tightly clasped together, every musical design corresponding to a literary idea. In this way the works which I had admired up to that time as models of pure counterpoint became for me a series of poems with a matchless eloquence and emotional intensity.

"The first result of our analysis was our recognition of the necessity for an edition of the chorales carrying the literary text above the music which interprets it, an edition which would respect the order desired by the composer and follow the festivals of the church year.

"The second result was the recognition that a study of the symbolism of these three books was just as necessary, and that if any person was indicated to undertake this task it was Schweitzer himself because of his theological, philosophical, and musical gifts." [1]

Thus Schweitzer was launched by this chance conversation on a new and important enterprise. The little study at first contemplated grew into an important and laborious enterprise. Merely to assemble the texts was difficult, since many of them were no longer used in the Lutheran liturgy. The study of the chorales became inseparably involved with the study of the cantatas; a chapter had to be written upon the history of religious music in Germany; the biography of Bach was necessary for the interpretation of the work. And when Schweitzer expressed to Widor his consternation, confronted by the constantly growing proportions of this subject, and knowing full well the obligations of his diverse undertakings and his university career, Widor simply replied: "You are right, but what can one not do with order and the will?"

So began a work which was to consume much of Schweitzer's time for the next half dozen years, one of the fruitful undertakings of a rich life. Schweitzer "grasped the skirts of happy chance," and by a strictly ordered life and an inflexible will produced a masterpiece in the literature of music.

The rôles of teacher and pupil were reversed in this interpretation of Bach, but in other respects Widor remained the incomparable master, helping the young man to improve his technique, to achieve

[1] From *J. S. Bach. Le Musicien-Poète*, by Albert Schweitzer. Leipzig: Breitkopf & Härtel, 1908, pp. vii–ix.

plasticity in his playing, and to catch a vision of the architectonic, which is perhaps the greatest gift to the world of French music. Schweitzer gratefully remembers also Widor's solicitude for his health, and how at times, when he feared that his young Alsatian friend was hungry, he took him to the Restaurant Foyot near the Luxembourg and let him eat the kind of meal his means did not usually permit.

The spring of 1899 found him back in Gunsbach for a month. The family had moved into the new presbytery in 1890. Then in April he was in Berlin for four months to study philosophy and the organ. He was not impressed by the Berlin organists, who lacked, he thought, the plasticity which Widor emphasized. Neither was he impressed by the Berlin organs, which lacked the rich and beautiful tones of the masterpieces of Cavaillé–Coll in Paris or the Silbermann organs in Strassburg. But he liked the intellectual life of Berlin and its social freedom. In July he was back again at Strassburg.

At the end of July he took his degree in philosophy, and a few months later published his thesis on the religious philosophy of Kant. He then began to study for his licentiate in theology.

The work which Albert Schweitzer had promised Widor to do on the interpretation of Bach had become possible because of Schweitzer's association with the Strassburg brother of his first organ teacher. Ernest Munch had been a student of music in Berlin with his brother Eugène, and then had settled in Strassburg as organist of the church of St. William. Schweitzer became acquainted with him immediately after his arrival in Strassburg in 1893, and remained closely associated with him until he (Schweitzer) left for Africa in 1913. Ernest Munch was a passionate admirer of Bach, and had undertaken the task of having, one after the other, all the vocal works of Bach rendered by his small but excellent church choir. Schweitzer a few years later wrote a tribute to this choir: "Every great work of art, like every great idea, needs an atmosphere of enthusiasm for the revelation of its perfect beauty: the singers in the St. William choir, with their fine director, so devoted to the cult of Bach, created this atmosphere around me." [1]

---

[1] From J. S. Bach. Le Musicien-Poète, by Albert Schweitzer. Leipzig: Breitkopf & Härtel, 1908, p. v.

A special program was issued for the twentieth anniversary concert of this choir, on January 15, 1905, and for this program Albert Schweitzer wrote a brief unsigned history of the organization. A longer tribute to its director was written many years afterwards. The story of Ernest Munch and his choir, as told in these two articles, forms an important chapter in the musical life of Albert Schweitzer.

❦

THE STORY OF THE CHURCH CHOIR AT ST. WILLIAM [1]

THE St. William church choir was founded in December, 1884, by the organist of the church, Mr. Ernest Munch, who had returned from Berlin a short time before. The establishment of the choir was the first step in the practical realization of the vision he had caught from his teachers.

In his petition to the presbytery he gives as the purpose of the newly organized choir the presentation of music in the service of worship. Bach's works are written for the service of worship. As his cantatas and passions have no place in our order of service, and yet are essentially and unchangeably ecclesiastical in character, there is nothing to do except to arrange services of worship with the works of Bach, if they are to be rendered in the atmosphere in which they arose.

So the program of the new choir was outlined. The choir has been faithful to it up to the present day. At the same time its special character and justification in relation to the choirs already in existence were determined: the *Chant Sacré*, Stern's Oratorio Society, which first brought honor to the great church music in Strassburg, and the church choirs of Old St. Peter under the direction of G. A. Merkling and Young St. Peter under the direction of Professor von Jan.

The new choir performed for the first time during the Passion Week of 1885. Its beginnings were modest. It numbered about forty

[1] *Zur Geschichte des Kirchenchors zu St. Wilhelm*, from *Le Choeur de St. Guillaume de Strasbourg, un Chapitre de l'Histoire de la Musique en Alsace*, compiled by Erik Jung. Strassburg: P. H. Heitz, 1947, pp. 13–17.

members, who had been gathered from the parish of St. William and from elsewhere in Strassburg and vicinity. At present there are from 100 to 120 members.

The performances of the choral and orchestral pieces took place at first under the bell tower, as there was no room in the organ loft. So in 1894 the *St. Matthew Passion* was performed in two separate locations: the big chorus stood under the bell tower, the little antiphonal chorus with its soloists and its orchestra beside the great organ. But in the long run this arrangement was impossible, since it was acoustically bad to have the choir singing behind the congregation with very limited assistance from the organ. In 1896 the church council, which has always had the warmest regard for the choir, decided to have the great organ, one of Silbermann's creations, renovated by the organ builders, the Brothers Walcker, and at the same time moved back to the rear of the choir loft, in order to provide space in front of it for the choir and orchestra. The city contributed generously to the costs, so that since 1898 the St. William choir has had a place in the organ loft that is ideal in every respect, in the sight of the congregation and under the best imaginable acoustical conditions. Widely traveled artists have declared that they have hardly ever seen another place as perfectly adapted for the performance of church music as St. William Church.

The performances in the church of St. William have been conceived as concerts for the people, and therefore in principle free. Until the middle of the nineties there was no charge for admission to any place, and to defray the costs the choir had only the freewill offerings left by people going out. That meant, however, that no distinguished soloists could ever be called in; and the lack of them became all the more noticeable as the work of the choir became more perfect. It seemed, therefore, to the leaders of the choir, President Küss, the General Secretary of the Board of Directors of the churches of the Augsburg Confession, and the director, an unavoidable necessity to reserve places in a part of the nave of the church at one mark each, and so to assure the choir of a fixed income. This measure turned out well, and did not injure the popular character of the performances. Nonetheless, for many concerts the costs were not covered. To meet this deficit the *Statthalter* Prinz zu Hohenlohe-

Langenburg made goodly contributions. The cost of giving a cantata runs each time to 600 to 700 marks, a Passion 900 to 1000.

The choir at St. William has a special significance for ecclesiastical music in Alsace–Lorraine, in that its leader is at the same time the teacher of Protestant church music at the Conservatory. A number of excellent young organists have learned to direct and accompany Bach's works in the choir of St. William, and choirs have been founded in a number of Alsatian cities, whose leaders got their inspiration from the St. William choir. The choir always offered its assistance to all projects for the rendering of church music. From 1889 to 1899 many of its members assisted in the concerts of the Chant Sacré, which at that time was being conducted by Mr. Munch, and produced the C major Mass of Beethoven, the Creation of Haydn, the Samson of Händel, the Paul and The Hymn of Praise of Mendelssohn, the Deluge of Saint–Saëns and the Manasseh of Hegar.

Together with the academic church choir the St. William choir gave in the presence of the composers the first performance of the Passion and the Harvest Festival of Heinrich von Herzogenberg and the oratorio Through Darkness to Light by Rauchenecker. It shared also in the perfomance of the sixteen-part Mass by Grell, given by all the church choirs of the city, seven hundred voices, under the direction of Mr. Munch at St. Thomas on July 27, 1902.

And now the choir of St. William looks back upon half a generation of work. Only a few of those who helped to found the society are still among its members; many of them who shared with joy in their early successes, advising and encouraging the director, have gone to their rest. The choir suffered a particularly heavy loss in the death of the organist, Eugène Munch of Mulhouse, who had played the organ part for the more important concerts from the beginning. He died in 1898. His successor as organist for the choir was Doctor Schweitzer, his pupil.[1]

Among the regular soloists of the choir at St. William may be named the following ladies: Miss Perrin, Mrs. Adels von Münchhausen, Miss Ast, Miss Kohlrausch, Miss Marais, Mrs. Hirn–Wolf, Mrs. Altmann–Kuntz, Miss Hedwig Mayer, Mrs. Geist, Miss Han-

[1] This article, written by Dr. Schweitzer himself, was unsigned, and so he speaks of himself in the third person. C. R. J.

nig, Miss Hackenschmidt; and the following gentlemen: Georges
Boeswillwald, Wolfgang Geist, Theodor Gerold, Ricard Fischer,
Robert Kaufmann, Epitalbra, Fritz Haas, Karl Weckauff, Anton Sis-
termans, Kalweit, Adolf Walter.

Special thanks are due the members of the municipal orchestra
who have participated with artistic devotion in the Bach concerts at
St. William, many of them since the organization of the choir.

Special thanks are due also to Mr. Frick, the member of the church
council who assumed responsibility for the arrangements and over-
sight of the concerts.

The church choir gave each year four or five rather important concerts. A Bach Passion was always given every Passion Week. Sixty of
Bach's two hundred cantatas have been given, a number reached in
very few cities. Besides the works of Bach, the choir has performed
pieces by Mendelssohn, the Psalms by Schütz, The Death of Jesus
by Graun, the Reformation Cantatas by Becker, the Dettingen Te
Deum and the Messiah by Händel, the Requiem by Mozart, and the
German Requiem by Brahms.

Thus it has been granted to the choir to give itself by its earnest
devotion to the popularizing of the noblest in church music. A de-
vout congregation always fills the church at its concerts, the press
supports the project with warm recognition, and the leader of the
choir has won honorable distinction by being appointed director of
music, and by being given the title of professor.

May it be granted to him and his faithful singers to continue in
the future with their great task, working incessantly upon our generation with the ennobling influence of pure art, with constant self-
criticism and selfless striving.

❦

ERNEST MUNCH, AS I REMEMBER HIM [1]

WHILE I was Eugène Munch's pupil at Mulhouse, I often heard him speak of his brother Ernest at St. William. I met the latter for the first time about 1892, when he came to a concert Eugène was giving at Mulhouse, where Eugène was an organist. The two brothers were very different. The Mulhouse brother [Eugène] was far from possessing the temperament of the Strassburg brother, but in his own way he was just as great an artist. His interpretation of music was based upon extensive and comprehensive study.

In the autumn of 1893 I came to Strassburg to study theology, after having been before that the pupil of the Parisian organist Widor. Ernest Munch received me with great kindness. In a very short time we were addressing each other familiarly. He was living at that time on the quai St. Thomas. I often went in the evening to visit him with his brother Gottfried, who was also living as a student of theology in the seminary of St. Thomas, and then we played music together well into the night.

It was Eugène Munch who accompanied in the St. William choir concerts, and came from Mulhouse for that purpose. At the rehearsals it was I who played. Later, when Ernest Munch's brother could no longer come for the concerts, I accompanied for those too. Munch had me play also as a soloist. This took place for the first time, if I remember correctly, in St. William at one of the concerts that were given regularly at this time for the ministers' conference at the beginning of the summer. The pastors from every part of Alsace, with hardly an exception, gathered for this occasion, and were grateful to Munch for these concerts.

During these years after 1894, the St. William choir began to realize the plan of its director to interpret, not only the few cantatas of Bach which were already pretty well known, but also to give little by little those that were not known. At that period the enterprise

[1] From Le Choeur de St. Guillaume de Strasbourg: un Chapitre de l'Histoire de la Musique en Alsace, compiled by Erik Jung. Strassburg: P. H. Heitz, 1947, pp. 51–62.

was a bold one, for it was necessary first of all to train the public just to understand Bach. One member of the municipal orchestra, who regularly took part in the St. William concerts, coined for Munch the sobriquet the "cantata man." It is probable that we produced in the course of those years a good many cantatas that had not been played since the death of Bach. Little by little our auditors arrived at the point where we were able to demand of them some comprehension of the serious and less accessible compositions of Bach.

The very first cantata of Bach played at Strassburg before 1870 was *Thou Shepherd of Israel, Hear* [1] (No. 104). The organist Théophile Stern of the Temple Neuf interpreted it with his choir, called, I believe, *Chant Sacré*. I know from my father, who was a student at that time, and sang in it, what difficulty the choir had in familiarizing itself with this style, which was so strange to it.

How many times during those days did Munch, his brother Gottfried, and I gather around a table in the evening to study together a volume of cantata scores in the great edition of Bach, regretting our inability to play them all at the same time! Before we separated for our vacations at the end of the summer we had chosen the four cantatas which were to be given in the concert on Reformation Sunday. It was often necessary to copy the parts, for we could not yet procure them in print.

One great difficulty arose from the arrangement of the participants. Choir and orchestra had to find places in the narrow space between the organ and the wall of the church on the St. William street side. The number of artists was therefore too limited. But the effect of the choir was marvelous from this location.

When a greater number of performers was necessary, only the space beneath the tower was available. This had one disadvantage: it was necessary to play behind the audience, and to be satisfied for the accompaniment with the little single manual organ which was there.

I remember very well the performance of the *St. Matthew Passion*, which took place about 1894. As is well known, this work requires two choirs and two orchestras. But Munch dared to separate the two

[1] *Du Hirte Israel, höre.* C. R. J.

choirs and the two orchestras—the first choir with its orchestra under the tower, and opposite them the second choir and orchestra beside the great organ. Gottfried Munch accompanied on the little organ under the tower, and I played on the great one. In spite of the distance we obtained a perfect ensemble. But the audience was still a bit disconcerted by listening to music coming from two opposite sides. For us the experience was very interesting.

The only satisfactory solution of the problem of arrangement involved the setting back of the organ—there was still room behind it—in order to make sufficient space for the choir and orchestra in front of the audience on the platform so enlarged. Unfortunately this solution involved the transformation of the fine old Silbermann organ. I personally regretted this very keenly. This organ, which had been maintained and finely restored by the Alsatian organ builder, had a marvelous sonority. I still remember the amazement of Pirro, a pupil of Widor, who acquired later a great reputation as a musicologist, when I had him mount the organ bench as he passed through Strassburg in 1895. He kept repeating, he who knew the splendid Cavaillé organs in Paris, "I have never heard such sonority!" Even in the forte the organ possessed a sweet and limpid sonority. It rendered the Bach fugues with marvelous clarity. I remember one evening going to the church when Munch was rehearsing for a concert. He was playing a mezzoforte passage on the flute stops. I was so entranced by the beauty of the tone that instead of going up to the organ loft, as I had intended to do, I sat down in a pew to listen in silence.

The cost of moving and changing the organ—they wished to enlarge and modernize it at the same time—was so high that the project could not be carried out without a subvention from the municipality. In the securing of this many difficulties were encountered, and it was not until 1896 that they were overcome. I can still see Munch when he brought me the long-awaited news: "Now, my little Schweitzer, it is going to be done; now we shall have the space we have needed so much."

For the first concert on the enlarged platform, the Bach B minor Mass was given, if I remember rightly. Munch of Mulhouse accompanied this performance (February 5, 1898).

Another difficulty in connection with our concerts arose from financial problems. In principle, the concerts had to be popular and free. But how were we to meet the expenses? How were we to cover the deficits? Therefore each concert brought discussions with Mr. Frick, the treasurer of the church. These were complicated by the fact that the consistory of the church wanted very much to have a choir to sing the church office on the festival days, but showed very much less interest in the numerous concerts the choir wanted to give. As both Munch and Frick had rather violent tempers, there were on several occasions collisions which threatened the activity, nay even the existence of the choir. Finally I was charged with the disagreeable negotiations with Mr. Frick.

I always let him talk, and then each time I would say to him, "From the point of view of the church and of the consistory you are evidently quite right. In your place I would talk exactly as you do. Nevertheless, from the point of view of the choir, Mr. Munch also has some justification. And we should take his views into account. Now we must reconcile ourselves to the fact that the choir, as Mr. Munch conceives it, is not simply a church choir, but a choir which also sings religious music apart from the church services. And St. William should be a little proud of a choir which sets such noble tasks before it. Where is there a church choir in Alsace of which the newspapers speak so often?" In this way the conversation would go on until Mr. Frick became a little more conciliatory, and with a little grumbling would agree to what we were asking. When we did not come to an agreement, we adjourned the deliberations to a more favorable moment, anticipating in this way the procedure now observed in international conferences. When a little later Robert Will was appointed to St. William, Munch found in him great understanding of the efforts of the choir, and a support so powerful that from that moment the discussions with the treasurer of the church, which continued to be my responsibility, became less difficult.

Moreover, financing the concerts became much easier, because it was decided to make a charge of one mark for the better places (about half of them), and to give free admission to the others. In this way the principle of free admission was preserved, and still an opportunity was given to those who wished to help with the expenses of the concert to assure themselves of a good seat. We continued to take a collection for expenses at the door, and the friends of our concerts had a chance to assist us with their gifts. We had at this time devoted supporters among the members of the teaching faculty at the University. The material support of the concerts was thus fairly well assured.

Naturally the means did not suffice for us to engage only soloists of the first rank. Nonetheless, even those of less reputation often gave distinguished interpretations, when they were wise enough to profit by the fact that Munch studied the scores with them. Neither did we have the means to engage only instrumentalists from the municipal orchestra, so we had to be content with the assistance of good amateurs—as was customary in the time of Bach. They were available in sufficient number.

Because our resources permitted us to pay for only two rehearsals with the orchestra—a first rehearsal and a general one—Munch arranged, on the three or four Sundays that preceded a concert, for what he called organ rehearsals between five and seven o'clock. The organ took the part of the orchestra to familiarize the choir with the instrumental accompaniment. At the same time the amateurs who were to complete the orchestra had an opportunity to practise their parts.

The members of the municipal orchestra who assisted at our concerts were full of enthusiasm. The orchestra soloists were excellent. I can still see them: Hofhansel the oboe player, Birkright the flutist, who was still playing with the wooden flute, the first violinist Benno Walter, and the violoncellist Schmidt.

What marvelous musical ardor prevailed at these rehearsals! Munch did not have to pay any attention to the choir, for the choir knew its business; he was able to concentrate exclusively on the orchestra. He conducted the rehearsals with much care and sensitiveness, and never wearied the performers. It was evident that he had prepared these rehearsals down to the last detail. He never lost time with secondary matters, but devoted all his efforts to the essential thing. This is the reason the attention of the performers never faltered, however long the rehearsals lasted.

We had a curious experience with one of the first concerts that followed the enlargement of the gallery. The performance, in our opinion, had been a great success. But the newspaper critics did not express an appreciation equal to our own; their reserve indicated that not everything had been perfect. As we thought it over we came to the conclusion that this might have been because the musical critics were all seated together, so that if one shook his head or puckered his eyebrows at some passage, none of his colleagues would risk giving a completely favorable report for fear of compromising himself. From that time on we saw to it that the critics did not sit together, and thus had their impartiality safeguarded; and this had a good result in their articles. The principle was once more proved that nothing must be left to chance.

The most important of the musical critics attached to the Strassburg newspapers at that time was Doctor Altmann. He had a mania for never expressing complete satisfaction, and for exaggerating the faults in detail, to prove that he was a connoisseur of music. This procedure irritated Munch, and more than once I had to come to Altmann's defence, when Munch became too angry with this quibbler, and proposed to tell him what he thought of him or have some one else do so. At heart Altmann was well aware of the worth of our enterprise, to which he owed after all his own excellent acquaintance with Bach. His wife, an admirable contralto, educated at the Conservatory of Strassburg, was one of the appreciated soloists at St. William.

We should not pass over in silence the excellent treatment we received from the Strassburg press. The newspapers took all the articles, even though very long, which we sent them to acquaint the public with the works we were going to play. For some years I was the accredited reporter for the St. William concerts, and many a time I sent to the papers veritable *feuilletons* upon the works of Bach. Never was one of them refused, even when it was delivered at the last moment. What this good press meant to us I did not fully appreciate until I became cognisant of the difficulties the John Sebastian Bach Society of Paris encountered in getting publicity for their concerts.

Let us render homage to Madame Munch also, who, at a time when her children were still very small and demanded all her attention, collaborated with the choir for years by taking care of the constantly growing musical library. On the days of the concerts she undertook still another duty. After the performance the soloists and the other participants were always invited to dinner at the Munches'. The final chord had hardly ceased to sound before Madame Munch hastened to return to her home to prepare for her guests. What did she not do to permit her husband to exercise this generous hospitality, which was for him a necessity! We, who had a chance to appreciate her activities close at hand, were filled with admiration for her gentle and distinguished manner in everything. Hers was a remarkable personality, with a great nobleness of soul.

The familiarity with the Bach scores and the practice in interpreting his works which I had acquired through association and collaboration with Munch, made it possible for me to accede to Widor's wish when he begged me in 1901 to undertake a study of Bach and his music with the French public in mind. It is to the St. William choir and its director that I am indebted for the ability to write this book, which appeared in French in 1904, and afterwards in German and English. I expressed my gratitude in the preface.

When I published in 1906 my work on the German and French organ builders, I dedicated it to Munch.

Somewhere around 1904 we journeyed together to Frankfort to get acquainted with Siegfried Ochs, who was giving Bach's *Mass B minor* there with the help of the Cecilia Society. Siegfried Ochs was trying to do in Berlin and Frankfort the same thing that we were trying to do in Strassburg, but with much superior resources. He had at his disposal choirs, orchestras, and soloists of the very first quality. He did not have to worry about the expenses incurred by his concerts, and could have as many orchestra rehearsals as seemed good to him. From one point of view, we were better off at Strassburg than he was: for the interpretation of the religious music of Bach we had the church which it required, while Siegfried Ochs had to interpret it in concert halls. The hours that we spent with this man, who was a remarkable connoisseur of Bach and shared our enthusiasms, were all too short. During the night of the concert, which was perfect in every respect, we had to take the train in order to be at our posts in Strassburg the next morning.

Some years before, in the neighborhood of 1898, Munch had gone to Breslau to play Bach there. An orchestra conductor from that city had been present at a Bach concert given by the chorus of the Strassburg Conservatory. Munch was at the organ, and his manner of accompanying pleased the visitor so much that he called him to Breslau to give a Bach concert. Munch cherished a very happy memory of this journey.[1]

Among the concerts of church music which Munch directed outside of St. William, I remember more particularly the Grell *Mass* at St. Thomas, and Händel's *Israel in Egypt* at the Temple Neuf. For the Grell *Mass*, this belated masterpiece in the purely vocal style, written for sixteen voices a *cappella*, all the church choirs of Strassburg came together under the direction of Munch. On this occasion he showed himself a past master in the art of directing a great vocal ensemble. Rehearsals were not spared, since we had no orchestral expense to consider.

For the performance of the *Israel*, the choir and orchestra were placed on a platform erected around the altar of the Temple Neuf. If my memory serves me, the concert was given in this church because there was not room enough at St. William. Although the exclusive study of Bach might have interfered with our appreciation of Händel, both of us, during the preparation of this work, came under the spell of this music, much more simple and direct, but still so expressive. As Munch did not want to dispense with the organ, I had to accompany at the great organ, at the opposite end of the nave from the altar. I could see the conductor of the orchestra only in a big mirror placed very close to the organ and brilliantly lighted, and I had to try in my playing to be always a little ahead of the time beaten by Munch, in order that the organ, in spite of the distance that separated it from the choir and the orchestra, should be perfectly synchronised with the ensemble. This *tour de force* succeeded to the satisfaction of the orchestra conductor, but it took days for me to recover from the fatigue resulting from the effort.

When the post of director of the Conservatory and conductor of the municipal orchestra became vacant upon the death of Franz

[1] Performance of the *St. Matthew Passion*, March 16, 1898.

Stockhausen, Munch became a candidate for the office, and as such conducted one of the concerts of the municipal orchestra. That evening he outdid himself. The way in which he rendered a Brahms symphony remains for me unforgettable. The public was carried off its feet with admiration. The next day the newspapers said, "If the choice had depended upon last evening's audience, Munch would have been selected." But we who were in touch with Mayor Schwander in this matter knew that he had other plans. A petition covered with signatures addressed to him in favor of Munch did no good. It was in vain that some of us, among others Doctor Pfersdorff and I, spoke to him in Munch's favor. He called Hans Pfitzner to the vacant post. But at the same time he created for Munch, as he had promised, a privileged position at the Conservatory, which gave him a great deal of freedom with respect to the director. Moreover, when Munch came to know Pfitzner he felt so profound an admiration for him and his work that he forgave him for having been chosen.

As for us, we were happy that Munch had come to know, during the weeks of his candidacy, in what esteem the people of Strassburg held him.

For some years I took his place at the organ of St. William's for marriages and funerals, when he was busy at the Conservatory and at the Protestant *Gymnasium*, where he was the singing teacher. In the same way I served as a substitute for the organist Schalz and his successor at the Temple Neuf, where I greatly loved the fine organs. They had been built by the Maison Merklin of Paris, and were sacrificed unfortunately for the sake of the church heating.

The advanced courses for organists, which were given for many years in the second half of July at Strassburg, made both of us a great deal of work and gave us much satisfaction. For these courses some fifteen teachers received a vacation, which permitted them to profit from the instruction of Munch for a period of two weeks. He insisted upon hard work. They had to turn these days to account in perfecting their organ work. I collaborated with Munch in giving some of the instruction, and in interpreting the works of French and contemporary organists. The evenings were given up to friendly gatherings, in the course of which Munch became the comrade of these teacher-organists. He had a gift for friendship. That was what attached so many men to him. I have always admired his simplicity, his naturalness, his cordiality.

From the beginning of the new century, I often had to give up my place at the St. William organ. The post of accompanist which I accepted, in succession to Guilmant, with the Jean Sebastian Bach Society in Paris, and other duties, monopolized more and more of my time. When in 1905 I began my medical studies, I had to husband my time and my strength still more, and so had to renounce many of the activities which I should have loved to continue.

Moreover, I thought it my duty to give place to the younger men, that they might have, as I had had, a chance to accompany the choir at St. William's and so gain knowledge and experience. Adolphe Hamm, who later became organist at the cathedral of Basle, was the first to succeed me. I have a vivid recollection of the remarkable way in which he accompanied the *Christmas Oratorio* of Bach. He was followed by others among the younger and better pupils of Munch.

Among the students of the older generation, Niessberger, the organist at the Reformed Church, was closest to Munch. Following the example of his master, he had founded a choir and organized distinguished concerts, which lent themselves to the progressive unfolding of his natural talent as an orchestra conductor.

One of the most remarkable among the Munch pupils belonged to this same generation—Émile Rupp, who was vitally interested in the manufacture of organs and possessed extensive knowledge in this field.

As an organist and as an orchestra leader Ernest Munch established a school in Alsace. It is thanks to him above all else that the Protestant churches have gifted organists and choir leaders. Others continue faithful to his ideal, because of the impetus they received from him. He accomplished the work to which he was called.

One incident at the beginning of a concert at St. William's impressed me very much at the time—I no longer remember in just what year it was. Munch was with us before the concert, in the room under the organ gallery where we left our vestments. He gave us the signal to go up and take our places. Upstairs the choir, the orchestra, and the soloists waited for him to mount his platform and to give the signal to begin. The time came, but he did not appear. As we continued to wait, one of the members of the choir asked me to play an organ number to quiet the impatience of the audience, which we began to feel. I did so. Finally twenty minutes later, Munch arrived and began the concert. He seemed pale and exhausted. Only little by little did he recover. We learned afterwards that he had been taken by a severe colic, and that this had not been the first time he had suffered such pains. This attack heralded, some years in advance, the malady to which he was later to succumb.

III

Vocation and Avocation

*O*N December 1, 1899, Schweitzer was appointed a deacon at the church of St. Nicholas. His mother's half brother, Albert Schillinger, for whom he was named, had previously been minister there, but had died young. His mother had been very fond of Uncle Albert. When he died he was buried in the cemetery of Saint–Gall, and later Uncle Louis, with whom Albert Schweitzer had lived in Mulhouse, and who spent his declining years in Strassburg, was also laid to rest there.

Strassburg had been converted to Protestantism in 1559. From that time on no mass was said even in the cathedral until Louis XIV restored it to the Catholic church. The city was therefore an important evangelical center. The church of St. Thomas, with its great square tower, was just behind the theological foundation where Schweitzer had been a student, and was the most important of the Protestant churches in the city, but St. William, where Schweitzer was collaborating with Ernest Munch, was not far away, and St. Nicholas, to which Schweitzer was called as deacon, was also rather near on the other side of the River Ill. St. Nicholas was not the most important church in the city, yet it was a significant post of service. It did not conform to any particular architectural style, and one who lived beside the building said that its tower was more like a great pigeon house than the spire of a church. To this church Schweitzer went. Technically he was no longer a student.

His second theological examination was passed on July 15, 1900, but not with great credit to Schweitzer, who was too busy with other things to review his studies. Schweitzer remembers his dismal showing in hymnody. When asked about the authorship of one hymn, written by Spitta, the famous poet of Psalter and Harp, Schweitzer said that he did not think the hymn was important enough for him to bother about the author. The poet's son, Professor Friedrich Spitta, was one of his examiners!

The licentiate in theology was conferred on July 21, 1900, and on September 23 he was ordained as curate of St. Nicholas. In addition to his preaching he had to conduct a confirmation class three times a week, but often he was free on Sunday, and would preach for his father back in Gunsbach. In 1901 he published an important study on the Lord's Supper; the same year he was made provisionally principal of the Theological College of St. Thomas, from which he had just graduated; in 1902 he received an appointment as Privatdozent and began lecturing at the College; and in 1903 he received a permanent appointment as principal.

With lecturing and writing and preaching the ordinary man would have been busy enough, but Schweitzer still found plenty of time for his music. There were no confirmation classes in the spring and fall, and by arranging for pulpit supplies when necessary Schweitzer could be away for three months in the year. At Easter he usually spent a month with Widor in Paris; in the fall he usually spent two months in the Munster Valley.

The Paris Bach Society was founded in 1905 by six musicians, two of them being Widor and Schweitzer. Gustave Bret, the conductor, insisted that Schweitzer should play the organ part in every concert; and from that time on he made many trips to Paris for the winter series of concerts. These were precious visits, bringing him the friendship of many distinguished people, including Romain Rolland; who was a musician as well as a writer, with notable books on Beethoven, Händel, early French music, and so on. It was he who organized the International Society of Music; and his great novel Jean–Christophe was a musical romance.

At the home of Uncle Charles and Aunt Mathilde Schweitzer most frequently met Widor and other members of Paris society; and the artificiality of that society depressed him. Its rigid conventions contrasted painfully with what was at that time the freer air of German life. His impressions he set down in an article which is included here because it gives a picture of the social conditions of that epoch.

Happily this day has largely passed, and what Schweitzer has written should be considered only as a historical socio-musical study.

❦

THE CHORUS IN PARIS [1]

WHEN my friends and I a few years ago started to organize a Bach Society in Paris to produce the Passions and cantatas, people everywhere expressed the opinion that sooner or later our enterprise would certainly go on the rocks, since it was impossible to keep a good choir together very long in Paris. When we said that what succeeded elsewhere should certainly be possible there as well, we received in reply only sympathetic shrugs of the shoulders.

The fact is that none of the choruses composed of society volunteers has enjoyed a very long existence in Paris. Usually they died with their founders, if not before. For the most part they were not purely Parisian organizations, but were undertaken by the Alsatian community resident in the capital city. This is the reason that Paris had the best mixed chorus in the middle of the eighties, when the Alsatian community and its adherents from the departments of the east, by virtue of the exodus from Germany after the year 1870, had achieved the greatest importance, and had taken a leading place in politics and intellectual culture. At that time the "Concordia," founded by the engineer Fuchs, was flourishing. Paris was indebted to it for its first acquaintance with the Bach passions and cantatas. The most distinguished musicians were interested in it and dedicated their talents to it. All at once, however, its splendor departed. The group which backed the organization was not important enough to bring to it in the long run the necessary vitality. The organization itself was not able to make the transition from the status of a personal creation to that of an independently organized society possessing objective stability. Its rich library of music was offered for sale at a ridiculously low price some years ago without finding a

---

[1] "*Warum es so schwer ist einen guten Chor in Paris zusammenzubringen*" [Why It Is So Difficult to Organize a Good Chorus in Paris] in *Die Musik*. Berlin: Bernhard Schuster, Bülowstrasse 107, Volume IX, No. 19.

buyer, which proves that no efficient chorus had taken the place of the "Concordia."

Only those choruses have survived that were composed entirely, or almost entirely, of paid professional singers. The best of them belong to the Society of Conservatory Concerts, the Colonne Society, and Vincent d'Indy's *Schola Cantorum*. They get their recruits from the church singers who at the same time belong to the choruses of the great operas.

None of those choruses has had a real success. Colonne had the greatest success with his Berlioz' *Damnation of Faust*. That at best they remain rather mediocre is not the fault of the voices available. These are at times even excellent, especially in the chorus of the Conservatory concerts. But money and time are lacking for the thorough study of the works. For each rehearsal one must count on from three to five francs a singer. That means for a chorus of from eighty to ninety people four to five hundred francs. Under these circumstances a profound analysis of the works is impossible. The *Messiah* or the *St. Matthew Passion* must be produced often after three or four rehearsals. The routine work of the professional singer is of course superficially good; gross mistakes seldom occur even after the hastiest study. But dynamic and depth are lacking.

The discipline is not very rigorous. It has always impressed me how little the conductor is heeded even in the chorus of the Conservatory concerts. More than three-quarters of the singers watch their notes from beginning to end for lack of discipline and skill. The director must make all possible concessions to them. The rehearsals are usually conducted with the singers seated. Men and women often keep their hats on. Intermittent pauses are numerous. And under no circumstances may the time agreed on be lengthened.

But it is morale more than anything else that is lacking. The sense of unity produced by a common goal is essential in a genuine chorus. There is no sign of this in the Parisian choruses of professional singers. Moreover, the deep emotion and inspiration that spring from the long and devoted study of a work and give warmth and fire to it are supremely wanting. Of the joy and pride which so often enable mediocre choruses to rise to artistic heights in their performances there is no trace here. In art, as in all places where the realm of the spirit begins, there are things which only the free man is able to accomplish.

Parisians are well aware that their choruses are only relatively good, and that the ideal is not to be reached in this way. When anyone comes back from Germany he praises, along with the railways of the neighboring country, its choruses. When a foreign chorus is heard in Paris, which does not happen very frequently, the public and the critics often give rein to an uncritical enthusiasm. The feeling is very widespread that the lack of good choruses means the loss of something of enormous worth to the musical life of the capital.

The need is felt, the enthusiasm is present, but the difficulties remain the same. They lie in the nature of Parisian life.

A young girl of a good family in proper Paris circles cannot belong to any chorus. She is not permitted to go out unaccompanied. Life is frightfully complicated by this. From the day when her daughter is fourteen years old, the Paris mother no longer knows any life of her own, but sacrifices herself for her child. She plans and plans to find the time to accompany her, and to make possible numerous excursions. Only those who have lived in these circles and have got an insight into such households can know how difficult life can be made by the rigid observance of the principle that a young, unmarried woman under thirty may not go out alone. If it is a matter of an evening engagement the difficulties multiply. Ordinarily this is possible only in houses where at least two servants are present. Parisians believe that a girl should be seen in the evening only in the company of her parents; it is absolutely unthinkable that she should be found alone in any other company. This is one of the horrors of that emancipation that "Americanism" brings with it.

It is evident, then, that a mixed chorus in Paris may not count on the younger women; they are still in a dependent status. Only such women can be counted on as have won their freedom through the years or through marriage. But even in such cases, going out in the evening constitutes such a difficulty that rehearsals must be held afternoons. It follows then that the chorus must get its recruits from such circles of society as are not averse to the cost of a carriage for every rehearsal. The Paris tramway system has, because of the topography of the city, developed badly, and will remain inadequate.

A woman who does not live in the neighborhood of one of the principal streets is always compelled to use a carriage in the evening.

One of the greatest hindrances in the development of choruses arises from something one would not suspect, namely, the strongly developed family feeling of the Parisians. Widespread social intercourse, so customary among the people of German cities, is unknown here. Of the coöperative movement there is no sign. Difficulties from this source in relation to chorus attendance do not arise, in the main, as they do in Germany. But the Parisian lives for his family; it demands everything of him. One evening in the week is from the outset rigidly set aside for the members of the family who live away from home. In the winter, January and February are largely filled with invitations to dine in the wider circle of relations. It is unthinkable to the Parisian that a chorus rehearsal should take precedence over such obligations; it would do violence to his sense of ethics. Whoever, then, has a large family circle and a large number of relations cannot even contemplate the possibility of joining a chorus. This agrees with the observation made daily in romance regions that wherever the family cult flourishes the taste for public enterprises in the main is less strongly developed.

The small and middle-class bourgeoisie can also provide few members for choruses. The society from which they must get their recruits —at least so far as the women are concerned—is in the highest degree untrustworthy. It is absent from Paris from the beginning of July to the end of October, so that there are really only six months available for regular rehearsals. From this one must again subtract half of January and February. At this time the conductor may make only minimum demands upon his ladies: their time is taken up with the after-New Year calls, which the Parisians make with exemplary conscientiousness. If the days when some of their friends receive fall on the days when there are afternoon rehearsals, their appearance at the chorus is quite impossible, since the visiting hours do not begin until late afternoon. I know the story of a woman who had been singing in a chorus, had had a falling-out with the conductor, and then had made his life miserable by choosing the afternoon of the rehearsal for her receiving day. Because of her intimate friendship with many of the chorus members, the director was made very unhappy worrying about the crucial rehearsals for a performance that was to take place in February.

Recently we have had to reckon also with the many invitations to tea which are becoming more and more fashionable.

The circle from which trustworthy chorus members may be drawn is therefore remarkably narrow. Moreover, the necessity of having rehearsals in the afternoon hours brings with it a multitude of difficulties which would not be present in the evening.

For the men's voices the situation is, if possible, even more unfavorable. Those who can regularly free themselves for an afternoon rehearsal are in the minority. The man who has an office or who is in business can do this only once in a while, perhaps only for an important rehearsal. The leader of the chorus finds himself therefore compelled to rehearse the women in the afternoon and the men in the evening, which is a great disadvantage in the study of the works. The rehearsals are far less interesting when the voices are drilled separately. The members do not hear the ensemble until the final rehearsals, and until then have to be satisfied with piece-work.

To be a member of a Paris chorus, then, requires enthusiasm, will and self-sacrifice. He who commits himself must make up his mind to carry on a fight with hostile circumstances.

This is particularly difficult, since there is no tradition to sustain the individual. Whereas in Germany it is taken for granted that a man with a talent for singing should belong to a choral society, in France he must first secure the approval of his family, in which effort he encounters all possible objections. In such matters we recognize the bearing of tradition upon cultural life, and the importance of the fact that an ideal has won acceptance in its time, and now without any discussion of its wisdom or its foolishness is recognized as reasonable and self-evident. The more closely one observes the more he becomes aware that the excellence of musical life in Germany is based in the last analysis on the fact that traditions and institutions were established in the eighteenth and nineteenth centuries, which provided the foundations for the regulation of our musical organizations today. These traditions sprang out of the artistic life of the free states and the little courts. In France the monarchy degraded all the cities of the country to the status of provincial cities. They possessed no cultural life of their own, but were dependent on the stimulus that came from the capital city. In the great city of Paris, however, the growth of traditions which put the individual at the service of the musical life were from the beginning impossible. They could arise only in small degree. This is the explanation also of the fact that no French city has an orchestra, whereas the little German cities very often have really excellent orchestras, at which French artists are always so astounded.

It is disastrous that the French school that came out of the Revolution does not cultivate singing. School choruses are a novelty. What the private schools have done for the art is also as good as nothing. The educational ideal of the great republican, Plato, who considered art as a part of general culture, is still without any influence in the most modern of republics.

The love of choral singing which the German carries with him from his school is not to be found in France. The idea of belonging to a chorus, and of becoming part of a whole, is strange to the Frenchman from the beginning; he must first familiarize himself with it through reflection.

In the existing choruses one notices that that indefinable something which is called "chorus discipline" is almost lacking in the members. Everyone brings to the rehearsals his full personality; he does not become a member of the chorus, a stop that the director pulls, but remains Mr. So-and-So, or Mrs. So-and-So, who wants to be recognized as such. The modern Frenchman has an instinctive anxiety about anything that is called discipline; he sees in it nothing but a submission that is unworthy of a free being. The higher conception, that discipline means the natural expression of the individual in a society united for a purpose, is in all circumstances foreign to the French spirit. He sees first of all in discipline the sacrifice of freedom and personal worth. The forming of groups—and not alone artistic groups—is made very difficult by this mentality.

Therefore the manifold difficulties combine in France to make the organization of a mixed chorus hard and to throw every imaginable difficulty in its way. A chorus organized after the German model is not to be thought of. Above everything else one should not start to assemble great choruses. Choruses of up to a hundred members are for Paris concert halls fully adequate. The Trocadero, which offers larger dimensions, is little adapted to musical performances because of its bad acoustics.

But quality makes up for what is lacking in quantity. Those who disregard the hindrances and agree to a chorus usually find excellent and well-trained voices at their disposal.

Only that chorus can expect to endure, however, which is recruited from a particular social group. If the members are not acquainted with each other, or are not bound together by common friendships, no coherence is to be expected. Through the peculiarity of the French mentality, the idea of corporate entity is in itself incapable of shaping a community.

First of all we must consider for possible recruits the Alsatian circles and those associated with them from the departments of the east, who are somewhat influenced by the German ways and pay homage to them in matters of organization. The French–Swiss community also provides good elements. Upon the genuine Parisians one cannot count very much at the beginning. They listen with passionate eagerness to choral music, but the way from enjoyment to coöperation is not yet for them a well-trodden path.

As for men's voices, one is still compelled for the time being to secure the coöperation of professional singers, since it remains hard to get volunteers in sufficient number.

If a conductor adapts himself to these circumstances, it is possible —provided he has good relations in the circles in question—to assemble an excellent chorus. He must realize, however, that he must begin small, and resolutely train his men and women singers to discipline, while preserving all the amenities. The leader of the Bach Society has pursued his goal in this way, and worked for three years in secret; whereupon the press, amazed at the performance of the small chorus, did their best to smooth the way for him.

It is to be regretted, for more than one reason, that choral music in the life of Paris is so shockingly retarded. Above all, a splendid literature remains closed to the Parisian. Until a few years ago I knew important musicians in the French capital who had never heard Händel's *Messiah*, or Mendelssohn's oratorios, or had heard them only in a very unsatisfactory rendering; to say nothing of the choral works of Bach, Beethoven, and Brahms. Even Mozart's *Requiem* is almost unknown. In the musical experience of the French the over-powering youthful impressions which the German receives from these works have no influence.

The composers are necessarily forced by these circumstances to neglect a whole category of music, in spite of the fact that as pupils in the Conservatory they have been trained in the composing of cantatas—this is a requirement in the competition for the *Prix de Rome*.

I have been much disturbed by the embarrassment which leading Paris conductors manifested when they were called to conduct a work with a chorus. It was evident that this was something utterly foreign to them. At a major rehearsal for César Franck's *Beatitudes* one of them had particularly to practise giving the signal for the chorus to rise. I have seldom found conductors who can manage the choral attacks in a way that is a matter of course to the German. Very often the rehearsing of the chorus is done by a coach; the conductor undertakes its direction for the first time in the rehearsals with the orchestra.

Most of all, however, the general musical education suffers from the lack of choruses. Only by rehearsing together and singing to-gether can we arouse an interest in polyphony. One who has never experienced a work of art which he has helped to create, in the midst of which he stands as it passes by, which he hears from within out, never emerges from the position of mere musical feeling to that of genuine artistic perception. The educational value of choral singing, which we may assume as a matter of course in the German people—at least for much the greater part of them—is lacking in the French. The feelings of the French are probably just as elemental and vital as those of the Germans, but the power of judgment that can be gained only through artistic activity is wanting.

Recently an organization has been formed—it calls itself the "French Society of the Friends of Music"—whose chief purpose is to naturalize choral singing in France. Among the founders we find almost none but people who know and prize from their own experi-ence the German and Swiss musical life. As one of the first tasks of this organization, the statutes propose the encouragement of choral singing in the schools. The immediate founding of a model chorus of professional singers in Paris is also contemplated. This chorus is to be at the disposal of the concert societies, and will supply good substitutes for the voluntary choruses.

Jules Ecorcheville, one of the most capable French writers on music, is in charge of the business of the organization; the training of the model chorus is entrusted to Gustave Bret, the director of the Bach Society.

As much courage is required for this undertaking as for the reforestation of heights which for hundreds of years have stood barren. It is to be hoped that the energy and enthusiasm of the new organization will succeed in laying the foundation for artistic traditions which will be of inestimable value in the musical life of France.

Concerning this, however, we may not forget that choral singing in France will never come to blossom and significance until the social attitudes and customs of the people from whom volunteer choruses are recruited have experienced a change. If an emancipation occurs which will permit a greater freedom to the young, unmarried women, so that evening rehearsals can be set, the major difficulties will be removed. If not, the circumstances will continue to remain abnormal.

A great artistic problem is therefore tied in the closest way to one phase of the woman question, which in other lands has long ago been solved. In France the fight will be long and hard, for paradoxical as it is, no other citizenry in the world is for good or bad as conservative as that of the modern French Republic.

❦

ONCE, in 1900, Schweitzer had seen the Passion Play at Oberammergau. Aunt Mathilde in Paris had invited him to accompany her and some friends on a carriage drive from Bayreuth to the Tirol. He had charge of the baggage of the party; this, he says playfully, was why he was invited. He did not like the Passion Play, though he felt that the players were putting their souls into it. It was not the simple peasant play acted by simple folk for other simple folk that he felt it ought to be. The play had surrendered to the demands of an eager public, and was being given on a huge stage with distracting theatrical effects. But the scenery of the Bavarian Alps was magnificent.

Bayreuth, however, he visited again and again, and always with a thrill of pleasure. In the cemetery of the town were the graves of the German satirist and humorist, Johann Paul Friedrich Richter, usually called Jean Paul, the French pen name he adopted, and Franz Liszt, the great Hungarian musician, who became towards the end of his life an abbé. But for Schweitzer the place was a Wagner shrine; for in the garden of Wahnfried the great composer lay buried, and in the theatre his genius lived on.

Schweitzer's enthusiasm for Wagner never faltered; perhaps in small part because the controversy over pure music and pictorial music came to rage around him as it had raged around Wagner. The Bach Society had published a monumental edition of Bach's works in the middle of the nineteenth century, and his music was claimed by the anti-Wagnerites as a supreme example of pure music. So they set Bach and Mozart over against Wagner, of whom Nietzsche once said with keen discernment, "As a musician Wagner should be classed among the painters, as a poet among the musicians, as an artist in the more general sense among the actors."

But Schweitzer couched his lance against these "guardians of the Grail of pure music," and described Bach as one who had something in common with Wagner, and even more with Berlioz. Wagner was to him a dramatic lyricist, for whom he had great admiration, and a fellow feeling in the controversy that raged bitterly about him. No man has ever been more hotly attacked or ever more zealously defended. He has been called the Carlyle of music and drama, with a passionate enthusiasm for the reform of art.

Almost fifty years after Schweitzer's first visit to Bayreuth, he wrote some burning words from Africa which showed that his veneration for Wagner had not dimmed with the years: "His music is so great, so elemental, that it makes Wagner the equal of Bach and Beethoven. Such assurance in composition, such grandiose musical architecture, such richness in his themes, such consummate knowledge of the natural resources of each instrument, such poetry, dramatic life, power of suggestion. It is unique; unfathomable in its greatness, a miracle of creative power!" [1]

With Richard Wagner's second wife, Cosima Wagner, Schweitzer finally became well acquainted in Heidelberg, Strassburg, and Bayreuth. He tells the story of this colorful and dominating personality in a vivid pen picture, with a glimpse of Richard Wagner's son Siegfried and his daughters.

❦

MY RECOLLECTIONS OF COSIMA WAGNER [2]

I SAW Cosima Wagner for the first time in Bayreuth, when in 1896 *The Ring of the Nibelung* was taken up again, twenty years after its 1876 *première*, which Wagner had directed in person. The musicians of the orchestra, with whom I used to lunch, spoke of her with great respect. But they were not unanimous in their opinion that it was a real advantage to have a woman of such an imperious will as Madame Cosima directing the performances.

It was about 1904, if I am not mistaken, when I made her acquaintance. It was at Heidelberg, on the occasion of an audition of Bach's *B minor Mass* executed under the direction of Philippe Wolfrum. Madame Wagner was there with her son Siegfried and one of her daughters. I acted with reserve, for her manner of receiving people who came to see her after the concert was lacking in simplicity and naturalness. She did not have the gift of putting people at their ease; she liked to have them approach her with the reverence due a princess.

A little while afterwards, when I was working on my book about J. S. Bach, she stayed for a time at Strassburg with her daughter Eva. Professor Johannes Ficker, whom she knew well, gave her as a guide one of his students in the history of art, and I joined them in their walks about Strassburg. Cosima Wagner had heard something about

---

[1] *Prophet in the Wilderness*, by Hermann Hagedorn. Copyright 1947 by Hermann Hagedorn, and used with the permission of the Macmillan Company, New York; p. 50.

[2] "Mes Souvenirs sur Cosima Wagner," from *L'Alsace Française*, Volume XXV, No. 7 (February 12, 1933), pp. 124 ff.

the book I was preparing, and she showed some interest in my idea that some of the music of the cantor of St. Thomas was descriptive. She asked me during our promenade to explain my views, and I noticed that she knew the work of Bach thoroughly. To demonstrate my ideas to her, I played for her on the beautiful organs of the Temple Neuf some of the most significant of the chorale preludes.

During our walks we talked about other things besides music. She told with great animation of the fight Wagner had waged in support of his art, so far as she had shared the struggle with him. I was surprised to find that still in that epoch, when Wagner's work had finally triumphed, she was haunted by the idea that the master's enemies remained active and formidable. This attitude seemed to me hardly consonant with the remarkable personality of Cosima Wagner.

Since I was a theologian, she touched also on religious problems. She once spoke to me of the religious instruction she had received, and of the questions she put to her professors. She had always thought that the great problem was how to reconcile the justice of God with His love, since, she said, love cancels justice, and as an attribute of God admits of no other. Therefore, she concluded, we may represent God only as a God of love, Who desires and achieves the salvation of all His creatures. In the course of this interview, which took place one beautiful, sunny afternoon, while we were walking along beside the Ill from the St. Thomas bridge to the University, I realized what a delicate and vital soul there was in this woman, at first approach so distant.

Her daughter Eva appeared very simple and natural. I conceived for her an extraordinary esteem, and we have always remained in excellent relations.

When, some time later, I went to Bayreuth to attend the performances, I paid a visit to Cosima Wagner, who received on certain days between eleven and one o'clock. On my first visit I had occasion to admire her amiability and *savoir-faire*. She was conversing with a gentleman who was pretending to know her quite well, although so far as I could see she did not remember him at all. She was floundering, but her floundering was that of a *virtuoso*. For me it was a very diverting spectacle. Finally her daughter Eva perceived her mother's embarrassment and rescued her.

Every time I was received at the Villa Wahnfried I admired anew the accomplished art and the perfect consideration with which Madame Wagner and her children devoted themselves to the visitors, who were often just curious people.

Two days after my first visit to the Villa I was invited to have supper with the Wagner family, during the second entr'acte of *Tristan and Isolde*, in the little hall of the Festspielhaus.

Also invited were the Prince of Saxe–Meiningen and Mademoiselle Grandjean of the Paris Opera, where the latter had played brilliantly the role of Isolde. The dessert consisted of a plate of magnificent peaches, which Mademoiselle Grandjean had brought from Paris. I was amazed at the skill which Cosima Wagner displayed in sustaining an interesting conversation. Moreover, she bore almost all the burden of it. I took some satisfaction in noticing that my fellow guests were as much overawed as I by this eminent woman.

As a matter of fact I was not at all at my ease during this supper. I was too much under the influence of the masterpiece that Felix Mottl had just been directing in such a sovereign manner. I should have preferred to go out into the country to sit down by myself, as I usually did at Bayreuth during the entr'actes.

In Cosima Wagner's activities at the theatre of Bayreuth she revealed a personality without an equal. With all her heart she was trying to conserve intact the traditions of the old Bayreuth.

I was able to take note of this during my different pilgrimages there. But in spite of the perfection with which the works of the master were executed, I was not wholly satisfied with them. I had the feeling that at no time could the interpreter give way to his own inspiration, and that his singing and playing had been too strictly ordered by Cosima. At the most moving moments there were lacking that spontaneity and that naturalness which come from the fact that the actor has let himself be carried away by his playing and so surpasses himself. Frequently, it seemed to me, perfection was obtained only at the expense of life.

I was very happy to know more intimately Siegfried Wagner. Rarely have I met a man more natural and more thoroughly good. As a stage manager and animator he was marvelous. He looked out for all the details of the stage setting. And how well he knew how to instruct and inspire the singers! He forced them to do nothing that went against the grain; he urged them to perfect and deepen their own conception of their role. I cherish an ineffaceable memory of the performance of The Flying Dutchman, which he had arranged and directed.

When I left for Africa in 1913 I promised myself to arrange my first leave in Europe in such a way that I could attend the performances at Bayreuth in the autumn of 1915. But then came the war, and afterwards the sad and troubled years that followed it!

It was not until the winter of 1923 that I was able to return to Bayreuth, on my way back from Prague, where I had been giving some organ concerts. The journey was not as easy as I had thought it would be. A special visa was necessary at that time to stop in Bavaria. Since my passport had no such visa in it, the gendarmes at the frontier station forbade me to take any train except the express which crossed Bavaria to the west. Luckily it was evening, and the guardians of the law were not performing their duties very conscientiously. I succeeded at the last moment in sneaking into the forbidden train, with a magnificent bouquet of white roses, which the admirers of Bach's music had presented to me on my departure from Prague, and which I intended to give to Cosima Wagner.

How sad to see again these loved places! At the Villa Wahnfried what dejection! They wondered if it would ever be possible again to stage the Wagnerian dramas at the Festspielhaus. The money was lacking to put the great theatre and the machinery into condition again. Was the international Wagnerian community still in existence? Or had the war shattered it?

At that time, as I learned when I arrived at the Villa Wahnfried, Cosima Wagner could receive only on those days when she was quite calm. But the news of my arrival (though she should hardly have remembered me at all) had disturbed her so much, that she had fussed for hours in advance about the dress she would put on to receive me. Finally, because her daughter feared the excitement would be harmful to her, I gave up the idea of seeing her and sent her the bouquet of white roses, which gave her a great deal of pleasure.

Afterwards I paid a visit to the widow of Hans Richter, the orchestral leader for whom I had so much respect. Cosima Wagner died a little while afterwards.

And now it is Siegfried Wagner who has passed away. . . . The Bayreuth that we knew, we the Wagnerian enthusiasts of my generation, exists no more. . . .

IV

Bach: The Musician-Poet

*T*HE new presbytery at Gunsbach was on the main street of the village, just east of the town hall, set back a bit and separated from the street by a lovely private garden. The main entrance to the house was on the other side. Albert's room was at the left of the door that led to the garden, and faced the sunny south. He had come home for the Whitsuntide holidays in the early summer of 1896; and one morning as the bright, warm sun streamed into his room and wakened him, and the birds sang in the garden before the house, he began to think of his favored lot, the happy family in which he lived, the privilege of books and music, teachers and loyal friends; and then he realized that he must give something for all these precious things that he enjoyed.

What should he give? Simply and clearly the answer came to him. He should give himself, after he reached the age of thirty, to the immediate service of humanity. He was then twenty-one. He had, therefore, nine years more which he felt he might rightly devote to his music and his studies. After that, service.

What was the service to be? He did not know. He thought it might be for destitute and abandoned children, perhaps for tramps and discharged prisoners.

His thirtieth birthday approached. A few months before the day came he found on his table a green-covered magazine, in which Alfred Boegner, the president of the Paris Missionary Society, pleaded for workers in the Gabun. This was the call. He would go.

He was in Paris again in the fall. On October 13, 1905, he dropped into the mailbox letters announcing that at the beginning of the winter term he would start his medical studies in preparation for work as a doctor in French Equatorial Africa. His resolve had not wavered. Neither did it falter when his family and friends argued with him about his decision. Romain Rolland was eloquently silent. Widor was eloquently vocal. He thought the general was deserting his command to fight at the front like a common soldier.

Nothing made any difference. He resigned as principal of the theological college, and towards the end of October began his studies in the medical school of Strassburg University.

Meanwhile he had completed his work on Bach, and in this same year, when his momentous decision went into effect, the book was published. It was high time for such a book. Bach's death in Leipzig in 1750 had created no stir whatever; his greatness was not recognized. At the end of the eighteenth century musicians thought that the great composer of the Bach family was Emmanuel, one of the sons. To all intents and purposes Johann Sebastian had disappeared. Then came Forkel's brief biography in 1802, followed in midcentury by the publication of the complete works of Bach by the Bach Society—a frightfully difficult undertaking in the face of an indifferent musical world—and in 1874 and 1880 by the two volumes of the detailed and almost exhaustive study by Spitta. In Germany, France, England, Belgium, Italy, Bach began to come into his own. It was almost like a rising from the grave, and indeed one of the chapters in Schweitzer's later German biography of Bach is entitled "Death and Resurrection." Yet when Schweitzer began his work on Bach much still remained to be done, as is evident from the conversation with Widor already reported. To help in the larger appreciation of the cantor of St. Thomas, to make his music understood for what it is, Schweitzer wrote his book. But in his characteristic modesty he disclaimed too much credit. What is needed, he said, to make Bach known and loved is not Bach festivals and books like his own, but the unheralded devotion of thousands of humble folk who should find food for their souls in his work, and then should tell others about it. Bach speaks to such men alone.

At the close of his epoch-making book, which for some time was a storm center among musicians, because of its contention that much of Bach's music was not of that pure, classical type that Spitta had declared it to be, Schweitzer says:

"The problem of interpretation is far from being solved. The work and the efforts of an entire generation of artists will be needed to establish the elementary principles for a modern rendering of the works of Bach. How can one speak wisely today, when the most beautiful and the most modern of the cantatas have never yet been given anywhere? We think we do sufficient honor to the master in giving from time to time the St. Matthew Passion, and we do not even suspect all the riches contained in the volumes of cantatas published by the Bach Society!

"Still, it seems to us that the day of the Bach of the cantatas has come, and that Bach, the musician-poet, will cease to be venerated as an unknown man as soon as musicians are found to perform his cantatas.

"It is both the grandeur and the weakness of music that it needs interpreters. A fine old painting commands the respect of the public today by its own merits. The older music, on the contrary, will remain strange as long as it is not rendered for us in a way that resembles a bit our modern music. The character of the work is necessarily corrupted by the spirit and the opinions of the man who undertakes to give it.

"But of what importance are these divergent interpretations? Whether the principles we employ are right or wrong the future will decide. The only thing of significance at the moment is that we should make known the great music of Bach. We cannot conclude in any better way than by citing the happy observation that Monsieur Gevaërt, one of the oldest enthusiasts for the cantor of St. Thomas, made to me: 'It is with the music of Bach as it is with the gospel. The people can understand it only according to Matthew, according to Mark, according to Luke, according to John, gospels which differ much, but which are always the Gospel. One thing only is needed, one thing indispensable: to stir discerning and sensitive souls!' " [1]

This is Schweitzer's humility speaking. But when Widor from Venice wrote his introduction to Schweitzer's book, on October 20, 1904, he was lavish in his praise. Listen to Widor:

"Better than all the speeches in the world, the pages you are about

[1] From J. S. Bach. Le Musicien–Poète, by Albert Schweitzer. Leipzig: Breitkopf & Härtel, 1908, p. 434.

to read will show the power of Bach's extraordinary brain, for they will give you examples and proofs. From Mozart to Wagner, there is no single musician who has not considered the work of Johann Sebastian Bach as the most fruitful of teachers. All right! If this was the opinion of the masters, while it was difficult to get the full meaning of his work, with a part of it lying unknown, buried in the dust of libraries, what will be our opinion today now that everything has been published?

"Until the present moment it was this writing, this polyphony, this technique that we have admired, astonishing mixture of ability and good common sense; not a note which did not seem to be the result of long cogitation and yet did not come to the point of the pen quite naturally as the only true, the only right note. And now in addition to these astounding qualities of workmanship, we are about to discover others of a higher order. Here is a thinker, a poet, a gifted interpreter of ideas, who reveals himself suddenly as a prodigious sculptor, the father of the modern school, the moving and graphic master.

"Bach died July 28, 1750; one hundred and fifty-five years, therefore, have been needed for us to penetrate his symbolism, to discover in him a descriptive and pictorial feeling like that of the primitives, to follow his thought step by step, and to contemplate in the clear light of day the incomparable unity of his art.

"As we read Monsieur Schweitzer's book, it seems to us that we are present at the inauguration of a monument; the last scaffolds, the last veils have fallen; we walk around the statue to study its details, then we withdraw a little to a point from which our eyes can survey the whole; and then we pass our judgment upon it." [1]

The moment the book was written a demand was made for a German translation. This Schweitzer attempted at once to do, but found it impossible for him to translate his thoughts into German. Therefore he wrote an entirely new book in German, the first pages of which were written in the Black Horse Inn at Bayreuth in this same year. It took him two years to finish it, but in view of the fact that he was having a heavy course of medical studies, lecturing regu-

---

[1] From J. S. Bach. Le Musicien–Poète, by Albert Schweitzer, Leipzig: Breitkopf & Härtel, 1908, pp. xiv f.

larly, preaching at St. Nicholas, making concert tours, and writing two other books, the marvel is that he was able to complete it at all, especially since the new book, to the consternation of the publishers, had 844 pages instead of 455. The German edition was published in 1908, and from this the English edition was made. The English edition in turn was largely altered and expanded at Dr. Schweitzer's request, so that it expresses Schweitzer's latest thought about Bach. And now there exists at Schweitzer's Alsatian home an interleaved edition of the German book, in preparation for that happy moment when the whole work can be revised again, in accordance with the latest knowledge of the great musician.

The following excerpts from the French edition include a study of the place of the chorale in Bach's work, a complete account of Bach's life and activities in brief compass, and an explanation of the symbolism which Bach employs. Here, then, is the heart of Schweitzer's interpretation of Bach—though all comment on particular works, whether instrumental or vocal, motets, Passions, oratorios and cantatas, is omitted. Those who wish to make a detailed study of these works are referred to the English edition.[1] It is a pity that the French version is not better known among the lovers of music. It has the tremendous advantage of brevity, and it is not a duplication of material in the German and English editions. As Schweitzer has himself said, the latter have an entirely fresh approach to the subject. The rhythm of the French sentence, the clarity and conciseness of the language, are qualities Schweitzer was unable to transfer to the German. He points out that there is something finished about French literature, in the good and the bad sense of the word, something unfinished about German literature in just the same way.

[1] J. S. Bach, by Albert Schweitzer. New York: The Macmillan Company, 1947.

❦

THE CHORALE IN BACH'S WORK[1]

THERE is a fundamental difference between Bach and Händel. Bach's work is based on the chorale, Händel for his part makes no use of it. With one of them free invention is everything; with the other, the author of the cantatas and the Passions, the work springs from the chorale and effaces itself in it. The most beautiful and the most profound of Bach's works, those where the deepest aspect of his philosophic thinking is expressed in the form of music, are his organ fantasies on the chorale melodies.

Is it not a strange thing that Bach, if he was a creative genius, should use as the basis of his work melodies already composed? The reason is that external circumstances constrained him. He was an organist and chapel master. As such he composed for the service of worship. His cantatas and Passions were destined to find a place in the liturgy, and he did not imagine that one day they would be given outside the service. Writing for the church, he felt himself compelled to attach his work to the chorale, the sole principle in the sacred music of Protestantism. Händel was free; he did not write cantatas, but oratorios for spiritual concerts.

From necessity springs power, it is precisely to the chorale that the work of Bach owes its greatness. The chorale not only puts in his possession the treasury of Protestant music, but also opens to him the riches of the Middle Ages, and of the sacred Latin music from which the chorale itself came. Through the chorale his music sinks its roots deep into the twelfth century, and so establishes a vital contact with a great past. It is not solely an individual phenomenon; in it live again the aspirations, the strivings, even the soul of former generations. Bach's art represents the blossoming of the chorale under the breath of a great genius. It is not simply a generation, it is the centuries that have produced this colossal work.

If, then, it is true that genius sums up in itself an entire generation, by giving adequate expression to the idea which fashions its time, and

[1] From *J. S. Bach. Le Musicien–Poète*, by Albert Schweitzer. Leipzig: Breitkopf & Härtel, 1908, pp. 1–4.

that it is necessary, therefore, for the understanding of that genius, to examine it at work in the age from which it has come, one consequence follows: we must base the study of Bach upon an even broader foundation. His great biographer Spitta understood this very well. Before painting for us his picture, he goes back into the past and retraces for us the history of Bach's large family. We see them spread out among the little villages of Central Germany, all of them organists and cantors, all upright and a bit stubborn, all of them energetic, all modest but with some appreciation of their value. We are present at the big family reunions, where they cultivate a spirit of solidarity and a common ideal. We run through what has come down to us from their works. And from this environment and from these works we see Sebastian Bach emerge. We are presentient of him, we understand him before we become acquainted with him. We foresee that the ideas and aspirations which are manifest in this family cannot stop there, but must necessarily be realized some day in a perfect, definitive form, in some unique Bach, where the different personalities of this big family reappear and survive. Johann Sebastian Bach, to speak the language of Kant, imposes himself upon us as a kind of historic postulate.

So the biographer proceeds in relation to the man; so the musician must proceed in relation to the work itself. A history of the chorale: such is the base that the study of the work demands. The evolution of the music, and the evolution of the religious poetry of the German Middle Ages, lead to the advent of the chorale in the Reformation. But they do not stop there. The final point, towards which both evolutions converge in their complexity, is Bach. Whether one follows one or the other, at the end of the road will be found Sebastian Bach.

The most beautiful flowers of German poetry from the Middle Ages to the eighteenth century, the strophes of the chorale, adorn his cantatas and his Passions. It is Bach who reveals their beauty; it is he who takes them out of the hymn collections to make them the property of the whole world.

Likewise, the efforts to harmonize the chorale, made by the former masters, come to their climax in him. It is he who achieves the ideal harmonization.

What the Scheidts, the Buxtehudes, and the Pachhelbels proclaimed from a distance in their fantasies on the chorale, becomes a reality in those of Bach: they are organ poems.

From the motet which is attached to the chorale comes, under the influence of Italian and French orchestral music, the cantata. This great foreign impulse follows its course and finds itself in the Bach cantatas. Just one fact: the chorus of the first cantata he conducted at Leipzig in 1714 (No. 61), is a French overture. Bach himself calls it Ouverture, and uses the word "gay" to indicate the movement in the middle part.

At the end of the seventeenth century, the biblical drama, which was in favor in the Middle Ages, comes back again in the form of the passion play in music to knock on the door of the churches. The fight begins between those in favor and those opposed. It is Bach again who puts an end to the struggle. He rehabilitates the ancient Passion by idealizing it: he writes the St. Matthew Passion.

From whatever direction he is considered Bach is, then, the last word in an artistic evolution which was prepared in the Middle Ages, freed and activated by the Reformation and arrives at its full expansion in the eighteenth century. The chorale is in the center of this evolution. Its story is, therefore, necessarily the prelude to a study of Bach.

❧

THE LIFE AND CHARACTER OF BACH [1]

1. BACH AND HIS FAMILY

BACH was born at Eisenach on March 21, 1685, and died at Leipzig on July 28, 1750. There is nothing particularly striking about his life; it is the life of a bourgeois, honest and laborious. An orphan at ten years, Bach found a refuge in the home of his oldest brother at Ohrdruff. At the end of some years, as his brother Johann Christoph's family continued to grow more numerous, he felt it his duty not to remain as an expense to his brother but to provide for his own wants. Because of his fine voice he was accepted as a chorister

[1] From J. S. Bach. Le Musicien–Poète, by Albert Schweitzer. Leipzig: Breitkopf & Härtel, 1908, pp. 105–170.

in the boarding-school of the lycée at Lüneburg, where he followed all the classes. Of course he could have desired nothing more than to continue his studies at the University and to complete his general culture; but one had to live before he began to philosophize. Bach was forced to accept the job of violinist in the orchestra of the Prince of Weimar. Some months later, in 1704, he was made organist in Arnstadt, where a new organ had just been constructed. He remained there four years. In the end, his stay was spoiled by the dissensions that broke out between him and the municipal council concerning a leave which had been granted him, and which he had prolonged by more than two months without even informing his superiors. Moreover, Arnstadt was really too little for him; he felt himself crowded there. It was therefore with real satisfaction that he accepted the post of organist at Mulhouse in 1707. He was immediately married there to his cousin, Maria Barbara Bach. In June 1708 he left Mulhouse for Weimar, where for nine years he fulfilled the functions of court organist and chamber musician. To these titles he added in 1714 that of concert master, that is, assistant conductor of the orchestra. But when the post of bandmaster became vacant, the prince, instead of offering the place to Bach, who believed he had good reasons for counting upon it, gave it to an entirely insignificant musician, Johann Wilhelm Drese, whose only qualification was that he was the son of his father, the former bandmaster. Under these circumstances Bach could not remain there longer. The Prince of Cöthen offered him the position of bandmaster at his court. Bach accepted, and continued to serve from 1717 to 1723. At length, however, his work ceased to please him, for it had little relation to the vocation which he felt within him. As a matter of fact, he was only the director of music in the Prince's chamber; the cantatas were not performed at all; for the court, like that of Prussia, was not Lutheran but Reformed; the organ of the court chapel was a small instrument with hardly a dozen stops, and moreover Bach did not have the title of organist. Let us add that Prince Leopold had married a woman who was not at all interested in music, and his love for art began to grow cold. Other reasons also decided Bach: his sons were growing up; it was necessary to give thought to their education. But Cöthen had hardly any educational resources to offer. Hamburg would have been the city of his choice, but the intrigues and the thalers [1] of his rival succeeded.

Nonetheless, when the position of cantor at St. Thomas, that is, chapel master for the Leipzig churches, became vacant on the death of Kuhnau in 1722, Bach hesitated for several months before announcing his candidacy. The cantor at St. Thomas was only a simple professor, the fourth from the top in St. Thomas School; he had to give certain lessons and to direct the choirs which the boarding pupils formed in the two principal churches. For a chapel master at a ducal court this was not at all an advancement. In the end, the father of the family decided: the bandmaster agreed to become a schoolteacher. He began his new duties May 31, 1723; he was to perform them for twenty-seven years.

Bach enjoyed very robust health. Except for some indisposition which prevented him from going in 1729 to greet Händel at Halle, we do not know of any serious illness that came to interfere with his work. His eyes were his one weak spot. He was myopic from birth, and it goes without saying that it did not help his sight to write music and to engrave his compositions on copper himself. During the last two years of his life his eyes became weaker and weaker. The operation performed on him during the winter of 1749–1750 by an English oculist who was passing through Leipzig, far from helping them, brought in its train the most disastrous consequences; not only did he become completely blind, but his health was also severely shaken. On July 18, 1750, he suddenly recovered his sight, but a few hours later an attack of apoplexy struck him down. He died in the evening of July 28, and was buried on Friday, July 31, in St. Jean Cemetery.

Such, with the exception of some minor episodes and some short journeys, was the life of the master. The obituary which was drawn up by his son, Karl Philipp Emmanuel, and his pupil Agricola, and appeared in Mizler's *Musikalische Bibliothek* in 1754,[2] hardly gives more than dates. Later, Forkel, the well-known historian of German

---

[1] A thaler is a German coin, formerly worth about three marks, but no longer minted. C. R. J.

[2] The Mizler *Bibliothek* was a musical review which appeared in Leipzig. The obituary notice is found in the 4th vol., 1st part, pp. 158–176 (1754).

music, in the biography he wrote of Bach in 1802, added to these dates some information he got from the two eldest sons of the musician, Friedemann and Emmanuel. Almost all the anecdotes about Bach go back in their original form to this biography.[1]

Then interest grew dull, and the study of Bach remained stationary for nearly sixty years. The first who undertook to publish a new biography, based on more careful research, was Bitter. His work, which appeared in 1865, was soon supplanted by a more solid and vaster work, the Bach Biography of Philipp Spitta. This work is the fruit of fifteen years of study, study singularly attractive doubtless, but fraught with extraordinary difficulty. Let one remember that hardly any letters of Bach exist, and that the information secured from contemporaries was insignificant and inadequate. It was necessary, therefore, to make the archives and the manuscripts speak. And Spitta made them speak. He leafed through the ecclesiastical registers in the localities where Bach had lived, scanned the acts of the municipal assemblies, and found more than he had ever hoped to find. In 1873 the first part of this work appeared, which, finished in 1880, was to be for the history of music what the book of Justi on Winkelmann was for the history of art.[2]

These more recent studies permit us to determine with more precision the appearance of the master. One is involuntarily tempted to trace a parallel between his life and that of Kant. Both lived a very simple bourgeois life, broken by no striking event; but though they lived within the confines of a modest and quiet environment, they were able to keep a vital contact with the world; both had the gift of letting the numerous impressions they received from the outside world ripen within them; neither had any great doubts about the road to take, nor any great difficulty in winning the esteem of his

[1] *Ueber Johann Sebastian Bachs Leben, Kunst und Kunstwerke. Für patriotische Verehrer echter, musikalischer Kunst* [Concerning Johann Sebastian Bach's Life, Art and Artistic Works. For patriotic admirers of genuine, musical art], by I. R. Forkel, Leipzig. Bureau de Musique, 1802. 69 pp. This work, inspired by an ardent admiration for Bach, is precious of its kind, and must be considered as the point of departure for every study of Bach. Nevertheless, it is not exact in all its details.

[2] *Johann Sebastian Bach*, by Philipp Spitta, Leipzig, Breitkopf & Härtel, 1st vol. 1873, 855 pp.; 2d vol. 1880, 1514 pp.

contemporaries; both, one may say, were greater and happier than other gifted men, because there was a complete identity between the ideal they followed and their daily occupations: Kant wanted to teach young people, Bach wished to enrich the Protestant service.

On the contrary, what a difference there was between the life of Bach and that of Händel! Händel was already a *virtuoso* and an admired composer at the time when Bach, his equal in age, was only a simple and obscure violinist in the ducal orchestra at Weimar; Händel was heard before Buxtehude, whom Bach a year later went to listen to with the respect and the curiosity of a pupil desirous of learning from such a master; Händel was applauded in Italy, Bach was an organist in a little German village. Händel lived at the English court and had at his disposition orchestras, choirs, and soloists of distinction; Bach was a schoolteacher and had only pupils to render his works. The *Messiah* had a resounding success; no one spoke of the *St. Matthew Passion*. Händel was buried in Westminster Abbey; we are reduced to conjectures as to where the remains of the cantor of Leipzig lie. And still, of these two destinies, which do we prefer: that of Händel, who for more than twenty years was mistaken about his true vocation and sought in the opera the glory that he was to find in the oratorio, or that of Bach, who discovered the way he was to take with such certainty and security?

Unfortunately, we possess very few details about Bach's intimate life, about the husband and the father of a family. He married twice. His first wife died suddenly at Cöthen in 1720, while he was at Carlsbad, where he had had to accompany Prince Leopold. She was already buried when he returned; he could only go and weep upon the still fresh grave of the woman who for thirteen years had shared his life and his work. Philipp Emmanuel in his obituary describes in a moving way the grief and prostration of his father; he was only six when his mother died, but the poignant scenes he witnessed left upon him an indelible impression. A year later the master married Anna Magdalena Wülken, the daughter of the trumpeter (*Hof- und Feldtrompeter*) of the Weissenfels orchestra. She was then twenty-one, Bach was thirty-six. This union was perfectly happy. Anna Magdalena was able to understand her husband and to follow him in all his work. She was a musician herself, with a beautiful soprano voice.

It was at the court, where she was a singer, that Bach doubtless came to know her. Let us add that she was endowed with remarkable musical intelligence, which her husband undertook to develop. We still have two books for the harpsichord that belonged to Anna Magdalena (*Klavierbüchlein*); the first is from 1722, the second from 1725. They contain, among other compositions for the harpsichord, French suites, sacred songs, and soprano airs. The second of these *Klavierbüchlein* is particularly precious to us, for in it Bach has written the fundamental rules for playing the figured bass. Anna Magdalena was not only an economical housekeeper—and economy was certainly necessary in such a numerous family—but more than that, she rendered great service to her husband in copying music. It was she, for instance, who copied the largest part of the *St. Matthew Passion*. A curious detail: her handwriting became more and more like her husband's; it was hardly possible to distinguish them.

What a charming family scene is called up, for instance, by the second oboe part in the cantata: *Ihr, die Ihr Euch von Christo nennet* [You who take the name of Christ], (No. 164)! The heading and the clefs are in Anna Magdalena's writing, but the notes, awkward and stiff, betray a child's hand. At the bottom is a primitive little monogram, where an effort is made to combine the three letters "W.F.B.": Wilhelm Friedemann Bach! The cantata is probably from 1723; the child was then thirteen years old; it was his first fair copy. Do you see the scene? Mother and son are sitting at the same table; a step is heard on the stairs: "Hurry up!" says the mother, "father is coming in."

On the other hand, how many sad scenes are evoked by the Weimar, Cöthen, and Leipzig registers! Bach had, in all, twenty-one children; seven by his first wife, fourteen by his second. Several died young, others at a more advanced age. Only eight were still alive, four girls and four boys, when the father died.[1] How many times he had to follow the coffin of someone dear to him: June 29, 1726, Nov. 1, 1727, Sept. 21, 1728, Jan. 4, 1730, Aug. 30, 1732, April 25, 1733— there were many days of mourning in the house of the Thomas cantor! Does the profound sadness of certain cantatas surprise us, when

[1] In the German version Schweitzer states that Bach had twenty children, of whom nine survived him. C. R. J.

we know under what sorrowful circumstances they saw the light of day? If the cantatas could only tell us of all these tearful days, we should understand to its full extent the anguish of which the inventory prepared after the death of the master hardly gives us a hint. The eldest of the sons of Anna Magdalena—he was called Gottfried Heinrich—is represented by a guardian, for he was mentally defective. Altnikol, the son-in-law of Bach, took him into his own home before Bach's death; the son did not die until 1763. It is precisely this Gottfried Heinrich who gave rise to the legend of David Bach, the deranged *virtuoso*, whose strange playing, it was said, brought tears to the eyes of the listeners. But Bach never had a son of that name.

The happiest epoch in Bach's family life was the years before the older sons had left the paternal home. Friedemann and Emmanuel had both received a very careful musical education. Bach had a talent that is not given to all fathers: he knew how to teach his own children. In 1720, when Friedemann had reached the age of nine, he had him begin his music, and wrote in succession the pieces which make up the *Klavierbüchlein* for Wilhelm Friedemann Bach. The *Inventions* (1723), and also the six sonatas for the organ, which come from the same epoch, were intended to serve as studies for the two older boys. But while he was encouraging his sons in their music, he insisted that they should take general subjects at the University of Leipzig; a certain amount of university culture was then, we used to say, indispensable to the artist. Emmanuel was not destined for an artistic career, but for the study of law, because his father did not think he had sufficient talent for music. It was not until 1738 that he decided definitely for music.

A letter written by Bach in 1730 to Erdmann, his former schoolfellow at Lüneburg, incidentally gives us some information about the family concerts. The motive of this letter is not the most happy one: Bach, disgusted with Leipzig because of various annoyances arising from his superiors, writes to his friend, who was then filling the important post of Russian representative at Dantzig, asking him to come to his help. After having set forth all the disadvantages of his present situation, he speaks of his family, and tells him that his children, big and little, are born musicians. "With my family," he says, "I can already organize a concert, vocal and instrumental, especially since my wife sings a very lovely soprano, and my eldest daughter also sings her part very well." Many of the compositions of the master, notably the concerts for one or more harpsichords with orchestra and certain solo cantatas, were doubtless written with these family concerts in mind.

Bach lived long enough to witness the success of his sons. Friedemann became organist at Halle; Emmanuel, harpsichordist for Frederick the Great, and later, in 1767, chapel master at Hamburg, where he succeeded Telemann; Johann Christoph Friederich held the post of chamber musician for the Count of Lippe at Bückeburg; Johann Christian, who afterwards in 1769 was to succeed Händel in the post of chapel master for the Queen of England, was only fifteen at the death of his father. Bach had a high opinion of Johann Christian's gifts; he even gave him at one time three pedal harpsichords, which did not fail to arouse the jealousy of the older brothers. This same Johann Christian was at one time (1754) organist at the cathedral of Milan.

Only one of the daughters of Bach, Juliane Friederike, married: she became the wife of Altnikol (1720–1759), organist at Naumburg, one of the favorite pupils of the master. In the postscript to a letter dated October 6, 1748, Bach announced with a certain pride to his cousin Elias Bach that Emmanuel was the father of two sons, but he regretted that the elder should have been born at the time of the Prussian invasion of Saxony (1745): *"Mein Sohn in Berlin hat nun schon zwei männliche Erben, der erste ist ohngefähr um die Zeit geboren, da wir leider! die Preussische Invasion hatten; der andere ist etwa 14 Tage alt."*

His son's compositions interested him vitally. He copied with his own hand Friedemann's fine organ concerto in D minor, and it is difficult to say to whom this copy—it is kept in the Berlin Library—does the greater honor: the father or the son.

Friedemann had always been his favorite son; his manner of writing for the harpsichord and the organ, indeed, resembles that of Johann Sebastian. But the thirty cantatas he composed at Halle do not at all resemble his father's; one would rather say that they were works composed before the time of J. S. Bach. Emmanuel was less gifted than his brother, but conscientious and assiduous in his work.

It is he who transmitted to his generation Johann Sebastian's principles of touch and style. He constitutes an epoch in the history of music, for it is with him that modern piano technique begins. In his cantatas and in his oratorios he is modern in the fashion of his time. If he had had ideas we might consider him in a certain way the hyphen between Bach and Beethoven. Johann Christian, the "Bach of London," wrote a number of commonplace little operas. To speak truth, it seems that the old stock of the Bachs was exhausted in producing Johann Sebastian; if the sons were remarkable artists it is due less to their talent than to the solid instruction they had received from their father.

As for Wilhelm Friedemann, he would have been the despair of his father if the latter had lived long enough to witness his downfall. Strange and irascible, he had, moreover, an unfortunate craving for drink. In 1764 he resigned at Halle, and afterwards led the life of a Bohemian. His friends, who picked him up drunk on the street, tried vainly to help him by paying his debts and by seeking jobs for him: he only sank deeper and deeper. He abandoned his wife and children, to drag himself around from one village cabaret to another with his violin. The precious manuscripts which had come to him as his share were lost, or sold to the first comer for ridiculous sums. Nevertheless there were times when he recalled with pride that he was the son of the great Bach. They say that one day in an inn, having heard a musician remark that the violin sonatas of J. S. Bach could not be played, he picked up his violin and played them from memory, drunk though he was. He did not die until 1784; Emmanuel lived until 1786.[1]

Anna Magdalena herself survived her husband for ten years, and this in a state of complete destitution. The sons by the first marriage abandoned her completely. The way in which they distributed among themselves their father's manuscripts before the inventory hardly testifies to a very tender regard for their stepmother. In 1752, two years after the death of Bach, in order that she and her three daugh-

[1] See *Carl Philipp Emmanuel and Wilhelm Friedemann Bach*, by C. H. Bitter. Two volumes. Berlin 1868. By the same author, *Die Söhne J. S. Bachs. Sammlung musikalischer Vorträge* [The sons of J. S. Bach. Collection of Lectures on Music]. Breitkopf & Härtel.

ters might live, she had to ask for monetary help from the municipal council. And her poverty became even worse after that. She lived by alms, and died in a miserable house in the Hainstrasse. No one knows where she is buried. Regine Suzanna, the youngest of the daughters, who was eight years old at the death of Bach, lived until 1809. Rochlitz, the great admirer of the works of Bach, learned of her misery, and made an appeal to the generosity of his contemporaries for the benefit of the last of Bach's children. The first to send a contribution was—Beethoven.

2. BACH'S SITUATION AND DUTIES AT LEIPZIG

Bach lived in the left wing of St. Thomas School: it was the residence assigned to the cantor. After long hesitation he had decided to accept a situation which was in no sense an advancement for him. Doubtless it was an honor to succeed the celebrated Kuhnau; doubtless the prospect of being able to devote himself entirely to sacred music was pleasing to him; but what constraints awaited him! As the fourth professor, he was under the rector and the council; as the teacher of the choir, under the consistory of the church. One anticipates the complications and the disagreements that will inevitably arise when his independent spirit begins to crash against all these barriers. One cannot avoid a certain feeling of resentment in reading the deliberations which preceded his nomination and the contract he signed. A man of the distinction of Bach had to submit to almost humiliating conditions: he is forbidden to leave the city without the permission of the Burgomaster-regent; he has to participate in the funeral cortèges and march beside the St. Thomas choristers as they sing the chorale or the motet; besides, he is enjoined "to arrange music for the church services which shall be short and not similar to operas."

Let us not forget in fairness that the municipal council was looking only for a schoolteacher capable of directing church music; and it did not find this schoolteacher in Bach. We read, indeed, in the deliberations that preceded the nomination of his successor: "The school needs a cantor and not an orchestra leader; Herr Bach was a great musician, but he was not a schoolteacher." Their experience had been unfortunate.

At first it seemed as if everything was going for the best. Bach declared his willingness to give the five Latin lessons each week which were his responsibility in the third and fourth classes. Afterwards, however, with the consent of his superiors, he freed himself from this duty, and had his place taken by a colleague, who agreed to give the lessons in return for fifty thalers a year. When this substitute was prevented from being there, Bach himself took the class, and was content to dictate to his pupils an exercise to be worked out (ein Exercitum zum elaborieren), and then to monitor the class.

Unfortunately, the St. Thomas School was then in a deplorable condition. It dated from the thirteenth century, and had been founded by the Augustinians of St. Thomas. When the schools were secularized during the Reformation it became a communal school and was considerably enlarged. It counted fifty boarding scholars. It was recruited from the young people and the poor children of the city and the vicinity who wanted a schooling; they were brought up gratuitously, but were required to sing in the church choirs. Twice a week they went out singing from house to house, divided into four choruses; they shared the gifts they received as well as the money they got from marriages and burials among themselves, after the rector, the professor, and the cantor, of course, had taken out the portion that was theirs by right.

This schola cantorum was, one realizes, at the same time a schola pauperum; and its organization was very antiquated. The "Thomaner" had a bad reputation; discipline was not very strong among them. There were even some among them who roamed the streets barefoot to beg. The bad condition of the rooms in the boarding-school, and the irregular life of the choristers, led to frequent epidemics in the St. Thomas School. In short, at the beginning of the eighteenth century the establishment, once so celebrated and so prosperous, was in a state of complete decay. The good families did not send their children there any more. Of one hundred and twenty boarders which the three lower classes formerly counted, there remained in 1717 only fifty. The council in vain made surveys and issued orders for the reorganization of the studies; its efforts had no result. The rector Ernesti was a tired old man who passively resisted the reform efforts, which sought, above all, to abolish the collections. These reforms would have diminished his income and the income of the professors.

It was at this time that Bach began his work; the situation was evidently hardly brilliant, and it grew worse until the death of Ernesti (1729). In 1730 Bach presented a statement to the municipal council, in which he made it clear that it was impossible for him to give sacred music worthily in the churches of Leipzig because of the bad condition of the choirs.

Very slender, indeed, were the musical resources at his disposal. The churches were supporting only eight instrumentalists. To have a complete orchestra—Bach in his statement demanded eighteen musicians—the cantor had to depend upon students who played an instrument, and who consented to give their help regularly, either for love of the art or in the hope of pay. But in the time of Kuhnau St. Thomas had been abandoned more and more by the students. Kuhnau lacked initiative, and, moreover, was an open adversary of "modern" music in operatic style. On the contrary, Telemann, who was studying at Leipzig at the beginning of the eighteenth century, and held at the same time the post of organist at the Temple Neuf, was a representative of the new music. His concerts won great success among the students; he finally attracted them entirely to his side in founding the *Collegium musicum*, to the great loss of Kuhnau. The best of the St. Thomas choristers left to go to him, hoping to be engaged later through his help at the Leipzig opera or at the opera in Weissenfels. Telemann's departure brought no change in this state of things: his *Collegium musicum* remained the center of artistic life in Leipzig, and it was not until 1729, when Bach himself undertook to direct the society, that he was able to secure the support of the students.

Let us add, however, that the position of cantor had its advantages. The daily work was not too absorbing. Bach gave a singing lesson from noon until one o'clock every day except Thursday. Saturday afternoon he rehearsed the Sunday cantata, and on Sunday he directed the choirs either at St. Thomas or at St. Nicholas. The professor therefore had abundant leisure, by which the composer profited.

The boarding-school of St. Thomas provided choirs for four of the city churches: St. Thomas, St. Nicholas, the Temple Neuf, and St. Pierre. The fifty-five boarding pupils formed, therefore, four choirs. For St. Pierre they chose the worst. "To St. Pierre we send the rubbish, that is, those who know nothing about music and can hardly sing a chorale." This is the way Bach himself expresses it in his statement of 1730.

The choir at the Temple Neuf was numerically very small, for at least three voices for each part were needed in the choirs of the principal churches. "It would be desirable," Bach says in the same statement, "if we could take four 'subjects' for each part and have sixteen persons in each choir." The fact is that he gave the *St. Matthew Passion* with two choirs, each composed of twelve, at the most sixteen voices, soloists included, since it was the first choristers who gave the solos.

Each choir was directed by a prefect (*Praefectus*); it was the cantor's privilege to choose the prefects from among the best singers. The positions were very much desired, the prefects having a special part in the income of the choir. The cantor himself directed only the choir which rendered the cantata, the *Figuralmusik*, as they used to say. For the cantata, as for the Passions, the two churches alternated. One Sunday the cantor directed the cantata at St. Thomas and the first prefect directed the motet at St. Nicholas. The following Sunday the cantata was given at St. Nicholas and the first prefect directed the motet at St. Thomas. This alternation was scrupulously observed. One year Bach wanted to give the Passion at St. Thomas when it was the turn for St. Nicholas. The programs announcing that the Passion would take place at St. Thomas were already in the hands of the public: it could not be helped; he was forced to abandon his project.

A cantata was given each Sunday, except for the last three Sundays of Advent and the six Sundays of Lent. Let us add the cantatas for the three festivals of Mary, and those for the New Year, the Epiphany, the Ascension, St. John's Day, St. Michael's Day, and the festival of the Reformation: in all fifty-nine cantatas each year. If we suppose that Bach composed five cycles of cantatas (*Jahrgänge*), as the obituary states and as Forkel tells us, he would have written in all two hundred and ninety-five; about a hundred must have been lost, therefore, since we have only one hundred and ninety.

The service at the two leading Leipzig churches was perhaps, of all the Protestant services, that which most resembled the Catholic mass. In Saxony they were very conservative in respect to the liturgy. The details of the service are known in part to us, thanks to the notes that Bach wrote on the cover of the cantata "Nun komm der Heiden Heiland" [Come now, Savior of the Gentiles] which he gave on the first Sunday of Advent in 1714.[1] The service began at seven o'clock and ended about eleven. It was composed of the following two parts: prelude on the organ; motet; introit, Kyrie, intoning of the Gloria, to which the choir replied with "*et in terra pax*"; often also in place of the choir it was the congregation which sang in German the chorale of the Gloria. Then came the Epistle, followed by the German chorale, and the Gospel, with the intoning of the Credo; after the Credo, the organist preluded, to permit the tuning of the instruments. Upon a sign from the cantor he stopped, and then began the rendering of the cantata, which lasted on the average twenty minutes. The winter cantatas were in principle a little shorter than the summer ones. After the cantata, the congregation sang the Credo in German; then came the sermon, which lasted at least an hour.

The second part of the service was centered in the Holy Communion. After the close of the sermon several verses of a German chorale were sung, then the words of Jesus instituting the Lord's Supper were recited. During the Communion the chorales of the Last Supper were chanted, the different verses of which were interluded with long organ passages. Several of the great chorales of Bach

[1] Here are these interesting notes: "*Anordnung des Gottesdienstes in Leipzig am 1. Advent Sonntag frühe:* 1) *Praeludieret,* 2) *Motetta,* 3) *Praeludieret auf das Kyrie, so ganz musiciret wird,* 4) *Intoniret vor dem Altar,* 5) *Epistola verlesen,* 6) *Wird Litaney gesungen,* 7) *Praeludieret auf den Choral,* 8) *Envangelium verlesen,* 9) *Praeludieret auf die Hauptmusik,* 10) *Der Glaube gesungen,* 11) *Die Predigt,* 12) *Nach der Predigt, wie gewöhnlich einige Verse aus einem Liede gesungen,* 13) *Verba institutionis,* 14) *Praeludieret auf die Musik und nach selbiger wechselweise praeludieret und Choräle gesungen, bis die Communion zu Ende et sic porro.*"

were written to be played during the Communion, among others, the admirable, mystical chorale "*Schmücke dich, o liebe Seele*" [Adorn thyself, dear soul], (VII, No. 49).

After the main service came a shorter one, in which the music did not have an interesting part. Finally, during the vespers, which began at a quarter past one, a motet was rendered. On festival days the part played by the music was even greater. During the main service the *Kyrie* and the *Gloria* were executed by the choir, the *Sanctus* during the celebration of the Communion. At the Christmas vespers the *Magnificat* was sung, and at the Good Friday vespers a Passion. There was preaching at all the services—not only at the two morning services, but also at vespers. The passions were done in two parts, the first before, the second after the sermon in the Good Friday vespers.

The Church of St. Thomas was for a long time opposed to Passions in the modern style. We used to say that Kuhnau was the adversary of everything in the nature of theatrical music. The Passion which he finally wrote, giving way to popular taste, in the new style, and which was presented in 1721, proves to us how ill at ease he felt in a manner which did not please him; the rough draft of it which we have is very mediocre. Let us note in passing that the musical Passions disappeared from the services in Leipzig in the course of this same eighteenth century. The last of them was performed in 1766, or sixteen years after the death of Bach. He had arrived just in time to write the *St. Matthew Passion.*

On the whole, Bach found himself in the most favorable conditions for musical creation. The petty difficulties and disagreements in his work were not such as to impede his artistic activity. Unhappily the master was not the kind of person to surmount lightly the smallest difficulties. He ran headlong into them, creating in this way troubles that another, more calm and flexible than he, would have avoided. Moreover, he lacked ability to fulfill his duties to the satisfaction of himself and others; organization was the least of his talents. When he undertook something, it was with the impetuosity of genius. If those around him were not won by his enthusiasm, Bach felt himself powerless and disarmed. He had no knowledge of the means which would have permitted a deliberate and methodical spirit to arrive at a goal in spite of everything. For instance, he was unable to preserve the respect of his classes and choirs, and from this arose all the later unpleasantness. He had only the authority of genius, of the man who pursues an ideal. When this did not impress his pupils he was helpless: the authority of the simple schoolteacher was missing. Then everything went wrong and discouragement came. At Arnstadt they had already found fault with him for neglecting the choir. It was the same at Leipzig. More often than was justifiable he turned over his singing lessons to the first prefect. And more than once, also, he had to have recourse to the authority of the rector to maintain his own authority over the choristers. Under the first two rectors, Ernesti the elder (who died in 1729) and Gesner (1730–1734), everything went relatively well; they upheld him to the full extent of their power. But the third, Ernesti the younger (1734–1759), quarrelled with Bach about the nomination of a prefect. Abandoned by his superior, the master after that was in a very difficult position.

Let us not think, because of this, that his superiors were ill disposed to him. Certainly they were unable to appreciate at its true worth the greatness of their cantor; but in fairness let us remember that they did not cease to esteem Bach, and nothing could be found to bear witness to any intention on their part that was frankly malevolent. It was not possible for them to avoid the inevitable friction, given the independent spirit and aggressive temper of the cantor. Whenever he felt his right infringed upon in the slightest way in the world, he flamed up, and out of a mere bagatelle made a great fuss. It is doubtless true that he never defended anything except what was his right in the numerous quarrels which he conducted; yet one cannot justify the almost fanatical frenzy with which he fought.

He had hardly been installed before he began the battle.[1] Görner, the organist of St. Paul's Church, which was the church of the University, had profited by the weakness of Kuhnau to detach this church somehow from the authority of the cantor of St. Thomas, who was director general of sacred music for all the Leipzig churches. Formerly, cantatas were given at St. Paul's only on the festival days under the direction of the cantor of St. Thomas, who received on these occasions a special remuneration. Later, cantatas were intro-

[1] See Spitta, II, pp. 36 ff.

duced regularly; and when Bach arrived at Leipzig the custom had
been established of having the cantor direct the cantatas on the
festival days, while Görner conducted them on the ordinary Sundays,
both of them sharing in the honorarium allotted by the University.
The first thing that Bach did on his arrival was to attempt the impossible—to reëstablish the full authority of the cantor of St. Thomas,
and particularly to secure the full honorarium for himself. In September, 1725, he even addressed a petition directly to the King, who
had an investigation made and supported the request of the master,
without, however, succeeding, it appears, in ending the debate entirely in his favor; the proof of which is that Bach alternated with
his rival afterwards in composing the odes rendered at the solemn
ceremonies of the University. Later in 1730 Görner was even named
organist at St. Thomas, and vexed the master more than once by
his ignorance and his arrogance. As a matter of fact Görner did not
at all consider himself Bach's subordinate but his equal. In one
anecdote Bach during a rehearsal was so impatient with the organist
who was accompanying the cantata, that he is said to have pulled off
his peruke and hurled it in his face, shouting: "You ought to have
been a shoemaker!" If this anecdote is true, it may very well have
been Görner who received in his face Bach's peruke. After a while,
however, the two men came to understand one another; later we
shall see Görner figure as a tutor for Bach's four younger children,
which would be difficult to explain if the relations between them
had continued bad.

In 1727 the schoolmaster Gaudlitz, who filled the office of preacher
for the afternoon services, drew in his turn the wrath of the master.[1]
It was customary for the organist to choose among the chorales de
tempore the one they were to sing. In order to make them fit his
sermon the schoolmaster Gaudlitz preferred to choose them himself,
and requested the consent of Bach and the consistory. Neither of
them caused any difficulty. But a year later Bach withdrew his consent, and without warning had cantatas of his own choosing sung,
pretending to be ignorant of those the preacher had indicated. This
procedure was, of course, not correct. Gaudlitz complained to the

[1] See Spitta II, pp. 57 ff.

consistory, which took his part. Bach, on his side, sent a statement to the council defending "his rights." We do not know the issue of this affair, so typical of the tactics of the master, which consisted in arousing the council against the consistory, or the consistory against the council, and then profiting by the ensuing discussions to advance his own ideas. Even at the time of his installation jealousy had broken out between the two authorities: the council insisted that the representative of the consistory had taken upon himself an importance which did not belong to him, and they exchanged any number of notes on this subject without being able to come to an understanding.

In 1729 and in 1730 the relations between Bach and the council were very strained. Bach had to examine the pupils who were seeking admission to St. Thomas boarding-school, and it was well understood that those he did not consider to be musicians were not to be admitted. But in 1729, at the reopening after Easter, several weeks after the first rendition of the *St. Matthew Passion*, several boys whom Bach had declared too lacking in musical gifts were admitted, and others whose request he had supported by a good certificate were refused. Moreover, the council had withdrawn certain funds which until then had been at the disposal of the cantor and which had served to compensate the amateur students who were willing to give him their help. The consequences were not long in coming. The rendering of the music in the churches became worse and worse, and the council thought they were justified in complaining to Bach himself about it. It was during the session of August 2, 1730, that the general dissatisfaction against the master came to an explosion. They complained, among other things, that the colleague charged with giving the Latin lessons had neglected his duties, that Bach had left Leipzig without notifying the Burgomaster-regent, and that his singing lessons were very irregular. No one of the councillors took his part. The Syndic Job even added: "The cantor is incorrigible." They thereupon passed a vote of censure; and because they anticipated that this censure would leave him rather indifferent, they decided to withdraw a part of his extraordinary income originating in certain foundations in which the professors of St. Thomas shared. And the records of St. Thomas School show that in 1729 and 1730 Bach did not share at all in the extraordinary remuneration from which his colleagues benefited.

These proceedings could not fail to wound him deeply. Greedy as he was in matters of money—the Görner affair provides proof of that —he cherished for many years a rancor towards his superiors for having wished to attack him by measures of this kind. As to their reproach that he had permitted the music of the churches to fall into jeopardy, he refuted it in a curt and trenchant *mémoire* of August 23, 1730; [1] the defense followed closely the accusation. The master proves in it (with reason) that these same superiors, who set themselves up as his accusers, are themselves responsible for the bad condition of the choirs. Is it not they that admit the boarding pupils without paying any attention to their musical abilities, and is it not they also that withhold the funds intended to secure the assistance of students? "Not only," he adds, "have I a great number of incapable choristers, but worse still I have to take for the orchestra from among the capable ones those who know how to play an instrument. What then is there astonishing about the fact that the choirs should be so small and so bad? If I am deprived of the means, how can I remedy the evil?" And so seriously does he take his rôle of accuser that he even neglects the most elementary rules of politeness and respect which should be shown to superiors. His *mémoire* ends with a sharp statement: "In the present choir are seventeen capable persons, twenty who are not yet up to their task, and seventeen entirely incapable." Signed: "Bach"—no more. Certainly the council was not accustomed to read such *mémoires*. The Syndic Job was right: the cantor was incorrigible.

It was in this mood that the master wrote to his friend Erdmann the letter full of bitterness in which he begged him to find another post for him. He complains particularly of the material disadvantages of his situation. This situation had been represented to him as very advantageous, and at first sight it seemed indeed to be so: in addition to the lodging, they had offered him a fixed sum of about seven hundred thalers, and every special fee would bring him from one to two thalers. But when he arrived in Leipzig he perceived that life was

---

[1] "*Kurtzer, jedoch höchstnöthiger Entwurf einer wohlbestellten Kirchen-Musik: nebst einigen unvorgreiflichen Bedenken von dem Verfall derselben.*"

extremely dear there. "In Thuringia," he said, "I go farther with four hundred thalers than here with twice that." And besides, the fees were very uncertain. In 1729, for instance, since the "air was healthy" he lost about a hundred thalers because of the small number of deaths.

With what little things the great ones are associated! This year of 1729 is for us a blessed year: it is the year which gave us the St. Matthew Passion. To Bach it was a year that brought only unhappiness. One feels through this whole letter that the shabby treatment given him by the council has cut him to the quick: in resentment he wants to seek his fortune elsewhere.

Yet his financial situation was not at all bad. The inventory made after his death, and the luxury he allowed himself in instruments of music prove clearly that, in spite of the family expenses, he enjoyed a certain affluence. The truth is that Bach was niggardly in matters of money. Is there any better proof of it than the following anecdote? His cousin Elias Bach from Schweinfurth, in gratitude for the hospitality he had received at Leipzig, sent him a small barrel of cider. But it happened that when it arrived at Leipzig it had lost a third of its contents. Bach, in a letter of 1748, thanks him very amiably for his kindness, but in a postscript gives a detailed account of what he had to pay for carriage, excise, and town tax, and begs him not to send any such shipment in the future, "for, in these circumstances," he adds, "the cider cost me too much to be considered a gift." [1]

Fortunately the new rector, Gesner, was an admirer of Bach's and sincere friendship soon bound the two men together. Using his influence with the members of the council, Gesner had the master liberated from his class work, and secured a restoration of his right in the distribution of the gifts. But the benevolence of the rector was in no way a sufficient guarantee in the mind of Bach. Already he had addressed himself directly to the Dresden court in the affair Görner; this time, to protect himself forever against these vexations,

---

[1] Here is the postscript: "Ohnerachtet der Herr Vetter sich geneigt offerrieren fernerhin mit desgleichen liqueur zu assistiren; so muss doch wegen übermässiger hiesiger abgaben es depriciren, denn da die Fracht 16 gr., der Überbringer 2 gr., der Visitator 2 gr., die Landacise 5 gr., 3 Pf. und general accise 3 gr. gekostet hat; als können der Herr Vetter selbsten ermessen, dass mir jedes Mass fast 5 gr. zu stehen kömt, welches denn vor ein Geschenke allzu kostbar ist."

he sought from the King–Elector, his sovereign, the title of Court Composer. Like his compatriots in general, he attached a certain importance to titles. Though Kuhnau, for instance, had been called simply "cantor," Bach, particularly in his relations to the council, felt it a bit humiliating to bear this subordinate title. He called himself preferably *Director Musices*, or *Director Musices et Cantor*; and at the top of his compositions he never failed to signalize his titles of Bandmaster to the Cöthen Court and the Weissenfels Court. But the titles which he had from these little princes hardly impressed his superiors. The important thing for the master, therefore, was to be attached to the court of the sovereign of the country. So we find him from this moment intriguing to obtain the coveted title of Court Composer.

In the request he makes July 27, 1733, of Augustus III, King of Poland and Elector of Saxony, he frankly confesses the practical reasons that lead him to seek the title in question. He dedicates to him the *Kyrie* and the *Gloria* of the *Mass in B minor*, the only parts of the great work which were then finished, begging him to deign to accept his "poor work" and not to judge him by this "bad composition" but in accordance with his celebrated kindness, and to take the composer "under his powerful protection." "For several years now," he continues, "I have been directing the music in the two principal churches of Leipzig; several times, without any justification, I have had to submit to vexations; they have even cut the incidental income which goes with my duties; all this will stop, if your Royal Highness will grant me the favor of conferring upon me a title which will attach me to the court chapel." In 1733, that is, he still remembers with bitterness the measures they had taken against him in 1730, though these had been rescinded for two years. Futile pains! In vain he reminded his sovereigns of his ambitions by many an occasional cantata written in their honor: he had to wait three years more before he received the nomination desired. The disorders in Poland required the presence of the King–Elector, who was absent from November 3, 1734, to August 7, 1736. Finally, on November 19, 1736, Bach received the decree which made him Court Composer for the Royal Chapel. This nomination arrived just in time to strengthen his case in a new strife with his superiors.

In 1734 Gesner had been called as professor to Göttingen, and a young scholar of great distinction—called Ernesti, like Gesner's predecessor—became rector of the St. Thomas School. The reorganization of the studies which Gesner had undertaken was very much on his heart. But he lacked his predecessor's tact. Besides, having no interest in art, he considered the time the students gave to music as lost from their studies—not without reason, of course. Everything went well, however, at the beginning. The rector and the cantor even became close friends, and Bach chose Ernesti as the godfather of his son Johann Christian, born in 1735. But in 1736 Ernesti inflicted a very grave punishment on the first prefect, Gottfried Theodor Krause, because he had corrected the choristers, perhaps too severely, for misbehaving during a marriage ceremony. Bach, who held Krause in great esteem, interceded in his favor, but in vain; Krause had to leave the school before he had completed his studies. In his place the rector promoted another Krause to the post of first prefect, Johann Gottlob Krause, of whom Bach did not think very highly; a year before, when the position of fourth prefect had become vacant and Ernesti had proposed him for this post, the master had observed that he was a scamp—in his energetic manner of expression "ein leiderlicher Hund"; but since he was in good spirits that evening, coming back in a carriage with Ernesti from a wedding feast, he interposed no objection to the nomination. Neither did he have anything more to say when Krause was promoted to be third and then second prefect. He even raised no objection—as he had a right to— when Ernesti made Krause the successor to his namesake. But several weeks later Bach abruptly dismissed him; and from this point an affair began which dragged on for more than two years. Ernesti rightly said that Bach should have made his objections earlier, at the time of the nomination; moreover, he was wounded by the uncomplimentary remarks Bach had made about him in the presence of this same Krause. Bach, on his side, insisted that it was for him and not for the rector to name the prefects. This was the way Bach had behaved in the Gaudlitz affair: he let things go, and then one fine day he remembered "his rights."

The rector restored Krause to his place; but when the latter presumed to direct the motet Bach drove him away in the midst of the service. At vespers the rector mounted to the organ loft and forbade the choristers to sing under the direction of any other prefect except Krause; but Bach chased Krause away again. And this was not the end. Bach began again his old tactics, arousing the consistory against the council; but this time he did it maladroitly, and the consistory remained on its guard. The Leipzig archives have preserved the innumerable letters and *mémoires* which Bach and Ernesti, one after the other, addressed to the council, during the two years through which this unfortunate affair dragged.[1] In them, Bach appears as hotheaded, blinded by his prejudice, but always right. Ernesti is prudent, and remains the master of the situation; profiting, perhaps too skillfully from the point of view of loyalty, from the blunders of the cantor. We wonder how Bach could have behaved that way in a matter of such little basic importance, especially since he was the first to suffer for it. The choristers exploited the dissension between the rector and the cantor, and it became almost impossible for Bach to maintain discipline. Even several of his ecclesiastical superiors, who at bottom wished him well, were vexed at the trouble he was causing them and withdrew their sympathy; among others the superintendent and president of the consistory, Deyling, a man of remarkable personality, who up to that point had had great regard for him and had always to the best of his ability upheld him.

In spite of his title of Court Composer, Bach therefore saw himself like Ernesti causing trouble to others. Since Krause was to finish his studies by Easter 1737 they kept him in his place until that time. But after his departure the undiscouraged Bach again began the fight. He wanted to have full liberty to make nominations at his pleasure. Even more: he insisted that Ernesti make official apologies to him in order to restore his authority over the pupils. On October 18, 1737, he addressed a petition to the King, who immediately sent an order to the consistory to make an investigation. By February, 1738, it was not completed; at Easter the King came to Leipzig with the Queen, and Bach directed some evening music in the square in honor of the sovereigns. We do not have this music, but we know from an article published in 1739 that it made an excellent impres-

---

[1] Spitta has reproduced them *in extenso*. See Vol. II, pp. 893–912.

sion. The King doubtless intervened at that time in favor of Bach, for from this time on we do not find any further reference to this affair. Ernesti remained rector, and made all kinds of difficulties for the master. The other professors took Ernesti's part, and showed a haughty disdain for everything that pertained to music in the school. When Ernesti found a pupil studying the violin, he did not fail to make fun of him; this is reported to us in the history of the Leipzig schools by the pastor Friedrich Köhler.

Thus the moral authority of Bach was done for at the school, with the pupils as with the professors. We may say with no fear of exaggeration that this affair spoiled for him the last ten years of his life. He felt himself abandoned and isolated at Leipzig; he would have looked for another situation had he been a younger man. He was compelled to resign himself to live in the milieu of St. Thomas as a stranger. What was being done at Leipzig did not interest him any more. Therefore he remained outside the great musical movement which took place in this city at precisely this epoch. In 1743—to cite only this one fact—a new concert society was founded, which had a great success, and which later, in 1781, gave birth to the society of the Gewandhaus Concerts. Bach showed no interest in this enterprise, which, as it developed, was to place Leipzig in the first rank of musical centers in the entire world.

3. The Amiability and Modesty of Bach

Let us not believe, however, that Bach had a mean character. The ferocious sensitiveness which he displayed the moment he felt his independence threatened did not prevent his being a very agreeable person to deal with. Of this there is unanimous testimony. He was above everything else upright, incapable of an injustice. No one, moreover, questioned his impartiality. In his organ appraisals he was severe and meticulous; no detail escaped him, and he pointed out, without deference to anyone, what seemed to him to be badly done. Forkel said very finely on this matter: "Whether it was a question of an organ appraisal or a competition of organists, he was so conscientious and impartial that the number of his friends hardly grew because of it." His strict justice, indeed, made enemies for him: Scheibe, for instance. The fact that Scheibe was the son of the celebrated organ manufacturer did not help him at all when he competed for the place of organist at St. Thomas, which had become vacant in 1729: the master, in his impartiality, was compelled to decide in favor of that same Görner with whom he had had a bone to pick in respect to the University church. Scheibe took his revenge later in a malevolent criticism which he published in the Hamburg "Kritische Musicus" in 1737. Stung though he was by the proceeding, Bach did not modify afterwards his most flattering praise for the organs of Scheibe, the father.

But Bach was more than impartial: he was benevolent. When he thought that an organ was well made, Forkel tells us, and that the profit of the constructor was not at all in proportion to his work, he sometimes requested for him a larger compensation. The certificates he gave as recommendations to young organists and to singers witness this benevolence. To this natural amenity was joined a modesty which made him sympathetic with all who approached him. If his pride made him haughty and even offensive towards people he suspected, rightly or wrongly, of considering him as some kind of subordinate, his simplicity and modesty were just as great, the moment this independence no longer seemed in jeopardy.

It was not at all that hypocritical and vain modesty which celebrated men sometimes affect, but a healthy and robust modesty, which was sustained by the knowledge of his worth. This is what gives his modesty its moral worth and grandeur. He never ceased to remain dignified even when writing to kings. The petitions he addressed to the King–Elector, his sovereign, are written in a very submissive style; but through the formulas of extreme deference which the times demanded breathes something of pride and resolution. We read between the lines: "I, J. S. Bach, have the right to make this request of you." Very different is the tone of the letter which accompanies the dispatch of the *Musikalische Opfer* [Musical Offering] to Frederick the Great. Bach speaks to him as to an equal, while respecting his royal dignity. He explains to him that, since his improvisation has not succeeded as he wished, he has felt the need of "elaborating the royal theme in a more profound way, and to make it known to the world with the sole purpose," he continues, "of enhancing, if only at one point, the glory of a monarch whose greatness and strength are admired by all the world, not simply in respect to the sciences of war and peace [*in allen Kriegs- und Friedenswissenschaften*], but also, and especially, in music." If we undress this sentence, and take off the refined politeness with which it is clothed, what have we left? Johann Sebastian Bach is proud to honor His Majesty Frederick the Great by publishing a fugue on a subject which he has devised.

With the exception of his pupils, he treated all artists as equals. Forkel tells us that he would not permit anyone to speak about the Marchand story before him. Here in a few words is the episode. Jean Louis Marchand (1669–1732), the "King's organist," had fallen into disgrace, and had been compelled to leave Paris temporarily. In 1717 he interrupted his travels at Dresden, where he had a great success. Some of the court persons, lovers of music, got the idea of organizing a musical competition between him and Bach. But on the appointed day they waited for Marchand in vain. Fearing defeat, he had left the city without a word, ceding the victory to his great opponent. Bach would not suffer anyone to allude to this triumph. Thus he honored himself, and at the same time respected his adversary.

When he was asked how he had attained such perfection in his art, he replied simply, "I had to apply myself; whoever applies himself in the same way will arrive at the same result."

Never, in his judgments of other people, did he depart from this kindly justice. There is no single instance of his having passed a severe criticism on the composition or the playing of a confrère, in spite of his pretentious vanity. One day he had a visit from a certain Hurlebusch of Braunschweig, a peripatetic virtuoso who was eager to be heard by Bach. The latter listened patiently; and when Hurlebusch left he gave a volume of sonatas, doubtless of his own composition, to the two sons of Bach, and urged them to study them well for their profit, not knowing how far advanced they already were in the art. The master must have smiled inwardly; but he never varied in the slightest from his amiability towards his visitor. Forkel lays great emphasis on all these signs of modesty. Doubtless the sons of

Bach were eager to have this side of the paternal character brought into view.

Even if these anecdotes were lacking, his attitude towards Händel alone would suffice to show how much Bach could admire all that was great and forget all personal vanity. If he never became acquainted with his great compatriot and contemporary, at least he did everything possible to meet him. Händel went from England to his native city of Halle three times, first about 1719. Bach was still at Cöthen, about four leagues from Halle. Bach immediately set out to visit him, but when he arrived Händel had just departed. The second time was in 1729; Bach was already at Leipzig, but he was ill. He sent Wilhelm Friedemann at once to invite Händel to come to see him. Händel sent his regrets that he was not able to accept the invitation. At the time of Händel's third sojourn,—in 1752 or 1753— Bach was already dead. It was one of Bach's regrets that he had never been able to make the acquaintance of his great rival. It was not that he would ever have thought of measuring himself against him; though in Germany they would like to have seen the two celebrated musicians pitted against each other, and discussed in advance Händel's chances on the organ, over the technique of which Bach had such superlative mastery.

But what better proof is there of this great modesty than the copies he made of Palestrina, Frescobaldi, Lotti, Caldara, Ludwig and Bernhard Bach, Händel, Telemann, Keiser, Grigny, Dieupart, and others—not only at the time when he considered himself still a pupil of these masters, but at the time when he had become a master himself? He disdained them so little that he took the time to copy their works; and, moreover, what has come down to us certainly represents only a small part of all that he copied. Seeing him copy the cantatas of Telemann, we wonder why he was not halted many times by his critical sense. The answer is that he was dealing with recognised masters; he respected them and copied them. A similar good fortune would not have occurred if the original score of the St. Matthew Passion had been lost; none of the contemporary masters had taken the pains to copy it.

4. Concert Trips; Criticisms and Friends

Modest as he was, Bach was eager to make himself known; each year as autumn came he undertook a kind of small concert trip. We have very little information about these expeditions. About 1714 we find him at Kassel, where he is heard on the organ. A pedal solo which he played before Prince Frederick so astonished the future King of Sweden that he took a precious ring from his finger and gave it to Bach as a souvenir of this occasion. The anecdote is told us by a certain Bellermann, rector at Minden, in his treatise on music (1743).

A year before, in 1713, Bach performed at Halle, with such great success that they wanted to make him accept at any price the place of Zachau (1663–1712), Händel's master, at the *Liebfrauenkirche*. Since they were constructing there a superb organ with sixty-three stops, Bach was easily persuaded to enter into negotiations with them. He even composed a cantata to show what he could do; but when the moment came to make a decision, he declined. The Halle council held a grudge against him for leaving them in suspense for more than a year; they went so far as to reproach him for having broached the matter for the sole end of obtaining a raise in salary at Weimar. We still have a letter from Bach which denies these insinuations very energetically, insisting that he had really refused, only because the information he had obtained showed that the proffered increase in salary did not seem sufficient to justify the change. Here is a new proof that Bach did not consider money questions as merely incidental in life—and did not conceal the fact either. This trait of character must have been very pronounced; for later Ernesti in a *mémoire* written about the Krause case was to go so far as to insinuate that a thaler never failed to have its effect when one wanted a certificate from Bach. The accusation, of course, had no justification; and it reacted upon the one responsible for it.

In December, 1714, Bach came to Leipzig to give his cantata *Nun komm, der Heiden Heiland* [Come now, Savior of the Gentiles] (No. 61); during the service he played the organ. We do not insist that this journey, concerning which there has been considerable discussion, actually took place. In 1717 we find him again at Halle.

The council had forgotten its grievance against him, and when at last the organ was finished they begged him to come and appraise it. Bach replied with a very polite letter, and considered it an honor to accept the invitation.[1] In 1715 or 1716 he had to appear at the court of Meiningen, but we lack precise information about this journey. We know of the journey of 1717, when he met Marchand at Dresden. Not only did this success make him famous in all of Germany, but at the Dresden court it also made a good impression which afterwards stood him in good stead at Leipzig.

The sojourn at Cöthen was interrupted by numerous journeys. His duties left him a great deal of leisure, and, moreover, his prince took him with him on his travels. In July, 1720, for instance, Bach had to accompany him to Carlsbad, and it was on his return from this journey that he learned to his sorrowful surprise of the death of his wife. Three years before, in 1717, he had been for the second time to Leipzig, having to make an appraisal of the new organ at the church of St. Paul. This organ had been constructed by Scheibe, who until then had passed as a rather ordinary organ builder; but the laudatory official report Bach wrote after the appraisal placed Scheibe at once among the first master builders of the sacred instrument. This organ at St. Paul was the most perfect and the most complete of all the Leipzig organs, and Bach used it by preference whenever strangers came to ask him to play for them.[2]

Once installed at Leipzig, Bach continued his custom of making an artistic journey at least once a year. He went on several occasions to play before the friendly courts of Cöthen and Weissenfels. In 1727 we find him at Hamburg; a little later at Erfurt.

The opera often attracted him to Dresden, where he was usually accompanied by Wilhelm Friedemann. When his favorite son was installed in his post as organist at the Ste. Sophie church in Dresden in 1733, he had one more reason for coming frequently to the "para-

[1] See this letter in Spitta, I, p. 514.
[2] Note the arrangements of the Leipzig organs in Spitta II, pp. 111–118. The great organ in St. Thomas had three manuals, with thirty-six stops; the organ at St. Nicholas also numbered thirty-six stops distributed over three manuals; but the new organ at St. Paul had fifty stops on three manuals. It had an excellent mechanical action, for Scheibe had an inventive spirit and had made several very happy discoveries.

dise of musicians," as they called Dresden, the German city where
artists were the most munificently paid. Bach doubtless did not lack
a certain envy of posts so generously remunerated. In one of his
letters addressed to the Leipzig council he complains, among other
things, about the inequality of treatment of the musicians of Leipzig
and those of Dresden.

Of all his good friends among the court musicians, those who
attracted him the most were Adolphe Hasse and his wife Faustina,
the noted *cantatrice*. Hasse in July 1731 had been called to Venice to
direct the royal opera. On the morning of the *première* of *Cléo-
phide* (September 13), an event of which all Germany was talking,
Bach, who had come to Dresden for the occasion, was heard on the
organ of Ste. Sophie before the entire *Kapelle*. In 1736, after his
nomination as Court Composer, he returned to Dresden and gave
an organ concert at the *Liebfrauenkirche*. A select and numerous
company came to hear him. How many times he must have compared
the singing of the admirable soloists in the Dresden opera with the
way the choristers of St. Thomas rendered his songs! We do not
know whether he heard one or more of his compositions sung by
Faustina; this was not impossible, in view of the friendship between
them. Hasse and Faustina went several times to visit him at Leipzig.

His last journey took him to the court of Frederick the Great.
The King, Forkel tells us, had on several occasions expressed to
Emmanuel Bach, who had been in his service since 1738, the desire
to see his father. Finally, in 1747, Bach set out with Wilhelm
Friedemann. Frederick II had the habit of looking every evening
through the list of the strangers who had recently arrived. One evening, when he was preparing to play a piece on the flute, he saw on
the report the name of Johann Sebastian Bach. "Gentlemen," he
said to the artists gathered for the chamber concert, "old Bach has
arrived." He put down his flute and sent for Bach, who, without
having had time even to change his costume, was forced to present
himself with his greatcoat and his dusty shoes. Then began, so
Forkel says, a long and lively conversation between the artist, who
wanted to excuse himself, and the royal host, who wanted to cut
short his excuses. The flute was not taken up again that evening.
Bach had to play on all the Silbermann pianofortes, of which the

King had fifteen. After having played several improvisations, Bach asked for a fugue subject. When the royal theme had been developed, Frederick wished to hear a six-part fugue. Bach remarked that not every subject could be treated properly in six parts, and begged that he might have a free choice. The fugue he thereupon executed stunned the King. The next day he had to make a tour of all the organs in Potsdam; they had him visit Berlin also. When he got back to Leipzig, he wrote the *Musikalische Opfer* [Musical Offering] on the theme given him by the King, and dedicated it to him.

His superiors did not regard with a very favorable eye the frequent absences of the cantor. "Herr Bach," it is stated in the records of the famous session of August 2, 1730, "has gone on a journey without asking leave of the Burgomaster-regent." It was another such journey, undertaken in July 1736, which helped to provoke the conflict with Ernesti; moreover, in his reports to the council the rector did not fail to mention the frequent absences of Bach; and we learn, incidentally, that at such times the organist of the Temple Neuf conducted the cantata in his place. We may presume that these observations made no impression whatever on Bach. He needed these journeys to get his breath again, and to escape from the petty troubles and restrictions from which he suffered at Leipzig.

The modesty and amiability of the man, as well as the skill of the virtuoso, made Bach universally famous. From 1717—that is, from the time of his triumph over Marchand—he was placed among the glories of Germany, and benefited by the jealousy the German musicians felt for the French and Italian musicians, who everywhere occupied the best places.[1] The Germans were proud of being able at last to set over against them an invincible adversary. German patriotism, which had not yet appeared in the field of politics, was awake in the field of art. Until that time the superiority of foreign music, and especially of foreign *virtuosi*, had never been questioned. Frederick the Great was not even willing to admit that good German *cantatrici* could exist, any more than, even in Lessing's time, he was willing to admit that there was a German literature. Bach therefore became a kind of musical hero. There were only two heroic figures

---

[1] Read the *Musikalische Quacksalber* [Musical Charlatan] of Kuhnau (1770) to see the state of mind of German artists towards their French colleagues.

yet in the eighteenth century: Luther and he; the third, the man who was to create German philosophy, Kant, was still unknown. Frederick the Great died without suspecting the greatness of the simple Königsberg professor.

National pride even silenced personal jealousies. Mattheson, who, far from celebrating the greatness of Bach, had always taken satisfaction in criticizing certain of his works in a manner which had in it little of kindness, could not help exalting Bach after his death as a representative of the national genius, exhorting all foreign artists to risk their *louis d'or* in buying *The Art of the Fugue*, which had just then appeared.

At a time when the great minds of Germany, the Goethes and the Hegels, fascinated by the appearance of Napoleon I, were still far from conceiving the idea of a German nation such as was to be born in the course of the nineteenth century, Forkel, the first biographer of Bach, dedicates his work to the "patriotic admirers of the true art of music"; and in the preface he speaks at length about the national character of his enterprise. "The works which John Sebastian Bach has left us," he says, "are a national patrimony of incommensurable value; no other people could match it with a similar work." And farther on, "To cherish the vivid memory of this great man—let me be permitted to say it once again—is not only an artistic duty, but a national duty." The personality of Bach plays, then, an important rôle in the revival of national feeling in Germany. The moment when the remains of the ancient Germanic empire were being reduced to crumbs, like the remnants of Wotan's sword, is precisely the moment when artistic Germany is inaugurating the cult of Bach.

This means that Bach did not have to strive to win the place in German thought to which he was entitled; his fame did it for him. Let us note, however, that the composer of the cantatas and Passions hardly enjoyed at all the celebrity of a *virtuoso*. No one, not even his enemies, contested the fact that he was the prince of harpsichordists and the king of organists; but no one either, not even his intimate friends, imagined the true greatness of the composer.

The adverse criticisms he had to endure while he was alive came from ill-disposed persons whom he had wounded without knowing it.

We may suppose that the remarks of Mattheson on the cantata "*Ich hatte viel Bekümmernis*" [I suffered great affliction], No. 21, did not affect him profoundly, if indeed he had any knowledge of them. But the criticism of Scheibe, which appeared in 1737 in the *Kritische Musicus* at Hamburg, and which stirred up a polemical literature that lasted for several years, did not fail to wound him to the quick. We cannot say that this criticism, so interesting in every respect, was stupid, for Scheibe did not lack intellect. He did not attack the greatness of the *virtuoso*, but criticized the composer for lacking gracefulness and naturalness. "Bach obscures the beauty of his works by an excess of art. Moreover," the critic continues, "they are too difficult; Bach judges only by his own fingers, and wants the singers and instrumentalists to do with their voices and their instruments what he does with his fingers on the keyboard. Again, he permits no latitude to the player, because he expresses exactly in his notes all the *manières* and all the little ornaments. In short, he is bombastic; which is what leads him from the natural to the artificial, from the sublime to the obscure. We admire the difficult work, although it comes to nothing, because he fights against reason." This criticism is in music what the famous criticism formulated by the Garve–Feder against the *Critique of Pure Reason* was to be later in philosophy. Both give evidence of unusual sagacity, but both also prove in the end only how little their contemporaries were capable of judging the greatness of a Bach or a Kant.

Scheibe is perhaps the first to become aware of the radical difference between Bach and his contemporary composers. Scheibe has sensed something irrational in this art, something that remains inexplicable, as long as one judges Bach from the standpoint of the musicians of his time. This clairvoyance does him honor; the criticism of that time was putting the master in the same class as Mattheson and Telemann, thinking thus to render him the highest praise. It is still with the same meaning that a year later Scheibe expresses his ideas about the Bach cantatas in particular. Unfortunately, in what follows he lets himself be dragged into purely personal invective, and the critic finishes as a pamphleteer. But in 1730, and later still in 1745, realizing that a procedure so little worthy of the great-

ness of Bach was in no sense an honor to himself, he made a kind of
amende honorable in the same Kritische Musicus.

As it usually turns out, these unjust criticisms were to redound to
the honor of Bach, and to make the musical world unanimous in
their admiration of him; Mattheson himself disapproved openly of
Scheibe. A certain Magister Birnbaum, professor of rhetoric at the
University of Leipzig, published in Bach's defense two writings
which bear witness more to his good will than to his real knowledge of
the subject. And it was thus with all the adulation showered on Bach
at the time: it teaches us very little; it is purely eulogistic. Gesner, the
former rector of St. Thomas, for example, speaking about Bach in an
annotated edition of the Institutiones oratoriae of Quintilian which
he published in 1738, pictures the master at the harpsichord, at the
organ and directing his orchestra, and then ends in this way: "For
the rest, I am a great admirer of antiquity, but I believe that in my
friend Bach, and in those who perhaps resemble him, there are contained several artists the equal of Orpheus and twenty singers like
Arion." This testimony of friendship and sincere admiration which his
former rector paid him must have at least comforted Bach; it came at
the time when the master was embittered by his fight with Ernesti.

A man named Friedrich Hudemann, a docteur-en-droit at Hamburg, and at the same time a remarkable musical dilettante, sang
Bach's praises in a poem he published in 1732. It plays among the
ancient allegories like the eulogies of Gesner, and like them also it is
addressed particularly to the organ virtuoso.[1] He knew Bach personally, and Bach must have had some esteem for him, judging by the
canon he dedicated to him in 1727.

Bach, then, was esteemed and fêted. Does this mean that he had
many truly intimate friends?

---

[1] Ludwig Friedrich Hudemann: Proben einiger Gedichte, Hamburg, 1732.
"An Herrn Kapellmeister J. S. Bach:
      Wenn vor gar langer Zeit des Orpheus Harfenklang
      Wie er die Menschen traf, sich auch in Tiere drang,
      So muss es, grosser Bach, weit schöner dir gelingen,
      Es kann nur deine Kunst vernünftge Seelen zwingen.
      Apollo hat dich längst des Lorbeers wert geschätzt;
      Du aber kannst allein, durch die beseelten Saiten,
      Dir die Unsterblichkeit, vollkommner Bach, bereiten."

He remained in constant contact with numerous people: Hasse and Faustina Hasse, Graun, Gesner, Birnbaum, Telemann, and many others; his pupils remained attached to him, and never missed an occasion to show their warm affection for him, in which was mingled pride in having been disciples of such a master; even princes, like Prince Leopold of Cöthen, the Duke Ernst August of Weimar, and the Duke of Weissenfels, treated him as a friend. Forkel, on the testimony of Bach's sons, states positively that these sovereigns showed him a cordial affection. Faithful to the traditions of the family, Bach kept in contact with all his numerous relations, and received into his home all the Bachs who came to study at Leipzig.

But these were not intimate friendships. Did Bach feel a more intense need of them? It hardly seems so. His intimates were in his family; his confidants were his wife and his elder sons. His greatness, the burden of his work, in which his thoughts were always immersed, hardly permitted him to have other friendships, and necessarily made of him a creature who was "distant" to others. His impetuous and irascible character, finally, made an intimate friendship with him somewhat dangerous. The real reason for the coolness that developed between him and Walther, as well as his rupture with Ernesti, was his cantankerousness and his stubbornness in never admitting that he was wrong. One cannot deny that the rector acted with loyalty, even with kindness, until the moment when Bach, without any apparent reason, attacked him personally.

5. THE SELF-TAUGHT MAN AND THE PROFESSOR

In the course of his polemic, Scheibe dared to say that Bach's general culture was not what one would expect of a great composer. What are we to think about this accusation?

Bach, let us say, was a cultured man. The lycée of Ohrdruff, where he began his studies, and even that of Lüneburg, where he finished them, had a great reputation. It is to be presumed that when he left Lüneburg he had completed the two years of rhetoric which would have opened the doors of the University to him, had it not been for the hard necessity of earning a living. Bach therefore had to rest content with what he had been able to get from the Gymnasium.

He was very familiar with Latin; his letters and his *mémoires* bear witness to that. Otherwise, when his appointment at Leipzig was being discussed, would he have declared himself ready to give Latin lessons to the third and fourth classes? We even get the impression that there was a certain pride in this declaration, after his rivals had admitted that they did not possess the requisite knowledge. His grasp of the vocabulary of rhetoric, to which the musical explanations he gave his students bear witness, prove that rhetoric as it was taught in those days was not at all strange to him. Moreover, *Magister* Birnbaum, himself a professor of rhetoric, taking up Bach's defence against Scheibe, insists that Bach, in his lessons and in his conversations, liked to dwell upon the analogies between rhetoric and musical theory. Therefore on the whole Bach possessed a good classical education. And like all cultured people of that time, he had a certain knowledge of French and Italian. The foreign words people were accustomed to misuse in those days when writing German are always employed by the master in the most correct way; the addresses of his letters are often written entirely in French. For example:

"A Monsieur A. Becker, Licencié en Droit, Mon très honoré ami à Halle."

Or again:

"A Monsieur S. E. Bach, Chanteur et Inspecteur du Gymnase à Schweinfourth."

But even in default of such proofs, the value which scholars like Gesner and Birnbaum placed upon his society and his conversation would have sufficed to establish the fact that Bach was in no sense solely a man of his art. Would he have attached so much importance to his sons receiving a good education, if he had not had himself the taste and the respect for intellectual culture?

Unfortunately, the best way of determining what books he read is missing. Since his eldest two sons had set aside beforehand all the books having to do with sciences in general and the theory of music in particular, as they had set aside also the musical scores, in order to divide them, the inventory mentions only the books on theology. But this little catalogue in itself witnesses to the scientific turn of Bach's mind. Besides the devotional books we find all the current theological publications; Bach therefore was interested in the religious questions that were being discussed around him. Moreover, the same little catalogue mentions two big editions of the works of Luther.

Should we be astonished, knowing Bach's character, that polemical literature should be abundantly represented? But we find here even Josephus' *History of the Jews!* Imagine Bach reading attentively the classic work of the friend of Vespasian!

The criticism of Scheibe, therefore, falls as false. Yet in reproaching Bach for being too little versed in the general studies related to music, he really expressed awkwardly an idea which at bottom was correct. Bach was a self-taught man, and as such he had a horror of all superfine theories. He had had no professor of the harpsichord, nor of the organ, nor of harmony, nor of composition; it was only by incessant toil and by constantly repeated exercises that he had learned the fundamental rules of his art.

This is to say that many of the theories and much of the reasoning on the art of music, strange or even new to others, had no interest for Bach, because he had seen to the heart of things. For example, he gave no weight to all the speculation on the mathematics and mutual relations of harmonics. This indifference of the master to these alleged discoveries must have been pronounced, for Mattheson says in one of his writings that in the lessons in harmony Bach gave there was certainly never any question of mathematical speculations. And indeed the teaching of the master at this point was summary: "Two fifths and two octaves may not follow each other; that is not only a *vitium* [1] but it also sounds bad." And that is all. This phrase is found in the copy of a course on the figured bass which he gave his students in 1738; he had doubtless dictated it as it stands. "But it also sounds bad." Can you not see him walking up and down in his class, his face illuminated with a superbly ironic smile?

His indifference to all the erudite enterprises in the field of music comes out clearly in his attitude regarding the Mizler Society. Lorenz Christophe Mizler, born in 1711, had studied at the University of Leipzig at the same time that he was studying the harpsichord and composition with Bach. To obtain the degree of *Magister* he published in 1734 a dissertation, "*Quod musica ars sit pars eruditionis*

[1] *Vitium* (Latin) means "fault." C. R. J.

philosophicae," which he dedicated to four musicians, among them Mattheson and Bach. In 1736 he inaugurated courses on mathematics, philosophy, and music, and founded at the same time a historical review called *Neu eröffnete musikalische Bibliothek* (1736–1744). The *Societät der musikalischen Wissenschaften* dates from 1738.

This Society proposed to reform the art by drawing up a system of musical science. Telemann became a member in 1740; Händel was made an honorary member in 1745; but Bach was so little interested in it that in spite of Mizler's urging he did not decide to seek a membership in it until June 1747. Since it was necessary to furnish some work in order to acquire the right of membership in the Society, he presented some canon variations on the Christmas carol *"Vom Himmel hoch, da komm ich her"* [From high heaven I come down], which he had engraved after he had revised them carefully.[1] The purpose of these variations explains their abstract and strictly scientific character. It is to this circumstance also that we owe the detailed obituary of Bach which appeared in the *Musikalische Bibliothek* of 1754, and a portrait in oil made by the court painter Hausmann. This portrait represents Bach holding in his hand a paper on which is inscribed the canon he presented at his entrance. Are we then indebted to this Society? Or rather is not the Society indebted to Bach? Without him, who today would know anything about the Mizler Society?

Self-taught Bach was, then, if ever an artist was that. He belonged to no school, and no preconceived theories guided him in his studies. He was the student of all the masters, the ancients and the moderns. Every time that distance and means made it possible for him, he went to visit the contemporary artists, to hear them and to study their way of working. He used to copy the works of others. Thus, without ever having left Germany, he was familiar with French and Italian art. Among the French, he was particularly interested in Couperin. During the Weimar period he studied especially Frescobaldi (1583–1644); Legrenzi (1625–1690), who was the master of Lotti; Vivaldi (died in 1743); Albinoni (1674–1745), a contemporary of Vivaldi; and Corelli (1653–1713).

[1] Bach V, pp. 92–102. *Einige canonische Veränderungen über das Weihnachtslied "Vom Himmel hoch, da komm ich her."*

Vivaldi interested him particularly. His concertos for violins and orchestra amazed Bach, and he transcribed sixteen of them for the harpsichord and four for the organ. But he was not content with merely transcribing them. In arranging them for another instrument he tried in some way to make them over: he made the basses more interesting, invented new intermediary parts, and introduced imitations which the author had not foreseen. It is regrettable that we do not have all the originals; a comparison with the transcriptions would have permitted us to examine the changes made by Bach—a very interesting study in any case; the ways in which he transcribed the violin effects on the harpsichord and on the organ deserve in themselves a special analysis. One thing is certain: he used the greatest liberty with the models, and many times he keeps almost nothing of the original but the theme and the general character. This should not surprise us; we know from other examples that he was in the habit of appropriating the ideas of others, and of treating them as though they were his own. He wrote an organ fugue on a Legrenzi theme (IV, No. 6), another on a theme from a violin sonata by Corelli (IV, No. 8), and two more (a major and a minor) on themes of Albinoni—all of them compositions that have nothing in common with the originals except the borrowed themes. They are greater and more developed; and one senses the pleasure the master surely experienced in finding that when treated in the right way these themes could yield much more than his predecessors had got from them. These are the efforts of a pupil who becomes dangerous to his masters.

At Leipzig Bach was particularly busy with the masters of Italian singing; he copied Palestrina (1515–1594), Lotti (1667–1740), Caldara (1670–1736), and others. His apprenticeship never ended; like all the great self-taught men, he preserved to his death an ardent desire to learn and a surprising ability to assimilate. Here again is another resemblance to Kant, who was always eager to be correctly informed about European literature.

As a self-taught man, Bach had also the mind of an inventor. Just as theories were repugnant to him, so everything in the way of practical experience attracted him. He knew thoroughly the structure and the nature of all the instruments, and was ceaselessly reflecting on ways to perfect them. From this arose his sympathy with Scheibe, the organ builder, who also had an experimental and inventive bent; Bach must have encouraged him more than once to carry on his researches and to penetrate deeper into the secrets of his art. The least detail in the mechanical structure of instruments had in his eyes an enormous importance. He never ceased to demand that the keys for the organ manuals should be made short, and that the superimposed manuals should be as close to each other as possible, for he was aware that slurring and easy changing from one keyboard to another depended in large measure on these details.[1] These are precepts which German organ builders have not taken into account; they are still building organs with keyboards far apart, and with keys whose proportions are copied from those of the modern piano, complicating to this degree the task of the musician who wants to execute the works of Bach with the desired perfection.

Bach was not at all content to form practical observations: he also invented. When the Mulhouse organ was to be renovated, he undertook the construction of a carillon of twenty-four bells which was to be connected with the pedals; we do not know whether it was constructed, because Bach had left the city before the organ repairs were finished.

At Cöthen he invented the *viola pomposa*, an instrument which occupied a place between the viola and the violoncello; it had five strings (*do, sol, re, la, mi*), and was intended to permit the rapid rendering of passages which were difficult to play on the violincello. The son of one of his pupils, Gerber, who lived close to the master from 1724 to 1727, states that the instrument was in use in the period when he was a Bach pupil. An instrument maker of Leipzig named Hoffmann had constructed it in accordance with the master's specifications. The last of the six suites for violoncello solos was intended for the *viola pomposa*.

The problem of perfecting the harpsichord always interested Bach. He was cognizant of the beginnings of the modern piano, for from 1740 Gottfried Silbermann had been constructing the *Hammerklaviere* [harpsichord with hammers]. Frederick the Great, as we have already

[1] See Adlung, *Musica mech. organ.*, 1763, where we find a multitude of interesting notes on Bach, the practical man.

said, had a whole collection of pianofortes from his factory. But though Bach encouraged Silbermann to pursue his experiments, he himself was not satisfied either with the mechanism or the sound of the new instrument. He dreamed of an instrument as sensitive and flexible as possible; and he had the organ builder Zacharias Hildebrand make for him in 1740 a harpsichord-lute which was to fulfil these conditions. To prolong the sound, he had planned two rows of catgut strings, and in addition one row of metallic strings an octave apart. In this way he had two sonorities at his disposal. When the metallic strings were pressed by the felt damper, he had a lute with a loud sound; without the damper, an instrument with a deeper sound. But this experiment still did not satisfy Bach; he was forced to continue to use the simple harpsichord. Forkel relates that in spite of the thinness of the tone he preferred it to all the other kinds of harpsichords, because it permitted him better than any other to get the exact shade of expression he wanted. He tuned his instruments himself; and with such skill that it never took him more than a quarter of an hour.

He was more successful in his attempt at touch reform. He was the inventor of modern fingering. Until the beginning of the eighteenth century harpsichordists did not use the thumb at all; they played with three fingers, or at most with four, which were held out straight and superposed and crossed at will. Bach told his son Philipp Emmanuel—who brings us the new proposal in his *Véritable Art de Toucher le Clavecin*—that in his youth he had heard great *virtuosi* who never used the thumb except in the last extremity, in long stretches. But growing technical complications called naturally for the use of the thumb. In France, François Couperin (1668–1733) established the theoretical necessity for it in his *Art de Toucher le Clavecin*, which appeared in 1717. But his fingering was much less modern than Bach's. Bach was the first to have the idea of normal and constant fingering of the scales.

Let us beware, however, of identifying too closely the fingering invented by Bach with modern fingering; Bach's fingering was richer in its resources—he combined the old method of fingering with the new procedures. Frequently he had recourse, for instance, to the expedient of crossing the second and third fingers, or the third and fourth, as is proved by two little fingered pieces in the *Klavierbüch-lein* of Friedemann. Our fingering does not offer these possibilities. Emmanuel Bach, the immediate author of modern fingering, simplified and modernized his father's fingering by renouncing the former procedures, that is, the crossing of the second, third, and fourth fingers.

This fingering reform proves how clairvoyantly and methodically Bach proceeded in all his researches. If true logic is the logic of induction, Bach was logical as very few artists have been. His theories and his principles always proceeded from facts; they were the quintessence of endlessly repeated experiments. He had the rare faculty that permitted him to see the ensemble in the details and to perceive all the details in the ensemble. Spitta points out, with justice, the difference between Bach's method of composing and Beethoven's. Beethoven accumulated his drafts, and experimented, so to speak, with his main idea, before finding the true form for its expression. The Bach scores, on the contrary, sprang up all at once. From the moment he began to write, the plan for the whole was already fixed, and the details began to group themselves quite naturally around the central idea. When later he happened to take up again one of his scores, he never failed to work it over, though without touching the plan itself. He did not upset the first idea, as Beethoven did: his modifications had to do only with detail. In short, he worked like a mathematician who sees clearly before him every step in a complicated operation, and is concerned only with expressing them in figures.

It was this sureness and really mathematical clairvoyance that give his official explanations their admirable clarity. Whether he is speaking about repairs to an organ, of preparing a *mémoire* on the condition of the St. Thomas choirs, or replying to an attack by Ernesti: the words and the sentences follow one another with a precision and a logic that nothing can stop. Never too much or too little; it is solid and closely packed. One cannot read Bach, even though only a short letter of recommendation, without real esthetic pleasure.

At heart Bach was an architect. The more one studies penetratingly his development, the more one becomes aware that all the progress the art of music owes to him can be gathered into a single word: a ceaselessly growing *perfection* in musical architecture. As for the fugues in particular, those of his youth are often admirable in invention and in richness, but they lack a plan; there is a superabundance of "subjective" climaxes. With time, however, his objectivity, that essential quality of architecture, seems to grow; the fugues become greater and at the same time more simple. In this respect the G *minor Fugue* for the organ is the most perfect; in spite of the abundance and interest of the details, there is nothing unexpected to shatter the unity of its great architectural lines. We stand before an ideal edifice, where strength and pliability unite to create the impression of grandeur.

There is something more here than parallelism and fortuitous harmony; Bach had a very unusual knowledge of architectural matters. During his sojourn at Potsdam he visited the opera house in Berlin, which had just been finished. When he arrived at the grand foyer, he went up into the gallery that surrounded it and looked carefully at the ceiling. "The architect," he said, "without knowing it, wanted to give us a surprise. If a person standing at the end of the room with his face turned to the wall speaks a word in a low voice, another person at the opposite end and also facing the wall will understand it perfectly; at any other spot in the room he will hear nothing at all." Just the conformation of the vault had revealed to Bach this acoustical phenomenon.

A man endowed with such clarity of thought could not fail to possess to a high degree the faculty of transmitting to others what he had acquired by his work. Bach was a remarkable teacher. His failures as a teacher at St. Thomas are to be attributed much less to a lack of teaching ability than to his inability to keep the respect of very young people. The member of the council at Leipzig who said after his death, "Herr Bach was a good musician but a bad professor," was right if by "professor" he meant schoolteacher. Kant, speaking of his long years as a tutor, loved to poke fun at himself: "Never," said he, "with the best intentions in the world was there a worse tutor." In the same way one might say of Bach: "Never with the greatest pedagogical talent has there been a worse schoolteacher." On the contrary, those who came to him to study under his direction found in him the best of guides. The distinction won by his pupils substantiates this: Johann Tobias Krebs, later court organist at Altenburg (dead in 1780); Johann Philipp Kirnberger (1721–1783), afterwards court musician for the princess Amelia of Prussia; and Kittel. It was Kittel who handed down to the nineteenth century the traditions of Bach's organ playing; he lived until 1809.

Forkel devotes a very interesting chapter to Bach as a professor. Doubtless Emmanuel had told him a great deal about this subject. Bach started his students with lessons in touch. We know that he had a peculiar method of fingering: to let the cord attacked vibrate to the full, he did not lift his finger directly from the key but drew it backwards and so performed a rapid *glissando*.[1] Forkel describes this touch without being able to explain its details. The students kept at these exercises for several months. To give them a rest, Bach had them play little pieces which he often composed during the lessons themselves. This is the origin of the *Preludes for Beginners* and the *Inventions*. Emmanuel Bach tells us that he would not let them linger too long on the easy pieces, but from the very beginning loved to inure them to difficulties. The *Klavierbüchlein* of Wilhelm Friedemann we have already mentioned offers the pupil very quickly indeed little pieces of some difficulty. For example, the master wanted to familiarize him at the beginning with all the kinds of ornaments: on the first page of the *Klavierbüchlein* of Friedemann all the indications for embellishments are illustrated with notes. It is a precious indication for us; these things show us how we must render the mannerisms and grace notes in the works of Bach.

To encourage his pupils he had the habit of playing for them, often several times, everything that he gave them to study. Gerber, who was his pupil from 1724 to 1727, tells us that Bach had played for him no less than three times the first part of the *Well–Tempered Clavichord*. "Among the happiest hours of my life," Gerber says, "I count those when Bach, pretending that he was not inclined to make me study, sat down in front of one of his admirable instruments, and so changed the hours into minutes."

But while he was teaching his disciples technique, he was instruct-

---

[1] This discription of Bach's method of touch is obviously not the modern idea of the *glissando*, which means running the finger over a number of keys in succession. C. R. J.

ing them in the elementary rules of composition. All the pieces he
had them play were presented to them at the same time as models of
composition, and he had them make an analysis of them. This double
purpose shows up clearly in the title of the *Inventions* and in the
title of the *Orgelbüchlein*. The *Inventions* are written to teach the
correct playing of two or three parts, to help the pupil to develop
for himself a fine *cantabile* style (*eine cantable Art im Spielen*")—
something that was essential in the eyes of Bach—and, finally, to give
him a "strong foretaste" of composition.

For special lessons in composition he had his own method, which
differed from every other course of lessons. Instead of beginning with
simple counterpoint, he had his pupils immediately harmonize chorales of four parts, and initiated them in composing a figured bass
correctly and interestingly. Every lesson in Harmony became at the
same time a lesson in counterpoint. His suggestions for the figured
bass have fortunately come down to us in different forms. The 1725
Klavierbüchlein of Anna Magdalena contains several brief explanations.[1] Moreover, we have a complete course on the same subject,
thanks to the copy that a certain Johann Peter Kellner made in 1738.
The original manuscript, we feel sure, was written from Bach's dicta-
tion to his class. Forkel does not mention this course, so precious for
the numerous examples it gives.[2] One cannot imagine more precise instruction. The introduction of material all by itself reveals the great
yet practical man. After having given some etymological information
and a few definitions, after having explained of what intervals the
perfect chord is composed, he immediately comes to the formulation
of a general rule: "The hands must always be made to move in contrary movements, in order to avoid successions of fifths and octaves."
Therefore from the very first lesson the pupil takes away experiments
to try.

Let us add another document no less valuable. Bach had the habit
of having his advanced pupils write out figured basses of strange

[1] They are reproduced in Spitta II, pp. 951 f.
[2] "*Des Königlichen Hof-Compositeurs und Capellmeisters in gleichen Direc-
toris musices wie auch Cantoris der Thomasschule, Herrn Johann Sebastian Bach
zu Leipzig Vorschriften und Grundsätze zum vierstimmigen Spielen des General-
Bass oder Accompagnement, für seine Scholaren in der Musik 1738.*" Spitta re-
produces this manuscript, II, pp. 913–952.

sonatas, which he afterwards corrected. So it was that Gerber, of whom we have already spoken, had to elaborate a sonata for the violin by Albinoni; his manuscript, with Bach's corrections, has come down to us, thanks to his son.[1]

As soon as his pupils had become familiar with the figured bass, they were set at the study of the fugue. Bach forbade them to compose on the harpsichord; and wanted above everything else to lead them to reason clearly.

He compared each part to a person in the act of speaking. It was forbidden to interrupt him or to silence him until he had said everything he had to say; it was just as much forbidden to let him speak when he had nothing to say. In correcting their essays, he urged them above everything else to avoid all "disorder." But with the personality of each part so respected he permitted them all kinds of liberties. There was no audacity which he would not tolerate, on the condition that there were reasonable ideas behind it. The pupils who had no imagination were eliminated at the beginning. All this, nonetheless, was in his eyes only the first apprenticeship; for genuine progress in the art of composition he knew only one way, that which he had followed himself: the study of the masterpieces. To become familiar with everything that is beautiful, that was for anyone the best way of teaching oneself; and he not only formulated the principle, he did better still—he applied it himself.

Still, among his numerous pupils, one cannot cite a single one who became a great composer; not even Friedemann, not even Emmanuel. They were only talented men. Even Julius Krebs, of whom Bach himself was the most proud, did not rise in his compositions above the level of honest mediocrity. They became orchestra leaders, cantors, or remarkable organists; but at bottom they owed their prestige and their distinction to the fact that they were former pupils of Bach.

There were only two of them in reality to whom posterity owed something: Emmanuel Bach and Kirnberger. Again, it is not to their compositions that they owe their celebrity—though the harpsichord compositions of Emmanuel are truly remarkable in some respects—

[1] The manuscript is reproduced in Spitta at the end of the second volume.

but to the theoretical works in which they formulated and popularized the master's principles of teaching. Emmanuel wrote his two volumes, *Sur la Véritable Façon de Toucher du Clavecin* [The True Method of Harpsichord Playing],[1] whose importance in the history of the modern piano we know. Kirnberger wrote his great work in two volumes on the theory of composition, in which he developed Bach's idea about teaching, and urged above everything else that one should begin with four-part harmonizations and not with little exercises in counterpoint; a work which stirred up long discussions in the world of the theoretician.[2]

Bach's pupils have added nothing, then, to the glory of their master; nor have they helped to make his works known. Though they played his organ and harpsichord compositions, they allowed the cantatas and the Passions to pass into oblivion. Emmanuel performed the cantatas and the Passions well at Hamburg; but his brother and he kept for themselves all their father's scores, and their friends even had to pay for the privilege of going through them. At Leipzig there remained only a very small number of Bach cantatas. Moreover, Doles, a pupil of Bach's, who was appointed cantor of St. Thomas in 1755, was not the kind of man to administer the great heritage that had come down to him. Already during Bach's lifetime he had tried to play a rôle as composer beside the master. His insignificant and sentimental works would never lead one to suspect whose disciple he was. He rendered some of Bach's works well, but without giving a thought to the possibility of establishing a Bach cult at St. Thomas.

And yet what difference does it make to the great geniuses if their immediate pupils are mediocre? They continue to instruct by their own works. When Bach recommended to his pupils above everything else the study of classic works, he did not suspect that his real teaching would begin when posterity should rediscover his Passions and his cantatas. It is told of Brahms that he awaited with impatience the appearance of each new volume in the *Bachgesellschaft* edition, and the moment he received it dropped everything else he was doing to

---

[1] Philipp Emmanuel Bach (1714–1788): *Versuch über die wahre Art das Klavier zu spielen.* Two volumes, Leipzig, 1753–1762.

[2] Johann Philipp Kirnberger: *Die Kunst des reinen Satzes in der Musik.* First part, 1774; second part, 1776–1779. The work has not been completed.

go through it; "for," said he, "with this old Bach there are always surprises, and one always learns something new." When a new volume of the great edition of Händel's work arrived he put it on the shelf, saying, "It ought to be very interesting; I will go through it as soon as I have the time."

6. Bach's Piety

One trait in the character of Bach is missing in this outline—the essential trait: Bach was a pious man. It was his piety that sustained him and kept him serene in his laborious existence. His scores, without any other document, would suffice to show us this; almost all of them carry at the head: "S.D.G.," *Soli Deo Gloria*. On the cover of the *Orgelbüchlein* the following verse may be read:

> Dem höchsten Gott allein zu Ehren,
> Dem Nächsten draus sich zu belehren.
> [For the honor of the most high God alone
> And for the instruction of my neighbor.]

This deeply religious spirit is disclosed even in Friedemann's *Klavierbüchlein*; at the top of the page where the first little pieces to play begin are the words, "*In Nomine Jesu*." With anyone else these declarations of piety, scattered at every turn, and under the most insignificant circumstances, would appear exaggerated, if not affected. With Bach one feels that there is nothing there unnatural. Certainly here was a profound spirit; but profound not after the fashion of those who in a sort of jealous fear anxiously disclose to the public their internal life. There was something frank about his piety. He did not withdraw from it; it constituted an integral part of his artistic nature. If he embellished all his scores with his "S.D.G." it was because music was something essentially religious to him. It was after all the most powerful means of glorifying God; music as a secular accomplishment occupied only the second place. This fundamentally religious conception of art is completely expressed in his definition of harmony. "The figured bass," he says in his course, "is the most perfect foundation of music. It is executed with two hands; the left hand plays the prescribed notes, and the right hand adds consonances and dissonances in order that the whole shall produce an agreeable harmony for the honor of God and for the proper delight of the soul. Like all music, the figured bass has no other purpose than the glory of God and the refreshment of the spirit; otherwise it is not true music, but a diabolical and repetitious prattle [*ein teuflisches Geplerr und Geleyer*]." It was therefore wholly natural that he should speak in a somewhat disdainful fashion of secular art. Witness the proposal he made to Friedemann when he invited him to accompany him to the Dresden opera: "What do you say if we should go again to listen to the pretty little songs of Dresden (*die schönen Dresdener Liederchen*)?" But this did not prevent him from writing secular music and even burlesque cantatas! In the last analysis this activity was less a work of art for him than a pastime and a recreation for his spirit.

This pious artist had a remarkable theological knowledge. The theological works mentioned in the inventory certainly enabled him to have opinions on the numerous dogmatic questions which were then agitating Protestantism. Did he not live in that troubled epoch which followed the Reformation, in the time of that second Reformation which arose, we know, at the turn of the seventeenth and eighteenth centuries, and in time was to produce a transformation in the spirit of Protestantism? The subjectivism in religion which had been restricted within definite limits by Luther reappeared at that time in all its strength in Spener, the leader of pietism.

Spener was by birth an Alsatian—he was born at Ribeauvillé in 1635; and he occupied ecclesiastical posts of great importance in turn at Frankfort a/M., at Dresden and at Berlin. He died in this last city in 1705. Without desiring to work an injury to the fundamental dogmas of his church, the leader of the pietists insisted however on the importance of individual piety; and by that very insistence put in doubt (without wanting to) the normative worth of formulated dogma. In any case Lutheran orthodoxy, which after the death of Luther had inaugurated a kind of new scholasticism, felt itself attacked. The struggle was engaged on all fronts. To speak the truth, it was never to end; the same strained relations still exist at this very moment between Protestant subjectivism and the dogma adopted by the Reformation, between pietism and orthodoxy.

This struggle between the orthodox and the pietists had at the time of Bach reached its climax. One might believe that the individual piety of the master had carried him to the new tendency. Numerous indeed in his works are the traces of pietism. The theological reflections, the turn of his sentences, and especially his use of diminutives—in short, his sentimentalism—all these are so many indications of the influence of pietism. His Passions can not disavow the date of their birth; one feels that they were born at a time when pietism begins to take root in the spiritual poetry of Protestantism. And still Bach was a member of the orthodox clan. The Weimar registers are there to attest to this fact; they show us that he chose as godfather for his first child the pastor Georg Christian Eilmar of Mulhouse. But this pastor Eilmar was the protagonist of the orthodox party in Mulhouse; he had attacked in a brutal fashion the pietist pastor Frohne, his older colleague. At the very time when Bach was at Mulhouse the council had even to intervene, to prevent a complete schism in the parish. Frohne—his attitude during the strife is ample proof—was a man profoundly pious, distinguished, sympathetic in every respect. Eilmar himself was the exact contrary; he was not only aggressive, but also spiteful, devoid of all intelligence and of every religious sentiment. And it was with this representative of orthodoxy that Bach was bound in friendship! Otherwise would he have chosen him as the godfather of his child, especially since he had already left Mulhouse when the baptism occurred?

How can we explain this dual religious attitude of Bach? At bottom he was a conservative spirit; quite naturally, therefore, he took his place with the orthodox, and saw in the pietists only inopportune innovators. Pietism, moreover, was antiartistic, in that it extolled the greatest simplicity in the service, was suspicious of art, and saw in its introduction in the church only a dangerous invasion of mundane pomp. The cantata and everything that closely or remotely resembled concert music was suspected by the pietists, who spared the chorale only because of its simplicity. This was why his sympathies at Mulhouse were with a man who in other respects little deserved them.

At heart Bach was neither pietistic nor orthodox: he was a mystic thinker. Mysticism was the living spring from which sprang his piety.

There are certain chorales and certain cantatas which make us feel more than elsewhere that the master has poured into them his soul. These are precisely the mystical chorales and cantatas. Like all the mystics, Bach, one may say, was obsessed by religious pessimism. This robust and healthy man, who lived surrounded by the affection of a great family, this man who was embodied energy and activity, who even had a pronounced taste for the frankly burlesque, felt at the bottom of his soul an intense desire, a *Sehnsucht*, for eternal rest. He knew, if any mortal ever did, what nostalgia for death was. Never elsewhere had this nostalgia for death been translated into music in a more impressive way. Many are the cantatas he wrote to describe the weariness of life. The moment the Gospels touch on the cherished idea, Bach seizes it and devotes to it a long description.[1] All the cantatas for bass alone are in this sense mystical cantatas. They

---

[1] Here are some of these cantatas:

> *Liebster Gott, wann werd ich sterben*, No. 8
> [Dearest God, when shall I die]
>
> *Liebster Jesu, mein Verlangen*, No. 32
> [Dearest Jesus, my desire]
>
> *Schlage doch, gewünschte Stunde*, No. 53
> [Strike, then, longed-for hour]
>
> *Ich will den Kreuzstab gerne tragen*, No. 56
> [I will gladly bear the cross]
>
> *Selig ist der Mann*, No. 57
> [Blessed is the man]
>
> *Ich habe genug*, No. 82
> [I have had enough]
>
> *Gotteszeit ist die allerbeste Zeit*, No. 106
> [God's time is the best time of all]
>
> *Ach lieben Christen seid getrost*, No. 114
> [O dear Christian, be comforted]
>
> *Ich steh mit einem Fuss im Grabe*, No. 156
> [I am standing with one foot in the grave]
>
> *Komm du süsse Todesstunde*, No. 161
> [Come, sweet hour of death]
>
> *Ach ich sehe, jetzt da ich zur Hochzeit gehe*, No. 162
> [Ah, I see, now that I go to the wedding].

begin with the idea of weariness of life; then, little by little, the expectation of death quiets and illumines; in death Bach celebrates the supreme liberation, and describes in lovely spiritual lullabies the peace that at this thought invades his soul; or again, his happiness is translated into joyous and exuberant themes of a supernatural gaiety. We feel that his whole soul sings in this music, and that the believer has written it in a sort of exaltation. How powerful, moreover, is the impression! What a penetrating charm is in the admirable cradle song, "*Schlummert ein ihr müden Augen*" [Fall asleep, you weary eyes], in the cantata "*Ich habe genug*" [I have had enough] (No. 82), or again in the simple melody "*Komm, süsser Tod!*" [Come, sweet death!].

So desired, so awaited, death did not at all surprise him. At the supreme moment his face must have been transfigured with that supernatural smile that we believe we can see in his cantatas and his mystical chorales.

7. BACH'S APPEARANCE, *Summa Vitae*

Four oil paintings have preserved for us Bach's features; one of them, the one executed by the court painter Hausmann for the Mizler Society, is at the St. Thomas School. Moreover, there exists a modern bust which has a very special value, having been modelled from a skull found in the St. Johann Cemetery in Leipzig, which without any doubt is the skull of Bach himself.[1] In 1894, when the church of St. Johann was being rebuilt, they dug up the old cemetery that surrounded it. We know from the registers that Bach was buried there in a rather shallow grave and in an oak coffin—the ordinary caskets were made of fir. Moreover, a local tradition had it that he was buried south of the church six paces in a straight line from the door. And indeed at this very spot they found an oak coffin containing the skeleton of an old man, whose skull had the characteristic features of Bach's head, as the oil paintings reveal them: prominent eyebrows, very marked nasal angle, a somewhat protruding lower jaw, very prominent chin. A renowned sculptor, Seffner, using as a

[1] See William Cart's study of Bach, pp. 252 f.

base a cast from this skull, made a bust of Bach with the valuable assistance of Herr His, professor of anatomy in the University of Leipzig, who gave him precise indications of the proportions which the fleshy parts and the muscles of the head would present at a given age. The bust obtained from these data confirms and completes to a certain extent the contemporary portraits of Bach.

Nonetheless, in spite of these portraits and this bust, the real appearance of Bach remains an enigma. We see easily a certain energy in the forehead, between the eyebrows something severe and sombre, and in the mouth a certain kindliness. But what the artists do not picture at all is the ensemble of his physiognomy. They have tried to seize his face in a state of repose, but this state was not at all natural to him; they combine and express simultaneously the different aspects of his face, but without accentuating his characteristic expression par excellence. These composite portraits are therefore to some extent impersonal ones, which assemble on the same canvas the different traits of the master without even attempting to catch the personality behind his face.

Only an artist of the first rank could have made a true portrait of Bach. The portrait painters of that day, considerable as they were, have in reality supplied us with only the elements of a portrait of him; and it is only when our imagination animates the features, lending a smile to them or letting the light play on them, that we can evoke the true Bach.

In general, let us say in conclusion, Bach was a happy man. Certainly his long career was a weary one, certainly he was not spared vexations; he lived in an environment too narrow for him not to be frequently wounded; and the last years of his life went by in a certain isolation. But he did not know the supreme sadness of the artist—the indifference of his contemporaries; justice was his lot even during his lifetime. His contemporaries revered him; he was able to render all his works himself; he lived in the midst of a large family, protected from material anxieties, having as his confidants and as his artistic companions his wife and his elder sons. What more could the man and the artist desire? Compare this calm existence with the tumults and the internal discords of Beethoven, or the stormy life of Wagner, full of strife, of assaults and of despair!

❦

THE SYMBOLISM OF BACH [1]

BACH was a poet; and this poet was at the same time a painter. This is not at all a paradox. We have the habit of classifying an artist according to the means he uses to interpret his inner life: a musician if he uses sounds, a painter if he uses colors, a poet if he uses words. But we must admit that these categories, established by external criteria, are very arbitrary. The soul of an artist is a complex whole, in which mingle in proportions infinitely variable the gifts of the poet, the painter, the musician. Nothing compels us to set forth as a principle that the sort of thing that issues from a man must always express an internal dream of the same order: that, for instance, one can transcribe a dream of a musical nature with the help of sound. There is no impossibility in conceiving a poet's dream expressed in color, or a musician's dream taking the form of words, and so forth. The instances of such transcriptions abound.

Schiller was a musician. In conceiving his works he had auditive sensations. In a letter to Körner May 25, 1792, he expressed himself thus: "The music of a poem is more often present in my soul, when I sit down at my table to write, than the exact idea of the contents, about which I am often hardly in agreement with myself." Goethe himself was a painter to this extent, that he was for a long time haunted by the idea that that perhaps was his true vocation. He studied design with assiduity, and suffered from not being able to render things as he saw them. We know how he sought to consult fate, in the course of a journey on foot which took him from Wetzlar towards the Rhine, in order to put an end to these uncertainties and to decide upon his future. "I was following the right bank of the Lahn," he says in Dichtung und Wahrheit, "and I saw at some distance below me the river shining in the rays of the sun, and partly hidden by a lush growth of willows. Then my old desire to be able to paint such things worthily awakened in me. By chance I held in my left hand a fine pocket knife; and at the very moment I heard

[1] From J. S. Bach. Le Musicien–Poète, by Albert Schweitzer. Leipzig: Breitkopf & Härtel, 1908, pp. 325–341.

resounding in my soul an imperious command to hurl this knife immediately into the stream. If I saw it fall into the water, my artistic aspirations would be realized; if the fall of the knife were hidden by the overhanging branches, I should have to renounce my wishes and my efforts. I had hardly thought of it when this fancy was executed, for without any regard for the utility of the knife, which had a number of parts, I threw it immediately with all my strength and with my left hand into the river. Unfortunately, this time I also experienced the deceitful ambiguity of oracles, of which the ancients have already so bitterly complained. The plunge of the knife was hidden from me by the last branches of the willows, but the water was thrown up by the shock like a powerful fountain and was perfectly visible to me. I did not interpret the incident to my advantage; and the doubt it awakened in my mind had subsequently this unhappy consequence, that I applied myself to the study of design in a more desultory and negligent manner. Thus I myself gave the oracle the chance to fulfil itself."

He became a poet, therefore, while he remained a painter: his work is composed of portraits and landscapes. Visual evocation—in this lie the originality and the secret of his narrative talent. His letters from Switzerland are sketches; and in his letters from Italy he congratulates himself "on having always had the gift of seeing the world with the eyes of a painter, whose pictures were present to his mind." In his gondola trips, Venice seemed to him like a succession of pictures from the Venetian school. His characters are portraits; in Faust, it is himself that he paints. All the idyllic scenes in this vast drama, naïve, tragic, burlesque, fantastic, allegoric, are so many backdrops on which the portrait of Goethe stands out at different moments of his life. Even music he perceived in a visual form: in listening to Bach he saw tall people in their finery descending with solemn steps a great staircase.

Is there any reason for recalling the classic case of Taine, this painter in literature? Gottfried Keller, author of Romeo and Juliet in the Village, began in the same way with painting. Conversely, Böcklin is a poet who has gone astray among the painters. His poetic imagination carries him away to mythological distances, and calls forth before his painter's eyes, in the form of concrete images, this

world of elementary forces dreamed of by the pantheistic poets. From
that moment on what does the poet care for lines or colors? Pictorial
composition, exactness of design—he holds them cheap; the essential
thing for him is ever more and more to express his ideas. Nothing
is more significant in this respect than Böcklin's last work, that formless but dramatic picture in the museum at Basel of the pestilence.

Nietzsche was a musician. He even made some attempts at musical
composition, and submitted his drafts to Wagner. They are still more
mediocre than the designs of Goethe. But at one time he thought he
had the gifts of a composer. He did possess them, in effect: it was
he who created in literature the symphonic style. His method of composing a literary work is that of a writer of symphonies; study from
this point of view his *Jenseits von Gut und Böse* [Beyond Good and
Evil], and you will find even little fugues like those in the symphonies
of Beethoven. To read a work without rhythm was for him an ordeal.
"Even our good musicians write badly," he cried peevishly. Is not
this affinity strange between Nietzsche, the musician among the
thinkers, and Wagner, the thinker among the musicians? Their fate
was to meet only to separate, to love each other only to hate each
other. Yet nevertheless, of all the Wagnerians Nietzsche is the only
one who understood the soul of the master of Bayreuth. It was he
who found this formula, so perfectly true, to characterize the artistic
spirit of Wagner: "Wagner as a musician should be classified among
the painters; as a poet among the musicians; as an artist, in a more
general sense, among the actors."

It is from this coexistence of different artistic instincts in the same
personality that we must start to establish those reciprocal relations
which unite the arts. In esthetics we have too long delighted in
formulating definitions borrowed from the nature of the different
arts, and then in piling up on this arbitrary base theories and con-
troversies. From this there have usually resulted axioms and judgments whose solidity was only illusory. What has not been said or
written about descriptive music! For some it is nothing less than the
final goal of all music; for others, it represents the degeneracy of pure
music: affirmations diametrically opposed, neither of which may be
called false, but which contain only parts of the truth. How resolve

this antinomy? By studying the question, we would say, from the point of view of the psychology of history.

Every art teaches us psychology, manifesting "descriptive" tendencies in so far as it wishes to express more than its own proper medium of expression will permit. Painting wants to express the feelings of the poet; poetry wants to evoke plastic visions; music wishes to paint and to express ideas. It is as if the soul of "the other artist" wants also to speak. Pure art is only an abstraction. Every work of art, to be understood, should suggest a complex representation, in which are mingled and harmonised sensations of every kind. He who, before a picture of a landscape filled with heather, does not hear the vague music of the humming of bees, does not know how to see; just as the man for whom music evokes no vision knows not how to hear. The logic of art is the logic of the association of ideas; and the artistic impression is all the greater when the complex associations of ideas, conscious and subconscious, are communicated through the medium of the work, in a way more intense and more complete. Art is the transmission of the association of ideas.

The painters do not simply copy nature, they reproduce it; so that we may share the surprise and the emotion that they themselves, seeing her as poets, experienced in her presence. And what do they teach us, if not to look at nature everywhere with the eyes of the poet?

Descriptive music is, then, legitimate; since painting and poetry are like the unconscious elements without which the language of sounds could not be conceived. There is a painter in every musician. Listen to him, and this second nature will immediately appear to you. To express the simplest idea, the musicians could not get along without pictures and metaphors. Their language is a kind of word painting; from which arises the attraction of their writings, so original, so picturesque, often also so odd and incoherent. Nothing could be more interesting than their letters in this regard: they show their minds ceaselessly agitated by visual images.

The descriptive tendency appears already in the works of the primitives. It is a very naïve, imitative tendency; they wish to reproduce the song of the birds, laughter, lamentation, the sound of a spring or a cascade; even more, they pretend to represent entire scenes, and end with musical narrations where the climaxes in a composition are supposed to correspond to those of a story. It is precisely in the two generations before Bach that we see the simultaneous appearance in Italy, Germany and France of this rudimentary descriptive music. So it is in characteristic pieces of Froberger and the French harpsichordists, with which Bach was acquainted; in the orchestral descriptions of the Hamburg masters, the Keisers, the Matthesons and the Telemanns; and especially in the biblical sonatas of Kuhnau, which are a kind of classic expression of this tendency.[1]

This primitive descriptive music has not come to an end; on the contrary, it reappears with all its pretensions in our program music. In the hands of Liszt and his disciples, great and small, who travel in this direction, the symphony becomes a symphonic poem (*Symphonische Dichtung*). The climaxes cannot be explained by themselves; they necessitate a commentator to announce what the music is going to represent. Make no mistake: however great the means it employs and the clarity of expression it attains, this descriptive music is nonetheless primitive and marginal in art, just because it cannot be explained by itself. And when it is practised by musicians of the second order, it is in vain that they multiply the explanations and comments on each measure; this primitive character becomes only more accentuated. Such were the old painters, who used to represent the utterance of their characters by garlands of words issuing from their mouths, instead of being content with gestures and expressions.

The story of primitive descriptive music is divided into two periods, therefore: ancient and modern. Here and there we are in the presence of normal tendencies, which in view of the way they appear and develop have resulted only in a false art.

In pictorial art we notice an analogous anomaly: biblical painting. Seduced by episodes known to everybody, the painters, ancient and modern, allow themselves to be carried beyond the natural limits of pictorial narration. They think to represent such and such an episode in sacred history by assembling on the same canvas the people who figure in it; they never think of asking if the action in the episode could be concentrated in a single scene and be interpreted in a con-

[1] The beginnings of descriptive music merit a special study. It would be necessary to assemble all the material in question, which has not yet been done.

crete way by the attitude of characters, as the logic of every pictorial composition requires. Like the biblical scenes in Kuhnau's cantatas, their works can be explained only by their implications. A man with a knife, a child with bound hands, a head which appears through the clouds, a ram in the bushes: all these brought together on a single canvas represent the story of Abraham's sacrifice. A woman and a man sitting beside a well, a dozen men coming two by two along the road, in the background people leaving a village: this is Jesus and the Samaritan woman.

Biblical painting provides an abundance of examples of this false pictorial narration, which in truth is only pretty imagery. However finished the execution, it does not make us forget the complete absence of composition. In reality there are only a very few biblical scenes that lend themselves to painting; the others are not such as to fulfil the desired conditions.

The only man who really showed discernment in his choice of subjects, and who never made a false biblical painting, is Michelangelo. Let us compare with his powerful evocations of sacred history the simple illustrations that Veronese has given us. Admirable and enchanting as The Marriage at Cana is in form, should we not think this was an ordinary banquet if it were not for a kind of tacit understanding between the painter and the public?

Biblical painting and historical painting are the two aspects of false description in the history of painting; and these two chapters in the history of plastic art have their parallel in the history of music. The two supreme representatives of the descriptive genre are, in plastic art Michelangelo, in music Bach.

Bach was a poet; but he lacked the gift of expression. His language was without distinction, and his poetic taste was no more developed than that of his contemporaries. Would he otherwise have accepted so gladly the libretti of Picander?

Nonetheless, he was a poet in his soul, in that he looked in a text first of all for the poetry it contained. What a difference there was between him and Mozart! Mozart is purely a musician; he takes a given text and clothes it in a beautiful melody. Bach, on the other hand, digs in it; he explores it thoroughly, until he has found the idea which in his eyes represents the heart of it and which he will

have to illustrate in music. He has a horror of neutral music, superimposed on a text with nothing in common with it except the
rhythm and a wholly general feeling. Often, it is true, when he finds
himself in the presence of a text which has no salient idea, he is
forced to make the best of a bad situation; but before resigning
himself to it he does his utmost to discover some germ of music in
the text itself. The musical phrase he applies to it is already born
from the natural rhythm of the words. In this he goes beyond Wagner. In Händel we often perceive a latent antagonism between the
words of the poetic text and the musical phrase superimposed on it.
For instance, he sometimes divides long periods into several phrases,
which cease from that point to form a whole. In Bach, on the other
hand, the musical period is modelled on the phrasing of the text;
it springs from it naturally. The longest phrase is rendered by one
of those magnificent musical periods of which he has the secret.
From passages without any structure, which at first sight seem un-
suited to any declamation, he draws the most beautiful musical
phrases, and with such a natural skill that one is surprised he did not
suspect this phrasing before.[1]

His greatest concern was to give the text the lustre that music
requires. It does not matter much to him that he amplifies the feeling expressed by these words; contentment readily becomes exuberant
joy, and sadness extreme anguish. Often he seizes upon a single
word which for him gathers up all the musical substance of the text,
and in his composition gives it an importance it actually does not
have. This is evident in the text of the cantata *Es ist ein trotzig und
versagtes Ding* [It is an insolent and discouraging thing], No. 176,
where he has given musical expression only to the word "trotzig" [in-
solent], though the whole passage has rather to do with contrition.
Often he presents the text in a false light; but he always brings into

[1] Let us cite, for instance, the first chorus in the cantata *Die Himmel erzählen
die Ehre Gottes* [The heavens declare the glory of God] (Psalm 19:2, 4), No.
76, and the cantata *Nach dir Herr verlanget mich* [I long for thee, Lord], No.
150. One appreciates this art particularly wherever Bach has set to music biblical
verses. These are the ones, indeed, which present the most difficulty in musical
declamation, never having been intended for music, and characterized, because of
the various translations to which they have been subjected, by a strange and
incoherent style.

the foreground the idea that lends itself to musical expression. The composition brings this out, as in repoussé work.

His dramatic instinct is not less developed. The plan of the St. Matthew Passion, so admirably conceived from the dramatic point of view, is his own invention. In every text he seeks the contrasts, the opposing elements, the gradations, to be brought out by the music. In the little collection of chorales (Orgelbüchlein) he brings out most clearly the importance he attaches to the contrasts: he arranges the chorales there in such a way that one sets another in relief. In the same way, in the mystical cantatas he opposes the fear of death (Todesfurcht) to the joyous nostalgia for death (Freudige Todessehnsucht). He often enriches a text by commenting upon it with a chorale theme which one hears in the orchestra. To the text "Ich steh mit einem Fuss im Grabe" [I am standing with one foot in the grave] is added the chorale, "Lord, deal with me according to Thy mercy" (Cantata No. 156); in a recitative from the cantata "Wachet, betet" [Watch and pray], No. 70, the trumpet suddenly sounds the chorale of the last judgment, "Es ist gewisslich an der Zeit" [Surely it is the time]; in the cantata "Sehet, wir gehen hinauf nach Jerusalem" [Come, we are going up to Jerusalem], No. 159, rises the passion chorale, "O Haupt voll Blut und Wunden" [O Head, covered with blood and wounds].[1][2]

But that which occupies the most prominent place in his work is pictorial poetry. Above everything else he seeks the picture, and in this respect he is very different from Wagner, who is rather a lyric dramatist. Bach himself is nearer to Berlioz, and nearer still to Michelangelo. If it had been possible for him to see a picture by Michelangelo, doubtless he would have found in him something of his own soul.

But his contemporaries remained unaware of his painter's soul. His pupils and his sons did not perceive his pictorial instincts, any more than they suspected that his true greatness was as a musical poet. So too with Forkel, Mossevius, von Winterfeld, Bitter, and Spitta. Spitta, whose profound acquaintance with the works of Bach

---

[1] Usually translated "O sacred Head, now wounded." C. R. J.
[2] For other examples of texts illustrated with chorale melodies see cantatas Nos. 14, 23, 25, 48, 75, 106, 127, 161.

put him in a position to see things clearly, has a fear of carrying his researches in that direction. When he cannot do otherwise, he confesses that such and such a page contains descriptive music; and is always sure to add that it is there purely by accident, to which one would be wrong to attach any importance. These examples are curiosities for him, nothing more. On every occasion he insists that the music of Bach is above such puerilities, that it is pure music, the only kind that is classic. This apprehension leads him astray. The fear that one day someone would find descriptive music in Bach, and that this discovery would injure his reputation as a classic writer, prevents Spitta from recognising the rôle which it plays in his compositions.

Let us watch Bach at his work. However bad the text, he is satisfied with it if it contains a picture. When he discovers a pictorial idea it takes the place of the whole text; he seizes on it even at the risk of going contrary to the dominant idea of the text. Preoccupied as he is exclusively with the pictorial element, he does not perceive the weakness and the flaws in the libretto.

Nature itself he perceives, so to speak, in a pictorial fashion. The poetry of nature in his work is not at all lyrical, as it is with Wagner: it is seen rather than felt; it is the tornadoes, the clouds that advance along the horizon, the falling leaves, the restless waves.

His symbolism also is visual, like that of a painter; that is how he expresses ideas that are completely abstract. In the cantata No. 77, for the thirteenth Sunday after Trinity, he deals with the verse from the Gospels, "Thou shalt love the Lord thy God with all thy heart, and with all thy soul, and with all thy strength, and with all thy mind, and thou shalt love thy neighbor as thyself" (Lk. 10:27), Christ's reply to the scribe who asked him what was the greatest of all the commandments. These commandments, great and little, are then represented by the melody from the chorale *Dies sind die heilgen zehn Gebote* [These are the holy ten commandments], which the organ basses sound forth in minims and the trumpets in crotchets, while the choir renders the words of the Savior, who proclaims the new law of love.

Was Bach clearly conscious of this pictorial instinct? He hardly seems to have been. We have not found among his confidences to his pupils any allusion that allows us to say so. The title of the *Orgelbüchlein* announces that the pieces contained there are model chorales; but he does not say that they are typical just because they are descriptive. And besides, are not all the parodies he made of his own works, that suppress in this way the pictorial intent of his music, there to show that his descriptive instinct was unconscious? Then where in the genius is the dividing line between the conscious and the unconscious? Is he not one and the other at the same time? This is true of Bach: he is not conscious of the importance in his work of descriptive music; but in his way of seeing the subjects to be treated, and in his choice of the means, he is thoroughly clairvoyant.

The great mistake of all the primitives consists in wishing to translate into music everything they find in a text. Bach avoids this danger. He is well aware that the climaxes of a text should be, if one is to risk retracing them with sound, both simple and strongly accented. Hence the times when he uses this means are very rare.

Moreover, when he follows the indications of a text he does not insist upon it in the pretentious fashion of the primitives. We must admire the way in which, in the recitatives of the *St. Matthew Passion,* he underlines one word in this way, and another word in that. These are light musical inflections, destined to pass unobserved. It is the same with the cantatas and with the chorales. On the other hand, when a new motif appears in the text the music changes immediately, since for Bach a new picture requires a new theme. In some choruses two or even three themes occur successively, because the text demands them. So in the cantata *"Siehe, ich will viel Fischer aussenden"* [Behold, I will send out many fishermen], No. 88, based on the text in Jeremiah: "Behold, I will send for many fishers, saith the Lord, and they shall fish them; and after will I send for many hunters, and they shall hunt them." The music of the first part paints a picture of waves, because the word "fisher" brings to Bach's mind a lake; in the second half (*Allegro quasi presto*), it is hunters climbing over the mountains: we hear fanfares. Many of the airs show the same peculiarity: the theme of the middle part corresponds to another image than that of the principal part.

What is there to say except that the music of Bach is descriptive only as far as its themes are always determined by an association of pictorial ideas? This association is sometimes energetically asserted, and sometimes is almost unconscious. There are themes whose pictorial origin would not at first be suspected, if it were not for the fact that in other works is to be found an entire series of analogous themes whose origin is not at all doubtful. There are then more accented themes that explain the origin of the others. When one brings together the Bach themes, one discovers a series of associations of pictorial ideas that are regularly repeated when the text requires them. This regularity in the association of ideas will not be found in Beethoven, or in Berlioz, or in Wagner. The only one who could be compared with Bach is Schubert. The accompaniment to his *Songs* depends on a descriptive language whose elements are identical with the language of Bach—without, however, attaining to his precision. Schubert hardly knew the works of the Leipzig cantor; but desiring to translate into music the poetry of the *Songs*, he had to agree with the man who had translated into music the poetry of the chorales.

The musical language of Bach is the most elaborate and most precise in existence. It has, after a fashion, its roots and derivations like any other language.

There is an entire series of elementary themes proceeding from visual images, each of which produces a whole family of diversified themes, in accordance with the different shades of the idea to be translated into music. From the same root we often find in the different works twenty or twenty-five variants; for to express the same idea Bach returns constantly to the same fundamental formula. Thus we encounter the walking themes (*Schrittmotive*), expressing firmness and hesitation; the syncopated themes of weariness, themes of quiet, represented by calm undulations; Satan themes, expressed in a sort of fantastic violence; themes of serene peace; themes consisting of two slurred notes, expressing suffering nobly borne; chromatic themes in five or six notes, which express acute pain; and finally the great category of themes of joy.

There exist fifteen or twenty of these categories, in which one can catalogue all the expressive motifs characteristic of Bach. The richness of his language consists not in the abundance of different themes, but in the different inflections which the same theme takes in accordance with the occasion. Without this variety of nuances, one might even find fault with his language because of a certain monotony. It is indeed the linguistic monotony of all great thinkers, who find only one expression for the same idea because it is the only true one.

But Bach's language permits him to define his ideas in a surprising fashion. He has a variety of nuances at his disposal to describe pain or joy, which one would seek in vain among other musicians. When the elements of his language are once known, even the compositions that are not associated with any text, like the preludes and the fugues of The Well-Tempered Clavichord, become vocal, and announce, after a fashion, a concrete idea. If we have to do with music written for words, we can, without looking at the text, and with the help of the themes alone, define the characteristic ideas.

But the strangest fact of all is that the language of Bach is in no way the fruit of a long experience. The different motifs that express pain are already found in the Lamento of the Cappricio, which he wrote between the ages of eighteen and twenty. When he composed the Orgelbüchlein, which dates from the Weimar epoch, he was about thirty. But at this time all his typically expressive motifs are already formed and fixed, and are not afterwards subjected to any change. While trying to represent in music a whole series of chorales, he found himself forced to seek ways of expressing himself simply and clearly. He gives up description through musical development, and adopts the procedure of expressing everything by the theme. At the same time he fixes the principal formulas of his musical language.

These little chorales are therefore Bach's musical dictionary. One has to begin with them if one is to understand what he wants to say in the cantatas and the Passions.

But in his effort for precision in language he sometimes transgresses the natural limits of music. It is not to be denied that we find in his works many disappointing pages. It is because a goodly number of his themes proceed from vision rather than from musical imagination, properly so called. In trying to reproduce a visual image he permits himself to be carried away into the creation of themes which are admirably characteristic, but which have nothing left of the musical phrase. In his youthful works such examples were rare, because his melodic instinct was still stronger than his descriptive instinct. But later the instances of this ultra-pictorial music become frequent. Among the great chorales of 1736, some, like the chorales about the Last Supper (VI, No. 30) and about the baptism (VI, No. 17), have already passed beyond the limits of music. It is the same with all the airs constructed on the theme which pictures the steps of a stumbling man. It is so with the cantata *Ich glaube Herr, hilf meinem Unglauben* [Lord, I believe, help thou mine unbelief], No. 109, which is almost impossible to listen to, because it describes a faith that swoons with themes of this kind. Did Bach, when he played or directed these pieces himself, know how to make them agreeable by the perfection of his execution? Did he have some secret of interpretation that we have not yet discovered?

However that may be, the fact is indisputable: his pictorial interest sometimes overbalanced his musical interest. Bach then exceeded the limits of pure music. But his mistake is not comparable to that of the great and little primitives in descriptive music, who sinned through ignorance of the technical resources of the art; his error has its source in the unusual loftiness of his inspiration. Goethe in composing *Faust* thought he was writing a piece appropriate for presentation in the theatre; but the work became so great and so profound that it can hardly stand dramatic representation. With Bach, also, the intensity of a thought he desires to express without reticence and in all sincerity is sometimes so great that it injures the purely musical beauty. Mistakes were possible for him; but his errors were those which only a genius is capable of making.

V

Organs and Organ Building

*T*HE two Bach books, for there were two, were a stupendous undertaking for this young man, Albert Schweitzer. Once in later years he picked up the German edition and turned the pages thoughtfully. "Did I really write this?" he asked, with a look of bewildered wonder on his face.

But this achievement was no greater than the stupendous labor of the next eight years: student of medicine and intern, professor at the University, settled pastor of a church, organist in demand for concerts in many places, and writer of extraordinary books on medical, theological, and musical subjects. The story of these years is an amazing record of endurance and erudition.

Immediately after the French Bach, and while he was working on the German Bach, he published in 1906 his first important book in the field of religion. It was a history of research into the life of Jesus, called Von Reimarus zu Wrede. The ink of the printing presses was hardly dry before his book on organ construction appeared. The book on Jesus was the fruit of long thought and study, which had begun when he was a soldier in the Kaiser's army in 1894 and carried a Greek New Testament around with him in his knapsack. The second book was also the fruit of long study and research, which had begun in 1896 when he stopped at Stuttgart on the way back from Bayreuth to hear the new modern organ in the Liederhalle. From that moment he began to say that the new organs were not as good as the old ones.

He was not contending for the organ of Bach's day. That organ was only a kind of forerunner of the wonderful instruments built between 1850 and 1880, and best exemplified by Aristide Cavaillé–Coll's organs in St. Sulpice and Notre Dame. The organ at Notre

Dame had been exposed to the weather during the First World War, when the stained glass was removed from the church; but the organ at St. Sulpice, Widor's organ, was functioning as well when Schweitzer became acquainted with it as when it was completed in 1862, and Schweitzer felt confident that if it were properly maintained it would be equally good two centuries hence. Indeed, he thought that Gabriel might still find it useful in the last days for the "wakeful trump of doom."

Often in the years before 1899—when the venerable Cavaillé-Coll died—Schweitzer used to meet him. On many a Sunday the two would climb the high flight of steps to the great organ and watch Widor play. Cavaillé-Coll would sit on the organ bench and run his hands affectionately over the console of this, the most beautiful creation of his musical genius. Then they would go with Widor into the organist's little room with the wonderful gravures and talk.

But not always was Schweitzer in such sympathetic company. Most organists and organ builders scoffed at his strange ideas, and thought him prematurely senile. And the mad destruction of the old instruments went on. For thirty years Schweitzer carried on the fight, until he felt at last that the principles for which he contended had conquered. But what sacrifice in time and energy, what incessant travel, and unending correspondence, and ceaseless argument it cost! A few of the old organs he was able to save, in France and Denmark and Holland, the first being Silbermann's magnificent instrument in St. Thomas at Strassburg. Later, when he was working in the jungles of Africa, his friends used to say of him, "In Africa he saves old Negroes, in Europe old organs." But there were many he could not save, sacrificed because of their mechanical defects, though with the proper restoration the defects could have been removed and the beauty of tone retained. All over Europe there was a craze for size and modernity, the largest number of stops, the greatest number of gadgets, the most imposing organ case. To a Swedish organist who was much more interested in the external adornment of his instrument than in its intrinsic beauty, Schweitzer once remarked, "An organ is like a cow; one does not look at its horns so much as at its milk."

As one climbs the staircase in Schweitzer's home in Gunsbach he is reminded of Schweitzer's passionate concern for the organs of Europe. For the walls are lined with framed pictures of fine old instruments. It is no accident that some twenty-five of these pictures are of Dutch organs, while only ten or so are of organs in other countries. For Holland as a whole was never tempted by the product of the modern factory; it preferred the marvelous tone of the old organs. It is not strange that Schweitzer has gone back to Holland again and again for concert tours, and that he has a host of friends and admirers in that country.

That modern organs can be built with the lovely tone of the old instruments has been proved by the Alsatian builder, Fritz Härpfer, of Boulay; and the little organ in the Gunsbach church, restored by his artistic ability, gives forth today under the inspired fingers of Albert Schweitzer as beautiful organ music as can be heard in the greatest of cathedrals. Not the biggest instrument for the available money, but the best one; that is the ideal.

The reader should remember that these writings on organ construction and organ playing were written a good many years ago, and do not reflect Dr. Schweitzer's present opinions concerning these matters. They are included here because of their importance in the history of the organ during the past forty-five years. Dr. Schweitzer intends to comment in the near future upon recent tendencies in organ construction.

The book which follows was dedicated to "Professor Ernest Munch, teacher of Alsatian organists, in heartfelt friendship."

❦

THE ART OF ORGAN BUILDING AND ORGAN PLAYING IN GERMANY AND FRANCE [1]

EVEN if it be true that the signature of our time is travel, it must still be conceded that this travel has not brought equal benefit to all domains of art, and that certain indications might almost make one doubt whether art had entered the sign of travel at all. One may ask himself candidly whether a kind of itinerant virtuosity has not profited almost exclusively from it, and whether the art of learning,

[1] From *Deutsche und französische Orgelbaukunst und Orgelkunst*, by Albert Schweitzer. Leipzig: Breitkopf & Härtel, 1906.

which seeks to appropriate the best in the lands of all the masters, has not rather gone backwards because of it. It almost seems as if art in the time of Bach was in a certain sense more artistic in its internationalism than it is today, in so far as people used to travel at that time to learn and to teach, whereas today they travel more often to perform.

That artistic ramparts exist, in spite of the sign of travel, to a greater extent than one might suppose, becomes clear to me each time I talk with a French organist about German organs and the German art of organ playing, and with a German organist about French organs and the French art of organ playing. It is something more than total ignorance about conditions on the other side that comes to light; it is almost an impossibility to understand one another even with the best will imaginable. It does not help to intercede in Paris for Reger and others among our promising young organists, and in Germany to call attention to Widor's organ symphonies. What purpose does this serve? Reger's works cannot be performed on the organ of Notre Dame or on the organ of St. Sulpice, and Widor's symphonies can be rendered on German organs only by doing a kind of violence to the nature and arrangement of the instruments.

"Therefore," each party says, "the other organ is no good." This shows that neither side knows the other organ. In order to bring this judgment, from which nothing of value issues, into a field of intelligent discussion that can be advantageous to the organ and to organ playing, and in order to acquaint the quarreling parties with each other, I take the floor as one who has had the advantage of both the German and the French schools, as one who by force of circumstances has felt for more than twelve years at home with both German and French organs, as one who defends the German art of organ playing in Paris and the French art of organ playing in Germany, and as one who is convinced that an agreement between the two types of organs and the two different conceptions must be reached; and that with such an understanding, with such an interpenetration of the German and French arts, a new period, rich in ideas and mastery of forms, will dawn in the history of organ playing. If the signs of the times do not deceive, the moment has come to learn from one another.

The rather sharp differentiation between the German and French organs began about a generation ago. When old Hesse played upon the new organ of St. Clothilde, he felt at once at home on it, and declared that it was his conception of the ideal organ. Today no German organist would find himself immediately at home on a French organ, and no French organist would ever give a recital on a German organ without rather long practice and intelligent assistance in registration.

The differentiation springs from the ways in which organ building in the two countries has been influenced by the new factors of electricity and pneumatics. French organ building remained more conservative. The organ of St. Sulpice, which will soon be fifty years old, remained the type of all French organs. German organ building followed the inventive path, utilized fully every technical advantage of pneumatics, and used electricity for the generation of unlimited wind volume and wind pressure.

There is in addition a purely superficial difference. In French organs the couplers and composition stops are arranged exclusively for the feet. The development in Germany led to the almost exclusive use of pistons.

But even the inner artistic principle is different. The artistic quality of an organ, and still more the whole nature of organ music, is determined by the way in which one proceeds from *piano* to *forte*, and from *forte* to *fortissimo*, and then back again to the initial tone color. In the German organ the revolving drum or cylinder prevails. It dominates the organ, as the playing of our *virtuosi* shows. It rules organ literature and composition, as a glance at any new work for the organ makes sufficiently clear. In other words, we [1] produce a crescendo by bringing all the stops into play one after the other without a break, so that they all operate in the same way upon the great organ; we sacrifice in this crescendo the artistic individuality of the stops; we take it for granted that every increase means at the same time a change in tone color; we reconcile ourselves to the mo-

[1] Albert Schweitzer was until the end of the First World War a German citizen. C. R. J.

notony which necessarily results from the fact that the sequence of the stops is always the same; we resign ourselves to the fact that we cannot determine when to introduce into the tone blend the sixteen-foot pipes, when the eight-foot, when the four-foot, when the two-foot, when the mixtures, when the reeds; we become the eternal slaves of the organ builder who designed the revolving drum, and give up all our independence in the execution of the *crescendo*, at the very moment when freedom is so closely allied to artistry: and all this in order to be in a position to achieve a *crescendo* by the simple movement of a wheel or a pedal.

It is otherwise with the French organ. It chooses the second alternative. It gives up the possibility of a *crescendo* executed with a single movement, and is reconciled to the necessity of a number of motions. In this way, however, it preserves at all times its freedom to introduce the stops in just the way indicated by the character of the particular *crescendo*.

The *crescendo* in a French organ depends upon the use of the couplers. In this way, the three persons which constitute the divine trinity of the organ are fully appreciated. If this, however, is to be really accomplished, the player must not be limited to the coupling of his second and third organ (choir and swell) to his first, but must be left absolutely free to start with any organ at all and couple the others to it. So in all the French instruments the first organ is called the great organ, as well as the neutral, nonspeaking, coupling organ. Its stops, that is, the stops that are pulled on the first manual, sound only when the pedal marked "G. O." (that is, great organ) is pressed. One can therefore couple to the nonspeaking manual (great organ), first the swell organ, then the choir organ, then by the use of the G. O. pedal the great organ, following at will the sequence II I III, II III I, I III II, or the one familiar to us, I II III.[1] All possibilities are provided.

It is the same way with the retiring of stops. It lies within the power of the player to keep till the end the I, the II, or the III organ without leaving the great organ.

There is for each organ a ventil for reeds and mixtures, that is, a

[1] I II III designate great, choir, swell organs. C. R. J.

pedal by which the mixtures and reeds arranged for that organ are made to speak at the discretion of the player, so that the player has it in his hands—or rather in his feet—to introduce into the tone color of the foundation stops the mixtures from the three organs in any sequence he chooses, before, during, or after their coupling, or in alternation with it.

The three couplers and the three combination pedals represent a multitude of crescendo possibilities; and at the same time offer the advantage that one can bring in the necessary crescendo at a designated climax, on its characteristic strong accent—which is not possible with the revolving drum, inasmuch as the drum introduces one register after the other, never a whole group of them, and therefore requires a certain period of time.

A third method of producing the crescendo and supplementing the other stops is the swell organ of the III manual. The III manual of the French organ is more significant than the II. The swell box encloses not only the soft-toned little stops, but also a mass of sound as important in number of registers as in intensity. The tone characters are represented in it in all pitches as completely as—almost more completely than—in the I organ. That means that crescendi can be produced with such a III organ, its shutters serving not only to make certain nuances possible upon the III organ, but also to develop the crescendo of the entire instrument up to a certain point. I remember an organ of Cavaillé–Coll's where one could alter the character of the full, coupled instrument by the swell box of the III organ.

The crescendo in the French organ depends, then, upon the couplers, the introduction of mixtures and reeds, and the use of the swell shutters.

For instance, we have the III organ, its shutters closed, coupled to the nonspeaking I. We have drawn the foundation stops on all three, sixteen-foot, eighteen-foot, four-foot, two-foot; we have prepared the mixtures and the reeds. The same in the pedal. We couple the II organ to the III; at the next climax we bring in the foundation stops of the I, while we play on the G. O. Thereupon we couple the pedal organ to the other organs when we need it. How, then, shall we proceed without a jolt from the foundation stop character to the tone color of the mixtures and reeds? By bringing in the mixtures and reeds first in the III organ. With closed shutters this can be done almost unnoticed. Now we open the shutters slowly. The tones of mixtures and reeds float along above the tones of the foundation stops in long, delicate waves, and blend with them. This introduction of the tone color of mixtures and reeds, previously only virtually present behind the closed shutters, is the climactic moment of the crescendo. Since in the III organ all tone qualities are represented, the full power of the whole instrument is felt from the moment of the introduction of the mixtures and reeds, which had been muffled in the swell box of the III organ. From this point on there is only the question of its unfolding. The subsequent introduction of the mixtures and the reeds of the II organ, of the I organ, and of the pedal organ, and the introduction of the suboctave coupler and the superoctave coupler (octave grave and octave acute) do not alter this tone color in any way; they make it only more intensive.

The dynamic indications in French compositions are to be explained accordingly. The sign for crescendo or decrescendo refers only to the handling of the swell box, even when the musician is playing on the first organ. At the top of the piece it is expressly indicated whether in addition to the foundation stops (jeux de fonds, or for short fonds) the reeds and the mixtures also, and which of them, should be prepared on the different organs. Their introduction is then definitely indicated, as well as the coupling and uncoupling. Crescendo poco a poco in an increase leading in a short line to fortissimo means that the player, when he has permitted the full III organ to develop with the foundation stops of the first two, should introduce at the climactic strong accents the mixtures and reeds of the other organs and of the pedals. Only this last crescendo corresponds to the increase we get with German organs with the register cylinder. The signs < >, no matter how many measures they stretch over, refer always to the swell box only.

I point out this fundamental difference in dynamic indications, because I have found that almost all German organists, when they are playing on the first organ, produce their crescendi and decrescendi by habit with the register cylinder, and so destroy completely the effect desired by the composer, who was not reckoning on a change in tone color.

The basic principle of the French system is the arrangement of all the resources of the instrument in the pedals. The French organs have no pistons under the keyboards. What system shall we decide upon?

I do not sit for five minutes beside Father Guilmant on the bench of his beautiful house organ at Meudon without his asking me, as if he had just remembered where we left off the last time: "And in Germany do they still build pistons? That I can't understand. See how simple it is when one has everything under his feet," . . . and the short, agile feet press couplers and combination pedals silently, then in a trice let them up again.

On another day Widor, for the twenty-fifth time, begins on the same subject. "Tell my friend Professor Munch at Strassburg that he must point out for me a single place in a Bach prelude or fugue when he has a hand free for a moment to reach for a piston! He must name someone for me who can play on the manual and at the same time press the piston on the key strip with his thumb."

I keep my silence, for the first German organist into whose hands I fall a few weeks later, and to whom I put this controversial question, answers me invariably, "The French are very backward. Formerly we too had all this in the feet; now, however, we have our beautiful pistons."

It is first of all a matter of habit. The French organist sits helplessly before the pistons; the German organist finds the pedals awkward. The question is nonetheless one of principle. Should one rather have a hand free or a foot free?

In principle one must concede the case to the French. One seldom has a free hand, but often a free foot. And experience corroborates the principle. I am always hearing on German organs the hesitations, the unrhythmical dislocations, which result from the fact that the player at the particular climax can not find the right moment to press his pistons. I know *virtuosi* who to avoid this sit between two helpers who push the pistons for them. But that means to sacrifice one's independence. And who has ever played with helpers without some untoward thing happening? And besides, when one has a chance to observe the pedal system one becomes conscious of the great complexity of the system of pistons. Let one see Guilmant, Widor, Gigout, or Vierne at their organs! They need no helpers. Quietly, serenely, and infallibly they do everything themselves. Whoever has observed this will cherish no more doubt as to which system is better.

I myself, though I am at home on both organs and have become familiar with both systems, must testify to the fact that the resources of the French system are simpler and therefore better. First of all, because all French organs are the same. Under the left side are the three pedal couplers; in the middle the manual couplers; close to that the octave couplers; then usually comes the swell shoe; at the right of that, the combination stops for the introduction of the mixtures and the trumpets—everything always in the order I, II, III. When Saint-Saëns was commanded by the President of the Republic to take his place at the organ of Notre Dame on official occasions, which used to happen before Vierne was made organist of the cathedral, he did not need five minutes to feel as much at home there as he was on the organ of St. Séverin, where he used to improvise so wonderfully.

With us every organ differs from every other in the arrangement of its resources. In order to play successfully on one of them, one must spend at least a few days in familiarizing himself with it. One could still be partly content with this situation if this were merely a chaotic condition out of which the perfected organ type might come. But such a hope would be vain, for in these differences is neither rhyme nor reason, but only chance, habit, caprice. There can be only one really perfect organ type. Yet instead of moving in this direction we remain stuck in this formless multiplicity, and even believe that this must be.

Now German art, and particularly German music, are greatly—yes, infinitely indebted to the little German states; a fact one realizes first of all when he lives in lands that have never known these conditions. But the effect on organ building has been bad. May France be here the unifying power for good, as she once was in history for bad.

The advantage that a player on the French instrument is most vividly conscious of is his ability to regulate the tone strength and tone color of the basses at any time by coupling or uncoupling the pedal organ without changing anything in the manuals. He finds this almost more agreeable than the possibility which always exists of coupling the manuals together; though the greatest reproach of our new organ devices is exactly this, that they make the coupling and uncoupling of the organs—the regulation of the blending of the three personalities which constitute the unity of the instrument—the exception rather than the rule.

Which of us has not regretted with almost every Bach number his inability on our organs to make the bass speak now more softly, now more strongly? To which of us are not certain prolonged bass notes, especially when the left hand is busy in the lower register, a torture? This difficulty does not exist in the French organ. One should hear Widor increase the volume of the great pedal organ notes in the Bach *F major Toccata* without changing the manual tone color! One should hear him command the basses in the *G minor Prelude!* Before the held bass note begins, all his pedal couplers are released in five short, successive movements. Then, towards the end of the held note, each coupler at the proper time enters again on the strong accent, strengthening the stress: the V, IV, III, II, I organs! This procedure is repeated six or seven times. But, I assert, I have never yet anywhere else heard the *G minor Prelude* without "Bach troubles."

The control of the foot couplers and the combination pedals requires, of course, a very special technique, which is almost more difficult to learn than the pedal technique. How often under the inexorable eyes of Guilmant, Gigout, or Widor, the pupil practises a transition, until he finally gets it, exact to the hundredth part of a second, quietly, without contortion, with infallible assurance, pressing down a coupler or a combination pedal and at once in readiness for the next one! For almost every piece one has to practise the climaxes, where the sequence of movements attains a certain complexity. I stood beside Widor when he was studying his last symphony, the *Symphonie Romane.* How many times did he return to certain places, before the couplers and the combination pedals obeyed him as he wished!

But when the particular movements are once learned, one is completely free, and master of the crescendi he wants to produce. Let one take his place beside Vierne, the young organist of Notre Dame who has hardly a gleam of eyesight, and follow him as he brings his wonderful instrument from pianissimo to fortissimo with no help of any kind except that of his feet, now endowed with sight!

An organist once objected to me that only the more talented pupils could learn this second "pedal technique." But Guilmant and Gigout, the teachers of the modern generation of French organists, have proved that any pupil, even though but moderately gifted, can overcome these difficulties by means of diligence.

But what prevents us from uniting the French and German arrangements in a single instrument, introducing the main couplers and combinations as pistons as well as pedal levers in such a way that pistons and pedals should always correspond? Then one would be in a position to use at any time the particular member that was free. One could, for instance, set a coupler with the hand, and then, since it would be set automatically at the same time in the feet, be in a position to shut it off either with the hand, or, if more convenient, with the foot. We boast, and rightly, that there are no technical impossibilities for our pneumatics. The organ builder who would undertake to provide the player with the main resources in this double fashion would in the right way cut through this knot which no amount of discussion can untie. This double arrangement can be installed, moreover, on any organ, by a simple, unpneumatic, purely mechanical device.

In the same way can be solved the question of whether we should have a cylinder crescendo. I myself know very well the advantages of a revolving drum when, for example, accompanying oratorios with great choruses to consider; and I admit that in certain cases one can produce unique effects. But I do not like its exclusive domination, especially in an organ with fewer than thirty stops, where it operates in a barbaric fashion. I am afraid, too, that it has not had the best influence upon the artistic sensitivity of our younger organists, and especially of our organ composers, since it has led both away from the true, simple, selective registration, and into the temptation to regard the organ as an instrument on which one played "strong and weak," not as a manifold unity in which every crescendo must come from the blending of certain tone units. I believe that if one should institute a general inquiry among experienced organists, many of them would testify that for artistic reasons they had lost their exaggerated appreciation of the revolving drum.

Here again it is a matter of doing one thing without leaving the other undone. Let them leave us the revolving drum, but give us at the same time the French resources, so that we shall not be confined exclusively to it. Then the harmful influence the revolving drum has exerted on the ideas of our young organists and on modern literature will of itself disappear.

It is surprising that our German organs lack the thing we most need. We have the revolving drum, the blind combinations, the synthetic stops, the *tutti (sforzando)*, and so on—that is, all the resources in which one *ensemble* of stops replaces another. But while we hold an actual organ registration we are not able to introduce new stops at our pleasure. This most elementary of resources, the very first requirement of composers, actually does not exist.

It is really unfortunate that very often the organs are never once independent of each other, because the stop that activates the blind combinations, or the one that brings in the *tutti (sforzando)* and mezzoforti, works for the sake of simplicity on the three organs and pedals at the same time—otherwise we should each time have to have four movements instead of one! Our apparent wealth is really a frightful poverty. It is impossible, when *tutti (sforzando)* is on, to use the pedals with the third organ, since the pedals also are on *tutti (sforzando)*. One could write a book about the pedal emergency in these modern organs of ours, which smile at one with their numberless, glittering little stops so rich in promise; a façadal wealth that is really only a glittering poverty, since it lacks the simplest and therefore most artistic of all the resources needed.

And to meet this need, the organ builders offer us today a weaker pedal introduced automatically, a pedal which replaces the other as soon as one passes over to the II or III organ by putting off the *tutti (sforzando)*; but this is only a lamentable makeshift, more adapted to reveal the need than to bring it relief; for a genuine organist wants the particular pedal that he needs, not any pedal that the organ builder prescribes as good for him in the full II or III organ.

We must also find a way of adding and retiring new tone ensembles. Here too I believe a compromise between the French and German types will commend itself, namely, a compromise between our blind combinations and the French introduction of mixtures and reeds. The French arrangement has the disadvantage of providing only for the introduction of the mixtures and the reeds; the German, that the entrance of the blind combinations retires the chosen registration. Since anything is possible in pneumatics, the registration provided by the blind combinations should be arranged to replace the registration chosen by the organist, or to complement it (the blind combinations to be withdrawn again by the same action of piston or pedal), in accordance with whether the musician, before beginning to play, has pressed a pedal or pulled a stop to activate or annul the main registration.

We should have, then, as resources for a medium-sized organ: pedal couplers, manual couplers, super- and suboctave couplers, doubly available blind combinations of the kind described above for each organ and for the pedals, and along with them all the revolving drum. With the couplers, the stops of the first organ would be introduced in the manner of the French G. O.

The idea of this type of organ has been forced upon me by a year of reflection about French and German organs and by a continuous striving for a useful compromise between them. Stimulating conversations with organ builders here and there have given me valuable hints. If one reflects on these simple resources, he will find that their riches stand in inverse proportion to their simplicity.[1] Whatever is

[1] The organ just finished for St. Nicholas in Strassburg [Schweitzer's own church at the time—C. R. J.], the work of two young Alsatian organ builders, Dalstein and Härpfer at Boulay in Lorraine, is of this type.

All the couplers and composition stops are doubled, in the form of pedals or pistons, in such a way that the piston and the pedal are connected with each other by a simple mechanism invented by Mr. Dalstein. The cost of each coupler or composition has been raised about twenty marks by the addition of this device. The double availability of the blind combinations, which enhance or complete at will the hand registration, makes all other resources actually superfluous; and even those organists who at the beginning distrusted the modernization that did away with the *piano*, *mezzoforte* and *tutti* (*sforzando*) became convinced of this. The advantage of using the first organ as a coupling organ

possible on a French or German organ is possible on this one also. Bach, César Franck, Guilmant, Widor, and Reger might all play on it with equal success.

Indeed, one might perhaps take exception to this organ on the ground that it is too simple; for in spite of warning voices the complexity of our organs has gradually become a mania with us. If an organ does not look like the central signal room of a great railway station, it is from the very start worthless to a certain category of our organists. They want half a dozen blind combinations spread out one over the other, even though they must be arranged on a panel behind their backs with pistons for synthetic stops, tutti (sforzando), and composition stops—all of them in the greatest possible number. I am sure that I have never heard better playing on such complicated organs than on others, and have usually noted that these instruments, though rich in interrelated resources, are equally poor in other respects.

Of our echo organs I may not speak; for they have nothing to do with the organ itself, and are dangerous playthings, which destroy the taste of the listeners, and, even worse, of the organists.

The Organola represents in our modern organ building "the fall of man." When will enough voices be raised publicly to characterize the production of such an apparatus for mechanical playing as what it is, an insult to the art of organ playing! For me the Organola has only a social meaning: in the future cripples and war invalids may hold organists' positions.

How far good taste has already strayed is evident in the fact that our organ builders dare to offer us meaningless things like echo organs and Organolas!

Then, too, it is almost laughable to see how people seek modernity even for little organs by overloading them with pistons. On organs with ten or twelve registers we find composition stops for piano,

---

was evident after the first practical demonstration. The whole console cost about 200 marks more than usual.

For a two-manual organ of twenty stops, with two doubly connected pedal couplers, two doubly connected manual couplers, and three doubly available blind combinations (organ I, II, and pedals), the difference in cost might be only a hundred marks!

mezzoforte, forte, and fortissimo! In thoughtless indolence our organists are getting away entirely from planned hand registration.

It almost seems to me as if we were all being deceived by the phantom of the "concert organ." What, then, is a concert organ? Are there two kinds of organs? Or is there not simply a best organ, and is not this good enough for a church organ? What would old Bach say of our distinctions? What, indeed, would he say if he knew that we distinguish between organists and organ virtuosi? Can there be anything better than a "good organist," one who does not consciously seek his own fame, but tries to hide behind the objectivity of the holy instrument and let it speak as if it spoke for itself, ad majorem Dei gloriam?

"Just think," said Widor to me once, "I have been insulted. I have been called in a magazine an organ virtuoso. But I am a genuine organist. An organ virtuoso is only a savage among organists."

That the concert organ and the "organ virtuoso" are almost unknown in France is due to the organ builder Aristide Cavaillé–Coll, the creator of the simple, and, in its artistry, the perfect type of French organ. He was more than a great organ builder: he was, like Silbermann, a genius in organ building. I can never forget him; I can still see him today with his little cap, and with the good, true eyes in which so much of art and intelligence lay, sitting every Sunday beside Widor on the organ bench at St. Sulpice, and caressing with his hand the console of his darling organ.

In German organ circles it has been repeatedly taken amiss that in my French book on Bach I maintained that Bach would have found his ideal organ once more in the model created by Cavaillé–Coll, rather than in our own instruments. Since I reaffirmed this position in the German and English editions that followed the French, I should like to raise the subject for discussion here and give the reasons for my assertion.

The test of every organ, the best and only test, is Bach's organ music. Let one apply this test artistically to organ building, instead of trying to imagine how Bach would throw his peruke in the air for joy over our pistons, and then after catching it again, set off to find out from one of our modern organ *virtuosi* how on the modern organ one can bring everything out of his music.

As a mind always prying insistently into the nature of things, he would immediately ask about the mechanics of our organ.

At once the practical advantages of our organ pneumatics would appear: ease and rapidity of touch, simplicity of arrangement, the unlimited possibilities in all the resources. Are these, however, as great esthetic advantages?

No. Our organ pneumatics is a dead precision. It consists in the transmission of power solely through wind pressure. It lacks the vital and elastic quality of the lever. Not all the springs can replace this direct, elastic transmission. The player must exert himself to cover this dead precision. It requires an artist to play well on a good pneumatic organ. And the pneumatic systems of our Walcker and Sauer, to name only two of the most outstanding, are true masterpieces.

If one, then, considers the average of the many kinds of pneumatic organs, with badly regulated keys, without depth, without free play, without a contact point that can be felt, where the slightest finger substitution is a hazard because the adjacent keys speak with the slightest touch, with pedals on which it is impossible for the best of organists to play correctly and cleanly—if one considers this average pneumatic organ, which one leaves in a high state of nervous despair, one may well wonder if we have not gone far astray with our pneumatics. No organist wants any longer a mechanism.[1] And yet many who played well and cleanly on their old mechanical organs now smear on the new ones of which they are so proud, and play without precision; though they do not notice this, because they have not become accustomed to the demands of the pneumatic organ.

I believe that we in Germany have abandoned our blind enthusiasm for the pneumatic organ, and are beginning to realize that from

[1] I dare not speak of the pneumatic organs built by houses of second rank in the transition period. What sums would be necessary to redeem these victims of the first experiments, which shriek every Sunday to high heaven, and to give them a new and positive spirit!

And how many of our modest organ builders, who once constructed simple and beautifully sounding instruments, sometimes even artistically toned, have failed, because they had to participate in the inventions!

an artistic point of view pneumatics is only a makeshift in situations where the tracker is no longer feasible.

With the tracker the finger feels a certain tension exactly when the tone comes; it feels the contact point. And the depressed key pushes up under the finger, in order that, when the finger shows the slightest impulse to leave it, it may immediately rise with its own strength and lift the finger up with it. The strength of the keys coöperates with the will! With the tracker even the mediocre organist cannot smear. With pneumatics there is no such coöperation on the part of the keys. It makes the playing worse instead of better, and brings to light the slightest fault.

Only with the tracker does one come into really intimate relationship with his organ. In pneumatics one communicates with his instrument by telegraph—for even the Morse apparatus depends on a key with a spring. The tracker system of the organ in St. Thomas's in Strassburg is well over a hundred years old; but it is a marvel to play a Bach fugue on. I know no other organ on which everything would come forth so clearly and so precisely.

Besides all this, the pneumatic organ is affected by the smallest thing. Once, between a final rehearsal and a performance, the organ builder had to be summoned by telegraph, because something had gone wrong with the pneumatic system. The trouble was found. Triumphantly he showed me the mischief maker: a little grain of sand fallen from the ceiling. "Just a little grain of sand!" . . . "It's a bad thing," I replied, "that a little grain of sand should cause such a disturbance. If it had been an earthquake I would say nothing. As for that, you will see that the old tracker organs will not suffer even when the world comes to an end, but will remain standing there for the angels at the last judgment to play the *Gloria* on." He was so perplexed over this upsetting of values that he even forgot the speech about the hot summer, which one usually brings into the discussion in opposition to the tracker.

"But the pneumatic organ operates so easily!" The man who threw in this comment was a giant, who might have appeared as the strong man at any yearly fair.

That a good tracker organ is better in small ways than a pneumatic organ our organ builders know very well, and even admit. But a pneumatic organ is simpler and cheaper to build. And conditions compel them to favor the cheaper thing.

The French pneumatic organ, which depends upon the principle of the almost sixty-year-old Barcker chest, does not have even this advantage. It is almost half again as expensive as our pipe pneumatic system. But it is more artistic and more elastic, since it operates with the pneumatic lever, and so has carried over into the pneumatic organ to a certain extent all the artistic advantages of the pure tracker organ. When I play in Paris an organ of Cavaillé–Coll, or a beautiful Merklin organ, I am each time delighted anew with the elastic and certain precision of this action, and afterwards I always have trouble in accustoming myself once more to our pneumatic organs. But among us the question of cost is final.

In general we could learn a great deal about the details of arrangement from the French organ. Its keys are somewhat shorter than ours; the black keys cunningly rounded off; the manuals closer together than ours as they rise above each other. Everything is provided for the most exact blending, and for the easy and sure changing from one manual to another, on which, as is well known, Bach laid a great deal of stress. And as for the French pedals, they cost, indeed, about double ours. But what perfection! All arranged concave and radiating, recently reaching to g^1, and with a really ideal spring. Our demands are much more modest.

The concave pedal has not yet won its way among us, in spite of its apparent advantages, and in spite of the fact that everyone who has reflected upon the radiating movement of the foot in pedal work must mark it as the only one that makes sense. I might almost have made an enemy not long ago of an organist friend upon whom I forced concave pedals when his organ was being rebuilt, had I not promised to replace the concave pedals after the space of a year with straight ones if he were not convinced of the utility of the innovation.

When I was talking to one of our most distinguished organ builders about this matter, and said to him that he constructed beautiful concave pedals only for other lands, while almost always he built straight ones for Germany, he answered, "In foreign lands I have to build these pedals. In Germany they are not wanted, and since many inspectors have never had concave pedals under their feet, I get nowhere with them."

In a word, it is easier to play well on a French organ than on a German organ. Because of the simple, practical refinement of the arrangements, one there is not exposed to many things that can happen to us. We think more of external refinements installed to please the eye. Instead of drawknobs we are beginning to favor tilting tablets; we introduced elegant pistons, and find them entrancing to touch, instead of pulling real drawstops or couplers.

I had just ended a Bach fugue on a wonderful old Silbermann organ, and was still completely captivated by the magic tone of the old mixtures, when someone next to me, who had his modern organ for two years, remarked, "You know, it must be disagreeable to play on an organ that does not have a single tilting tablet." In his irritation over the old drawstops he had not heard the organ.

I should like to raise the question whether in general we have not paid more attention to the visible changes in our consoles, and less to the important thing, the effect upon the tone. Are the advances in organ building beneficial to the tonal quality?

No! Not at all! Our organs are indeed more powerful than the old ones, but no longer as beautiful. Our old organs, even those built twenty years ago, are more beautifully and more artistically voiced than those of today.

It is remarkable to me that the laity have noticed this before the organists have. Musical laymen have often remarked to me timidly, when an old organ has been replaced by a new one, "that the old one was still almost more beautiful." This recognition makes but slow headway with the organists. We must first of all arouse ourselves from this intoxication with inventions before we can get our hearing back again.

That the tone has not profited by the modern inventions results in part from the fact that one of the principal inventions, the possibility of getting unlimited wind production by the electrically driven bellows, quite naturally set us off on the wrong track—even the most thoughtful among us. We began to exchange tone richness for tone power. In the old organs we had to be economical with our supply of wind. When this was no longer necessary, we laughed over the narrow wind ducts of our fathers, and began to intone strongly and vigorously, ever more strongly, ever more vigorously, rejoicing in the roaring and blustering. The high point of our enthusiasm was reached with the introduction of high-pressure flue stops.[1] A distinguished organist wrote at that time, "We have succeeded now in making an organ of fifteen stops that produces the full effect that formerly an organ of thirty stops produced." The aberration could not describe itself better.

The disenchantment arrived; it grows stronger. But how long a time must still elapse before we strive once more for tone richness alone, renouncing the tone power which the electrical bellows offers us as a gift from the Greeks, and going back once more within the boundaries of art, where the difficulty of producing the desired volume of wind formerly kept us.

A fat person is neither beautiful nor strong. To be artistically beautiful and strong is only to have a figure with a perfect play of muscles. So in time we shall desert the modern organ inflated by wind pressure, seek the full, rich, and beautiful organ only through the collaboration of the normal, differentiated, and artistically toned stops, and give up trying to assemble a full organ by craftiness. Craftiness does not belong with art, for art is truth.

But even if we had had artistic insight, so that the mounting possibility of wind pressure would not have tempted us in the wrong direction, nonetheless our organ building would have been forced along this road. It is all a financial question. Our organ builders found themselves in the embarrassing position of having to accept those inventions which made possible a reduction in prices, and therefore success in competition. Everything else, the purely artistic, was compelled to stand aside. The past forty years, the age of invention in organ building, will not appear some day on the pages of history as the great years of artistic progress, as many among us believe, but rather will they be described in this way: "Battle between the commercial and the artistic; victory of the commercial over the artistic."

---

[1] In a very large church two or three artistically built, high-pressure stops may be added for a grandiose effect, and have a place therefore in the perfection of the instrument. In middle-sized rooms, however, they can only disfigure the organ tone, and must therefore remain the exception in organ building.

Any concern that placed the artistic above the commercial was from the beginning lost. The invention intoxication that gripped us organists in this period demanded external, epoch-making, cost-reducing discoveries. Our organ builders had to bow to this spirit; many of them, as I know, inwardly furious.

So we have come to the factory organ—the good old factory organ. For what is artistic in it we are indebted to the sacrificial spirit of our organ builders, who even for these reduced prices still did the best work they could, and were satisfied if generally they could "get by." In the righteous judgment of history they will some day be honored, in spite of the fact that their organs are only good factory instruments; but we, who decided what organs should be built, and supposed that art could profit from this undercutting competition, shall be dishonored, because we did not sufficiently comprehend, what as pupils of the old Bach we should have comprehended, that an organ builder can be an artist only when he is engaged as an artist by an artist. If this support is lacking, then circumstances force him to become a dealer in objects of art.

Of course there have been exceptions. But in general we organists cannot deny that we have followed the tendency of the times to-wards cheapness; and that we often gave the contract to that man who for the same price offered one or two more stops, even though they were only a little aeolina or a little piston, and that we did not ask if at the same time artistic work, that is, work that does not need to take either time or pay into consideration, was still possible.

A happy fate protected Cavaillé–Coll from being forced at the same time along this road. His principal activity fell in the last decade of the Empire, when money for ecclesiastical purpose was plentiful. Afterwards Guilmant and Widor, his artistic advisers, gave him such a reputation by their support that he did not have to lower his prices to meet competition. "Yes, the old Cavaillé," one of our sympathetic organs builders said to me not long ago, "when one of his men worked on something for three weeks and it did not please him entirely, he had him start again at the beginning; and if again it did not satisfy him, still another time. Who among us can do that? We should not last three months."

At last, however, fate overtook even him. In his last years he had to contend with financial difficulties. The firm itself in its venerable house, 15 Avenue du Maine, in the business district of the Gare Montparnasse, was, indeed, saved; Cavaillé, however, died poor, leaving nothing behind him for his family. But for this very reason the organs of St. Sulpice and Notre Dame will sing his praise as long as one stone rests upon another. Until some day Paris has become a heap of rubble like Babel, those who are susceptible to the magic beauty of his organs will leave Notre Dame and St. Sulpice thinking with deep feeling of the man who dared in spite of the times to remain a pure artist.

Cavaillé–Coll was convinced that he had found in the Barcker chest, which he employed for the first time in the Basilica of St. Denis, the ideal action to connect the keys with the pipes. For resources he was satisfied with couplers, and the ventil for mixtures and reeds. For large organs he provided a simple series of blind combinations; this is the way it is on the organs of St. Sulpice and Notre Dame. No efforts to go farther in this direction interested him: all his inventiveness and endeavor were directed towards the perfecting of the voicing and timbre of the tone, precisely that which in German organs had been neglected.

In the strength of tone he gave to a single stop he remained conservative. It is true that he constructed high-pressure reeds (trompettes en chamade)[1] for the swell organ; for the other stops he sought only beauty. Even his flutes—not simply his principals and gambas—are wonderfully beautiful; though they perhaps lack the interesting variety that certain German organ builders have achieved in the flute family.

In order to make clear the difference between German and French organs, let us draw on both of them all the foundation stops, sixteen-foot, eight-foot, four-foot and two-foot, in all the manuals. In the German organ the ensemble often sounds harsh, at times intolerable. I know modern organs on which even all the eight-foot foundation stops of the I manual produce an effect that is intolerable. Let us not speak of our double flutes. An organ builder confessed to me that he shuddered at the double flutes people forced him to build; and I

[1] Trompettes en chamade were originally horizontal pipes outside the case. Cavaillé–Coll revived them and put them inside the case. C. R. J.

myself in certain instruments hear the double flutes plainly even when the whole organ is sounding.

All the foundation stops are the basis of the entire organ. When the basis itself has no lovely unity of tone, what becomes of the whole instrument?

It is quite different with Cavaillé. The foundation stops are voiced with reference to the tonal unity they should form. Not only those in each manual alone, but also all of them together, form a well-balanced, harmonious whole, and indeed in such a way that the individuality of each of the three organs is fully brought out. The foundation stops of the great organ provide the groundwork. They are exceedingly weak, but have a full, round tone; those of the II organ introduce to some extent the brightness; those of the III furnish the intensity. The tone of the swell is much more intense than the tone of the great organ. With us the coupling of the third organ, when all the foundation stops are pulled, is not noticed. With Cavaillé, on the contrary, it is as if at every instant light—white, streaming light—came flooding into the mass of tone from the foundation stops.

And there is no harshness, not even in the highest registers. Since French compositions are prepared for such organs, they are intolerable on our organs. "How can Widor set down such sustained dissonances?" said a Berlin organist to whom I owe a great deal. Indeed they were unbearable on the organ in question, a torment . . . but not on the organ of St. Sulpice!

In order to avoid this, I take for French compositions on German organs only half the foundation stops, almost no four-foot and two-foot stops on the first organ, for the sake of the upper registers. In principle I draw only as many foundation stops on the I and II organs as will permit all the coupled foundation stops of the III to be plainly heard, and the swell to influence the ensemble. Only when one observes this practice can one make César Franck, Widor, Guilmant, Saint–Saëns, Gigout, and the others sound on our organs as they sound on their own.

The voicing of our foundation stops, which is not concerned with the ensemble, is such, then, that the mixtures do not blend with them, but only make them strong by adding their own overpowerful voicing. When one hears a modern organ, he hears the foundation stops and the mixtures rolling along unblended; whereas the mixtures are designed to enter into the tone color of the foundation stops to make them light and transparent, that is, adapted to polyphonic playing.

On our organs it is simply impossible to play a Bach fugue and prelude with foundation stops and mixtures, the latter now added and now retired; impossible, too, to bring out the climaxes by coupling and uncoupling the manuals or by changing them; impossible, in other words, to make the fugues and preludes stand forth as architectonic, vitalized musical creations. On Cavaillé's organ this is possible, because everything is based on the beautiful tonal unity of the foundation stops and the mixtures. Therefore the French organists play the Bach fugues in many respects more simply, clearly, and appropriately than we; because their organs are nearer to the Bach organ than ours.

We, however, have to adapt the Bach fugues to our organ. Our interpretations spring in part from necessity, which does not prevent most people from considering these interpretations as evidence of artistic progress. Since we cannot play them as simply as was intended, our registration and treatment are orchestral. We pour them into a new form, and introduce *crescendi* and *diminuendi* where none is foreseen in the fugue plan, because on our organ we cannot create the clear and satisfying tone color which Bach intended.

But in the end nothing helps at all, for on our organs one can hear only treble and bass; it is impossible to follow the figures of the middle voices. I will not speak of the bad taste which is current in the registration. I once heard the theme of the great G *minor Fugue* interpreted with the flutes of the III organ, in such a way that the whole fugue swelled up like the body of a fish. But whether the registration is in good taste or bad, fugues played in this way are untrue and unnatural, as though one wished for greater effectiveness to publish the Dürer engravings as colored chalk drawings.[1]

[1] Even our modern grand piano is unsuitable for Bach's music. The recognition of this fact begins to be felt everywhere. See concerning this matter, *Sur l'Interpretation des Oeuvres de Clavecin de J. S. Bach* [Interpretation of Bach's Harpsichord Works], by Wanda Landowska, Mercure de France, 1905.

I can still see today the surprised countenance of one of our most famous Bach singers, when not long ago she heard the G minor Fantasy take shape on the organ of St. Sulpice under Widor's fingers in its simple, tone-satisfying, and transparent form.

Back to the polyphonic organs desired by Bach; away with the orchestral organs! More delicate foundation stops! The harmonious unity of the foundation stops! Away with our few shrieking mixtures! Many soft mixtures!

Where is the mixture family adequately represented, even in some measure, on any manual of our instruments? Our II and III organs were for a long time denuded of mixtures. Slowly we are coming to the point of again adding a mixture even to small organs. But how long will it be before we shall have secured the right proportion of mixtures in all organs, before it shall become a dogma that an instrument is the richer, truer, and more beautiful the more lovely mixtures it has, that in general it can never have too many of them, and that even our swell organs must be filled with them? For the Bach fugue requires homogeneity in tone color on all three manuals! It is designed as a monochrome, like a copper plate engraving.

But this again is a question of money. An organ of forty stops with the right mixtures is at least as expensive as our present organ of fifty stops, if not more so. But there will surely come a time when we shall again think not of the number but of the tonal richness of the stops, when we shall prefer the true expensive organ of forty stops to the false one of fifty; when we shall look back on these instruments of ours, with their few, small, brutal mixtures in unresolved conflict with the gigantic, formless body of our foundation stops, as on something we have overcome.

Then, and not before, the problem of the pedals will be solved. Our pedals are at once so strong and so weak because the tone is not characteristic and not clear. When one listens to a pedal solo on one of our organs, he begins to think that the body of some dragon is twisting around in the background of the church in wild, ponderous writhings. When the manual is added to the pedal, however, one asks immediately, what has become of the pedals? Our whole organ stands on feet of clay, for in comparison with the full body of our coupled manuals our pedals are always too weak, especially since our greedy manual foundation stops, quicker to snap up the wind than the big, cautious sixteen-foot animals, take it away from them.

The adding of lovely mixtures to the pedals is the only answer to the pedal problem for the entire instrument. Now, however, we find hardly any mixtures in our pedal organs. Even the four-foot ones are usually lacking. And the one or two mixtures sometimes found there are unusable because they do not blend with the tones of the foundation stops, but make blurred figures with them in unresolved discord, sometimes even with acoustical distortion. On the other hand, in the increase of tone volume in our pedal foundation stops we are already far beyond the limits of artistic tolerance. Listen once to the F major Toccata on our organs. Who could think this rumbling forth of excessive tones beautiful? Who could find in it the wonderful Bach lines?

We must build pedals that are not excessively strong, but rich, intensive, and flexible, with tones that carry alone and carry also when the foundation stops and mixtures of all the manuals are coupled to them. That means sixteen- and eight-foot foundation stops, not excessively powerful and not too many, and almost as many beautiful and softly voiced mixtures. Such a pedal organ is never too weak and never too strong; it does not obscure or cover the middle stops of the manual.

This realization that we must go back to many and lovely mixtures made more and more headway with Cavaillé–Coll in the last period of his creative work. His pupil Mutin, who now directs the concern, follows in his master's footsteps, and accomplishes this purpose. I shall never forget when I first heard the ideal pedal of which I had dreamed. It was on the model organ that embellishes Cavaillé's studio, an instrument of about seventy stops rich in mixtures. In the pedal organ almost all the mixtures, even the septième, are represented. I played Bach's A minor Fugue with coupled manuals, all the eight-foot, four-foot, and two-foot foundation stops and mixtures drawn. The lines of the pedal figures stood forth clearly without any obtrusiveness, with intensive plasticity. "Play it once more," said Mutin, "without the mixtures." As I started to push in the pedal mixtures he said, "Stop, let them stay." And the same pedal that previously had been everywhere strong enough for the whole instrument without the reeds . . . was for the new registration, though unchanged, not too strong. Finally I made use of the same full pedal organ, and left in the manuals only the eight-foot and four-foot principals . . . and again it was not too strong. . . . Then I felt like one who had been permitted to look into the future; and I stepped down from the bench completely convinced that the time for the organ powerful in tone was passing, and that the time for the organ rich in tone, the organ of Bach, the old organ arising in new glory, was coming.

An organ rich in tone presupposes that the waves of the single tones should come to the ears of the hearer unmixed, not intermingled to any extent with the others, and that only there should they blend as independent personalities in the richest variety with the artistic unity.[1] Cavaillé–Coll had already turned his attention to the phenomenon of fusion (entrainements harmoniques), and had reflected on the means of preventing one pipe in the full instrument from devouring the same tone in other pipes—as the lean cattle of Pharaoh devoured the fat ones—so that when all fifty stops of an instrument were sounding we could really hear only twenty-five, the others only strengthening to a certain extent instead of enriching, because as physical individualities they no longer existed.

Mutin has carried his experiments to a practical conclusion, and turns them to good account on all his organs. Pipes with the slightest difference in dimensions never destroy each other's effect, but each stands forth as a personality whatever its volume of tone. If the diameters are the same, or if the difference is greater, then the entrainement is within the bounds of toleration. In installing an arrangement Cavaillé–Mutin always sees to it that the richest minimal differences in dimensions are observed throughout.

[1] From the first it has impressed me that certain splendid Silbermann organs sound rather bad near by, because the individuality of the different registers persists unbroken. All the more splendid, however, is their tone in the nave of the church.

It has been observed also that such old organs, even when they are weakly voiced, can be heard through the walls of the church! Every tone in the polyphony arrives clearly at the ears of the listener in the square before the church. How is it with the modern organ? With all its power it is able to send through the stones only a muffled howling and moaning. Thus even the stones bear witness against it, and furnish the proof that its tone does not carry.

Is the tone of our organs appealing, however? Yes . . . if one considers prompt speech of the pipe the same thing as good speech. Let one play rapid trills in the lower register of the manual, and quick passages with the sixteen-foot pipes in the pedal!

But prompt speech of the pipe is not necessarily good speech, for good speech means promptness plus quality,[1] that is, that the tone of the pipes is properly adjusted and to a certain extent articulate. On our organs the tone often blusters forth—is not adjusted. The right blending of the separate tones is therefore impossible. When one listens closely, one always hears an interval between two tones, or, on the contrary, they sound together for a small fraction of a second. There is no vital relationship between them; rather do they roll after each other like cannon balls. The organ is the ideal choir, to which only words are denied. Is it then comprehensible that so little value is attached at times to the artistic expression of the stops?

Here also, it seems to me, Cavaillé's pupil Mutin is on the right track. He proceeds from the observation that a wooden bellows gives a different wind pressure in his instrument to the different registers: below, a good deal of wind but with restraint; in the middle, moderately strong but in quantity less than below; above, very little pressure but intense—the quantity always therefore in inverse proportion to the intensity. If now the volume of tone in a wind instrument is very small in relation to that of an organ stop, and yet requires this difference for a proper tone, how much more is this true for an organ stop! Therefore the wind chest of the stop is divided into three or four parts, and each part receives the supply and pressure of wind that makes for the best tone in that register. The great model organ in the studio of Cavaillé–Mutin operates with wind chests divided into three parts, which are fed with wind of different pressures. Of course the construction is much more complicated and the costs appreciably higher; but listen to the result! Such a stop is worth three others; to say nothing of the fact that now the whole instrument also receives for its lower registers their proper amount of wind. Let one listen sometime to the middle voices in a Bach fugue played on organs so constructed! Not a tone, not one, is lost, since each has a

---

[1] Ansprechen heisst eben An-Sprechen.

different individuality from that above and below. I do not venture
to assert that this organ in the Mutin studio—with which the builder
will not part—is technically and artistically the most perfect one
ever built. But it certainly is an instrument that suits Bach's works,
in so far as it meets the requirements his organ music makes of the
ideal organ.

When will the time come when this most elementary esthetic requirement of differentiation in wind pressure is met on all organs?
Now, if all goes well, each organ has its wind—the first the strongest,
the second not quite so strong, and the third the weakest; which
means that the first is much too strong, because about the same pressure is provided for it as is required for the supply of the pneumatic
system. One should listen to the sounds produced in this way by the
principals and the flutes! How richly sounds, on the contrary, the
instrument in which the stops of the same manual are supplied with
two or three different wind pressures, in such a way that each one
receives the wind required for the most perfect tone, without having
to take into consideration whether it is in front or in back, high or
low! What a wealth of perfect tone individuality in such an instrument!

Instead of this we find among us excessively strong-toned mixtures, placed above in the very first rank, which seem to be particularly designed to destroy the beauty of the whole instrument. And
many organists—incredible as this seems—think they can accomplish
through a differentiation in the wind supply the same thing that is
accomplished by a differentiation in the wind pressure, though these
have to do with entirely different things. The collaboration of both
differentiations is required to give an organ a beautiful wealth of tone.

And the reeds? They are pleasing on neither the German nor the
French organs, because on both they are too strong and dominant.
When once I said to Widor that I considered the French reed, in
other respects so beautiful, as an artistic handicap, he admitted to me
that he had been carrying around with him for years the same conviction, and was of the opinion that we must go back to the building
of reeds which do not dominate the whole instrument, but harmonise
with the foundation stops and the mixtures, and to a certain extent
only beautify them. Gigout holds the same opinion. But what work,

what trouble, to build reeds that are at once beautiful, soft, and good sounding!

When we once have them, the other question of whether we should play Bach with reeds will be solved. With our reeds, of course not. But it seems to me certain that Bach was dependent on his eight- and four-foot reeds. And who would deny that a pedal organ, with delicate reeds which lead to the mixtures, is the perfect ideal? Yet let us not forget the four-foot pipes. Four-foot flutes, four-foot principals, and four-foot trumpets, not coarsely voiced, should be on any comparatively perfect pedal organ. No coupler can replace them in the entire *ensemble*. Without them the pedal figures roll to the ground, instead of standing upright in the range of the stops.

And this is all a question of money! With today's prices the technical, artistic problem, which constitutes the problem of the rich-toned organ—that is, the beautifully toned organ—cannot be put in the foreground. Instead, the builder has to offer the most stops for the least money, and sometimes against his better judgment deliver what the customer wants instead of what the builder knows is the best; he has to build for the eye and not for the ear—the useless instead of the useful!

If only the highly gifted inventiveness of our German organ builders, who in recent decades have had to go in almost exclusively for cheapness, could be turned loose upon purely artistic questions! But that will happen only when we no longer give thoughtless consideration to the number of stops, and reconcile ourselves to the fact that prices are going up a good third higher! Until then we shall live in the period of the good factory organs.

But even with these prices, who can get really first-class quality? How is artistic tuning possible under these circumstances? A tuning appropriate for the locale, done with conscientious art, takes four times as much time as is now customary, when each day's tuning expense must be anxiously reckoned; and even the effort to tune artistically would eat up all the profits.

Good tuners should be paid like ministers, and should occupy such a place in the rank of artists that one artistic tuner should be considered equal to six average *virtuosi*, since a half dozen of the latter are easier to find than one artistic tuner. Only the mistakes of ministers concern posterity; of the *virtuosi* it cherishes perhaps the names; the work of the tuners, however, just as it leaves their hand, edifies generation after generation.

Where at present-day prices is the organ builder to find the means for research, without which there is no progress? They say that we are about to become a wealthy land. The future will not know that from our organs, for the poor Germany of earlier days built better ones.

Let no one deceive himself: as the organs, so the organists. No other instrument exercises such an influence upon artists. Perfect organs train organists in perfection; imperfect ones train them in imperfection and in false virtuosity. No talent and no genius can prevent this. The art of organ playing is always the product of the art of organ building. Without the art of organ building, which for his time and in its way was perfect, the Bach art of organ playing would never have arisen.

So, too, the modern French school of the organ is the result of this perfected organ construction. We in Germany are unquestionably richer in talent. But we do not possess such a circle of extraordinary artists as that which is represented in France by the names of Saint–Saëns, Guilmant, Widor, Gigout and Vierne.

The French organist differs from the German in the simplicity of his playing. The virtuosity that is found among our leading organists is much less prevalent there. Above everything else they seek a quiet plasticity, which brings the tone pattern to the listener in all its greatness. It seems to me as if the French organist even sits more quietly on his organ bench than we do. With all of them one finds an absolute precision in pressing and releasing the keys, which results in blending and clear, natural phrasing. Of course there are many organists among us who have these qualities in the same measure; but in France they seem to be the product of the school itself. All, even the otherwise mediocre players, possess them; whereas we have outstanding players who lack perfect precision, whose hands and feet do not work together with mathematical exactness, so that the other qualities in their playing are spoiled for the listener who really listens. To be sure, it is even more difficult to play with perfect precision on our organs than on the French organs with their mechanical action. What always surprises me particularly in the French organists is the quietness and infallibility of their pedal playing.

I cannot express my feeling better than by saying that the French organist plays more objectively, the German more personally. This, too, comes from the school. We have no school, hence each man goes his own way: so many organists, so many conceptions. To a certain extent that is an advantage we have over the French. I often rejoice in the vital individuality of our German organists—when they are men of taste. But we go much too far; and out of sheer "personality" playing and composition introduce emotion into the organ —natural human emotion, but not the wonderfully luminous, objective emotion of the last great preludes and fugues of Bach; and thus spoil the works of our great master by trying to animate them with our personal feelings. The organ itself should speak. The organist and his idea should vanish behind it—s'effacer, as the French say. He is, with all his thoughts, too little for the quiet majesty of his instrument, which is evident even in its outward appearance, and which, as Bach teaches us, expresses gloriously all feelings.[1]

Perhaps the French, on their side, at times carry too far the objectivity of their playing. But the repose and greatness that lie in it are so beneficial that one does not profit by the appearance of any outspoken personal feeling. "Organ playing," Widor once said to me on the organ bench at Notre Dame [2] as the rays of the setting sun streamed through the dusk of the nave in transfigured peace, "is the manifestation of a will filled with a vision of eternity. All organ instruction, both technical and artistic, has as its aim only to educate a man to this pure manifestation of the higher will. This will, expressed by the organist in the objectivity of his organ, should overwhelm the

---

[1] For this it is also important that the organist should be invisible, which often is not the case in our newer Protestant churches. For me it spoils the most beautiful Bach fugue, when from the nave of the church I can see the organist moving convulsively about at his console, as if he wanted to prove to the believers ad oculos how hard organ playing is. A little man can be only grotesque in his playing before a great instrument. Let us be protected from this sight by a screen from the organ housing around the visible console.

[2] In the early period, after the nomination of Vierne to be organist of Notre Dame, Widor often played on the cathedral organ. At the time in question he was practising his latest organ symphony.

hearer. He who cannot master the great, concentrated will in the theme of a Bach fugue—so that even the thoughtless hearer cannot escape from it, but even after the second measure grasps and comprehends it whether he will or not—he who cannot command this concentrated, peaceful will imparting itself so powerfully, may be a great artist in spite of this but is not a born organist. He has mistaken his instrument; for the organ represents the *rapprochement* of the human spirit to the eternal, imperishable spirit, and it is estranged from its nature and its place as soon as it becomes the expression of the subjective spirit."

The same conception of the nature of the organ lies at the basis of Guilmant's playing, except that with him the objectivity is interestingly and peculiarly animated by a certain lyrical experience.

We may say that in the French art of organ playing the feeling for architecture, which is to some extent the basis of all French art, comes to light. The swell box has therefore an entirely different significance from what it has with us. Instead of expressing feeling, it serves an architectonic purpose. The swell organs are so important on all French instruments that one can model the foundation stop tones of the whole organ with the volume of sound shut up in them. Says Gigout to his pupils, "A player handles his swell organ rightly, if his hearers do not suspect that the swell is functioning at all, but only feel as necessary the unnoticeable opening and shutting of the box." Guilmant presents the same principle to his pupils.

In the French art of organ playing, the noble and the simple in the use of the swell box come ever more clearly to light. In César Franck, and in the earlier compositions of Saint-Saëns, one still finds the small but frequent use of the swell, where this device to a certain extent takes the place of the emotional expressiveness which is lacking in the organ. This is the handling of the swell box which is still current among us. As time goes on, however, the simple, economical use of the swell box, used only in a general way, prevails; as it triumphs in the last works of Guilmant and Widor. To their pupils, and no less to the pupils of Gigout, it has become flesh and blood. Let us read through with this in mind the first organ symphony of Vierne, and compare it with the indications in our modern organ compositions. It will be easy then to shed the prejudice that the French are foolishly seeking effects with the swell box, and admit that right here we can learn from them.[1]

But when shall we have such proper swell boxes? It was not very long ago that leading organists among us held the opinion that a small organ needed no swell box, any more than it was necessary to have the pedal organ extend to f[1]. But the swell and the complete pedal belong to the nature of the organ itself, just as much as four feet belong to the horse. Rather have two or three fewer stops, for with the right kind of a swell box one can make two stops out of each single one. It is in these small organs in particular that certain advantages possessed by the French instruments appear much more conspicuously than in the great ones.

In registration also the French are much simpler than we. Almost twice as many registration changes are prescribed in a German organ composition as in a French one. Saint-Saëns is a master of gifted registration. Guilmant's registration is extremely skilful and in very good taste. Widor gives up registration almost completely, and increasingly so. "I can no longer comprehend very well a registration which is intended only to change the tone color," he said to me once, "and I find only that change in tone color right which is unmistakably required by the climax of the piece. The simpler our registration is, the closer we come to Bach." In his *Symphonie Romane*—the only registration in the first ten pages consists in adding the mixtures and reeds from time to time to the coupled foundation stops. Of course one should not forget that the French swell, in its

---

[1] I cannot imagine what automatic swell boxes can be. They open and close automatically at times determined in advance once and for all, and thus under certain circumstances produce a *pianissimo* where the composer intends the climax of the *crescendo* to stand. This "epoch-making" invention will be practical only when it succeeds in setting in operation the same clock work in the brains of the organ composers, so that they cannot do otherwise than imagine their periods of *crescendo* and *diminuendo* in the manner of the automatic swell box. Until then the automatic *crescendo* must remain the prerogative of the harmonium, where it succeeds admirably in giving "expression."

One of the best known instruments in Berlin has an automatic swell in the echo organ.

We already have even automatically operating roller *crescendi*. This is the final consequence of our mechanical slavery.

effect on the entire instrument, makes a great deal possible which can be accomplished on our organs only through registration.

Among the formal advantages of French organ compositions I should like to include also the wisely considered, effective use of the pedals, and the avoidance of every unnecessary octave doubling, whether in the manuals or in the pedals. It seems to me that our younger composers have not sufficiently studied the use of the pedals in the preludes and fugues of Bach, otherwise they would themselves have become aware of the mistake of incessantly bringing in the pedals. Over eighty percent of the octaves prescribed so frequently in modern compositions are usually meaningless, cause loose playing, and are ineffective. One should study Widor's works for his use of the pedals both in single line and in octaves!

Close observation discloses really two French schools: an old one, not directly influenced by German art, and a younger one, which shows German influence. As specifically French I would count in the older generation Boëly (died 1858), Chauvet and César Franck. The younger generation is represented by Saint–Saëns and Gigout. Gabriel Pierné and Boëllmann—so prematurely dead (born at Ensisheim in 1862, died as organist of St. Vincent de Paul at Paris in 1897)—also belong here.[1]

This older school had to strive with difficulty after an organ style, without ever quite attaining it even in its best representatives. César

[1] The works of Boëly and Chauvet have hardly any enduring significance; César Franck's early compositions, Six Pièces d'Orgue [Six Organ Pieces], published by Durand, also have really none. But his Trois Pièces pour Grand–Orgue [Three Pieces for the Organ], and his great fantasies which he calls chorales, will endure as something peerless (published by Edouard Durand). These three chorales are Franck's final work. They come from the year 1890. When he could no longer walk, he still managed to drag himself to St. Clothilde's to complete the registration indications.

To prevent misunderstandings, let me remark that the chorale in modern French organ literature means simply a fantasy on a formal, noble theme, which, however, is freely conceived. This designation arose because certain organists of the older generation thought that the chorale themes in the chorale fantasies of Bach come from Bach himself.

Among Boëllmann's compositions I cite: Douze Pièces en Recueil. 2e Suite; Fantaisie [Twelve Selected Pieces. Second Suite; Fantasy] (Leduc); Suite Gothique, Fantaisie Dialoguée [Gothic Suite; Fantasy in Dialogue] (organ and orchestra; arranged for organ alone by Eugène Gigout) (Durand). Gabriel Pierné: Trois Pièces pour Orgue [Three Organ Pieces] (Durand).

Franck's and Saint-Saëns' works [1] are the improvisations of gifted musicians on the organ, rather than organ works, even though the content in the later works of César Franck makes one overlook certain violences done to the organ style. Boëllmann's compositions are interesting youthful efforts, which certainly would have led to something significant.

Gigout [2] stands all alone in this school. He is the classicist, who has attained a pure organ style. He has something of Händel's manner. His influence as a teacher is outstanding, and his playing marvelous.

This specifically French school cultivates the art of improvising— though not so much, of course, as that old organist of Notre Dame (may his name not be cherished by posterity) who boasted that he had never played anything on his organ from notes—but still to the extent of laying very special stress upon it. Saint-Saëns is first fully appreciated when his improvisation is heard at St. Séverin, where occasionally he substitutes for the gifted Perilhou. Gigout's strength also lies, above everything else, in this very domain.

Vincent d'Indy tells, in the masterly book which has just appeared about his teacher (ed. Alcan, Paris, 1906), of César Franck's improvising. As Franz Liszt was leaving St. Clothilde on April 3, 1866, he was so moved that he said to those around him that no one else since Bach had so improvised on the organ.

Guilmant likes to improvise. Widor not so much, "only when he feels forced to say something." Vierne's improvisations at Notre Dame excel by their perfection of form. Schmidt, also, belongs

[1] Among the works of Saint-Saëns should be mentioned Trois Rhapsodies sur des Cantiques Bretons [Three Rhapsodies on Breton Songs] (Op. 7, Ed. Durand), of which the first and the third are really wonder works, and have also the unusual advantage of pleasing the listener immediately; Trois Préludes et Fugues pour Orgue [Three Preludes and Fugues for the Organ] (Op. 99, Durand); Fantaisie pour Grand-Orgue [Fantasy for the Organ] (Op. 101, Durand). The last two opera are ingenious and substantial, but do not completely please in their organ style.

[2] Of Gigout's works let us name Six Pièces. [Six Pieces] (Durand); Trois Pièces [Three Pieces] (Durand); Prélude et Fugue en Mi [Prelude and Fugue in E] (Durand); Méditation [Meditation] (Landy, London); Dix Pièces en Recueil [Ten Selected Pieces] (Leduc); Suite de Pièces [Suite of Pieces] (Richault); Suite de Trois Morceaux [Suite of Three Pieces] (Rosenberg); Poèmes Mystiques [Mystical Poems] (Durand).

among the leading improvisers. He is one of the most talented of the younger generation, who, unfortunately, because of his appointment as Chapel Master at St. Philipp du Roule, is for the present lost to the organ.

In general, improvising and even playing from memory have a bigger place in French organ instruction, as Widor, Guilmant, Vierne (his assistant at the Conservatory), and Gigout have imparted it, than among us. In the competition for the organ posts at Notre Dame are required the improvisation of a fugue on a given theme, a free improvisation, and twenty modern or classic works for the organ played from memory. The pedagogical value of playing from memory on the organ is in fact extraordinarily great, because the pupil is compelled thereby to take account of everything. It may be that we too much neglect playing from memory on the organ.

The other French school, represented by Guilmant, formerly at the Trinity, and Widor, at St. Sulpice, had its origin in Belgium. Guilmant and Widor were pupils of Lemmens, who in turn in his time was a pupil of Hesse. From the very beginning, therefore, as their early works show, Guilmant[1] and Widor were acquainted with the organ style which emanated from Bach, and did not need to seek gropingly for it.

Guilmant is now not only one of the leading musicians, but at the same time the most universal teacher, with outstanding pedagogical talent and musical historical culture. He is the one who has made known in France the old organ music from the era preceding Bach. How much German organ music can learn from his works concerning form and construction has been constantly emphasized for years in German critical circles.

[1] Alexandre Guilmant: *Sieben Sonaten* [Seven Sonatas] (Durand–Schott) (Op. 42, 50, 56, 61, 80, 86, 89); *Pièces dans Differents Styles* [Pieces in Different Styles] (18th Volume, Op. 15, 16, 17, 18, 19, 20, 24, 25, 33, 40, 44, 45, 69, 70, 71, 72, 74, 75) (Durand–Schott); *L'Organiste Pratique*; 12 *Lieferungen* [The Practical Organist; 12 books] (Durand–Schott); *Noëls, Offertoires Elévations; 4 Lieferungen* [Carols, Offertory Elevations; 4 books] (Durand–Schott); *L'Organiste Liturgiste; 10 Lieferungen* [The Liturgical Organist; 10 books]; *Concert Historique d'Orgue* [Historical Organ Recital]. Guilmant deserves special credit for his edition of the French organ masters of the 16th, 17th, and 18th centuries. Up to date six annual volumes have appeared.

Widor is more of an introversive spirit. His ten symphonies [1] reveal the development of the art of organ playing as he himself has experienced it. The first are creations perfect in form, permeated by a lyric, melodic, sometimes even a sentimental spirit, which show however in the wonderful structure of their themes the peculiar endowment of the creator. With the fifth symphony he deserts this road; the lyric withdraws; something else strives to take form, first in the fifth and sixth symphonies, which are among his best known, and which are still in melodic form. The seventh and eighth are transition works; they are of the organ, and yet conceived in a boldly orchestral manner. What a marvel is the first movement of the eighth symphony! At the same time the austere appears ever more clearly—the austere that Widor brings back to sacred art in his last two symphonies. "It is noteworthy," he said to me in that period, "that except for Bach's preludes and fugues—or, rather, except for certain preludes and fugues of Bach—I can no longer think of any organ art as holy which is not consecrated to the church through its themes, whether it be from the chorale or from the Gregorian chant." Thus the ninth symphony (Symphonie Gothique) on the theme "Puer natus est" [A boy is born] is written as a Christmas symphony, and the tenth (Symphonie Romane), on the wonderful motif of the "Haec dies" [This is the day], is conceived as an Easter symphony. And when one May Sunday, still striving with technical problems, he played for the first time in St. Sulpice the Symphonie Romane, I felt with him that in this work the French art of organ playing had entered sacred art, and had experienced that death and that resurrection that every art of organ playing must experience when it wishes to create something enduring.

Louis Vierne, who was called in 1900 to the Church of Notre Dame while still hardly thirty years old, is the pupil of César Franck, Widor, and Guilmant. His two great and important organ symphonies have very much promise. [2]

I should not want to forget the good Dallier, a pupil of Franck,

[1] Charles Marie Widor: Symphonies pour Orgue (Hamelle), Nos. 1–4, Op. 13; Nos. 5–8, Op. 42 (2d edition 1900); No. 9, Symphonie Gothique (Op. 70); No. 10, Symphonie Romane (Op. 73).
[2] Ed. Hamelle.

formerly at St. Eustache, now at the Madeleine, where he became
the successor of Gabriel Faurés, the wonderfully gifted improviser
and student of Bach, who himself was the successor of Dubois. A
rendering of Bach's *E flat major Triple Fugue*, during a musical
festival at St. Eustache, I shall never forget.

Among the young men we should name are Quef, the successor
of Guilmant at the Trinity; Tournemire at St. Clothilde; Jacob, a
very outstanding player, at St. Louis d'Antin; Marti at St. François–
Xavier; Libert at the Basilica of St. Denis; Marquaire, the substitute
for Widor at St. Sulpice, whose very interesting organ symphony
has been published by Hamelle; Bret, who as the director of the Bach
Society now places all his gifts exclusively at the service of the works
of the old master; Mahaut, an accomplished player, and at the same
time an enthusiastic interpreter of the works of his teacher César
Franck; and Bonnet, the successor of Dallier at St. Eustache.

Common to both schools, and to the old as well as the young, is
their reverence for Bach. Even among us Bach is hardly played more
frequently and exclusively than in many a Paris church. During the
offering at Notre Dame, Bach's choral prelude on "*O Mensch
bewein' dein' Sünde gross*" [O man, mourn for thy great sins] flows
through the mighty halls of the cathedral.

Of the future of the French school I cannot speak. *L'Orgue
Moderne* [The Modern Organ], a collection of the more modern
and most modern efforts, which appears periodically under the
patronage of Widor, does not please me at all. In form everything
in it is good, and much more mature than the first works of our
young German organists. But the resourcefulness, the storm and
stress, the fermentation, that could give wisdom to this clever young
generation, in order that from it something more than cleverness,
something great and enduring, might come—these are lacking. The
contemporary works of the young German organists display less ability
in form, sometimes less organ style, less reflection and clarity; but
in place of these many of them have a very promising wealth of ideas.

But what in general will become of French organ construction
and the French art of organ playing? What will the separation of
church and state bring? Already the churches are preparing for the

separation, and are cutting the already small salaries as far as they can be cut. Most organists have already been notified that a fourth of their pay will be taken away. Dallier first lost a third of his income at St. Eustache and then a half. Thereupon he applied for the post at the Madeleine, which was just becoming vacant. The position of organist at Notre Dame may in the future pay hardly more than 1000 francs. Organ building stagnates. Splendid organs which once stood in the churches are to be bought for ridiculous prices. Often one asks himself if the most certain result of the separation will not be first of all the ruin of organ building and organ art. The crisis which both will pass through will in any case be very severe.

But let us leave the future alone. At the moment the point is that the partition between the French art of organ playing and the German should be razed, and each should learn from the other. German and French talents are destined to stimulate each other. In the art of organ playing especially, just as we Germans can learn a limitless amount in technique and form from the French, they on the other hand can be shielded by the spirit of German art from impoverishment in their pure and perfect forms. By the interpenetration of both spiritual tendencies, new life will arise on both sides. Up to this time only the American organists have really profited from the advantage of passing through the German and the French schools, inasmuch as they usually passed half of their period of learning in Germany, and the other half in Paris. In the future may it be that both the German and the French, in order to enjoy the same benefits, may be seized by that urge to travel and learn which characterized the old organists. Perhaps when that time comes a French organist will acquaint his colleagues with the art of Reger, Wolfrum, Lang, Franke, De Lange, Reimann, Egidi, Irrgang, Sittard, Homeyer, Otto Reubke, Straube, Beckmann, Radecke, G. A. Brandt, and the rest; even as I have tried herein to make better known to the German organists the nature of the French organ and the French art of organ playing.[1]

[1] This treatise first appeared in *Musik*, Volumes 13 and 14, 1906. Fifth Year.

❦

*T*HUS Albert Schweitzer launched the campaign for the new
organ; an organ which should preserve the lovely tone of the
old instruments, but somehow avoid their mechanical defects. The
factory organ was not the answer; another answer had to be found.
The publication of Schweitzer's small book brought down on him
an avalanche of correspondence—mingled praise and blame; bitter
criticism; constructive suggestions. The following years were filled
with many things, but his interest in this question never wavered.

The great opportunity to advance his cause came with the invitation to address the Third Congress of the International Society of
Music at Vienna in 1909. In preparation for his appearance there
Schweitzer wrote a questionnaire which was sent out to organ players and organ builders in half a dozen European countries. Some
hundred and fifty detailed answers were received. The labor involved
in analyzing the replies was enormous; Schweitzer states that he
spent on each report an average of six hours. Months were consumed
by the study; but the report made to the organ section of the International Congress was an important milestone on the road to the
better organ. In the previous booklet we have Schweitzer's own ideas;
in the report to the Congress we have a cross section of informed
opinion in Europe at the beginning of the twentieth century concerning this burning question of organ construction. The questionnaire and report form an appendix to this book. (See pages 253–289.)

After hearing Schweitzer's report the organ section went to work
through days of intensive application to draw up the International
Regulations for Organ Building, which were later sent to organ
players and organ builders throughout Europe. These detailed and
elaborate specifications, containing at great length the recommendations of the organ section, are sometimes attributed to Schweitzer
himself. He had a major hand in framing them, but of course they
are the work of all the faithful members of the organ section. Because they are too technical, and because they are not exclusively the
work of Albert Schweitzer, they are not included in this book.

VI

Medicine, Theology and Music

*S*CHWEITZER describes these early years of the century as a "continual struggle with fatigue." No wonder! His medical studies were exacting enough, but there were all the other things too. He loved his preaching, and he had not been able to make up his mind to resign from his pastorate at St. Nicholas. He kept on, moreover, with his lectures at the University, made still more burdensome because he was giving new lectures on Pauline problems. He was trying to follow the development in Paul's thinking, as he passed from primitive Christianity, with its extreme eschatological emphases, to a new and strange mysticism, characterized by the central idea of dying and being born again in Jesus Christ; a mysticism which prepared the way for the hellenization of Christianity with its doctrine of the Logos. He had hoped to finish this study before the end of his medical course; he succeeded only in completing the introduction. But what Schweitzer called his "introduction" was a large volume in which he had surveyed all important previous interpretations of the writings of St. Paul from the Reformation on. The book was published in 1911. It was almost twenty years later before the rest of his study was ready for publication.

The delay was in part caused by the fact that he was working on the greatly enlarged second edition of his history of research into the life of Jesus, which was published just after his departure for Africa in 1913. It was delayed also by the enormous amount of work he had to do in preparing his thesis for the doctorate in medicine—a study of the mentality of Jesus from the point of view of psychiatry. And lastly it was delayed by his music.

He was going to Paris regularly now for the concerts given by the

Bach Society. That meant three days of absence each time. The Bach Society, founded in 1905, had already taken an important place in the musical life of Paris. It was composed largely of professional singers, and was led by Gustave Bret. The competence of conductor and chorus made it possible for them to render each season a goodly number of Bach's choral works.

Dr. A. T. Davison, Professor Emeritus of music at Harvard University, gives an interesting glimpse of Albert Schweitzer as organist for the Bach Society. In contrast to what he calls the mechanical and heartless perfection of the chorus and orchestra, Schweitzer's work at the organ was easily the most distinguished of all.

"I was struck, first of all, by Schweitzer's indifference to any 'effectiveness' in registration or manner of playing, the entire process being concentrated in the presentation of the music in its proper setting without the slightest effort to make it 'telling' of itself. And it must be remembered that the question was not of the great organ compositions; it was solely of the organ background to, let us say, one of the cantatas. My early studies had centered about the instrument as a vehicle of display, and from Widor I was discovering that the organ and the organist were the servants; the music, especially that of Bach—the master. The unpretentious accompanimental parts must always be a pretty routine affair to the organist who loves his playing better than the music he plays. Schweitzer, however, never once obtruding himself, lavished upon them all the scrupulous attention they deserve but all too seldom receive. I realize now that my feeling about his skilful and appropriate support was primarily a technical one, albeit an as yet undiscovered clue to the impulse that converted these stylistic marvels into an almost biographical record of Bach himself.

"As far as I can remember, Schweitzer, in spite of his authoritative knowledge, was never consulted—publicly, at least—regarding any of the questions involved in the performance of Bach's music. In fact the only occasion upon which I remember his forsaking the near-anonymity of the organ bench was at a rehearsal when the conductor, wishing to judge an effect from the rear of the hall, put his baton in Schweitzer's hand, and asked him to direct the chorus and orchestra. At that time, at least, Albert Schweitzer was in no sense a conductor, and it is significant that he made no pretense of being one. Turning his back squarely upon both orchestra and chorus, one hand thrust in his trousers' pocket, his head back, staring up into the dark of the Salle Gaveau, his arm moving in awkward sweeps and unorthodox directions, it was quite obvious that if he gave himself a thought—which I doubt—it was only to consider himself the agent who should bring the music to life. Beyond that he had no responsibility. It was for the conductor to judge whether the balance of tone or the seating of the participants was satisfactory. Above all, there was complete detachment; entire absorption in the sound of the music. To this day I can remember the intense admiration I felt for Schweitzer's indifference to externals. How I swelled with indignation at the pitying smirks of the orchestral players as they condescendingly shrugged their shoulders and ostentatiously disregarded the vague gestures of the conductor pro tem. It was then, I feel sure, that I first sensed the stature of the man." [1]

In addition to his regular appearance as organist for the Bach Society in Paris, Schweitzer was traveling also to Barcelona to play for the Bach concerts given by the Orféo Catalá. He liked and admired the conductor, Luis Millet, and greatly enjoyed these engagements, though they were very exhausting.

On one occasion an organ and orchestra concert was given for the king and queen. After the rehearsal Señor Millet insisted that Schweitzer leave his music book on the organ. "No one will touch it," he said. Very reluctantly, Schweitzer did so. An hour before the concert they came back again; the book was gone. The director and the assistant director hunted everywhere for it in vain. The time for the concert came; the king and queen arrived; and still there was no book. Schweitzer was in despair. Finally someone suggested that they look in the room where the cleaning-woman kept her things. And there they found it.

After the concert the king and queen expressed their deep appreciation to Schweitzer. "Is it difficult to play the organ?" asked the king. "Almost as difficult," replied Schweitzer, "as to rule Spain." "Then you must be a man of courage," laughed the king.

[1] The Albert Schweitzer Jubilee Book, edited by A. A. Roback. Cambridge, Mass.: Sci-Art Publishers, 1945, pp. 200 f.

Other concerts called him away from Strassburg frequently. They had become a financial necessity, for the loss of income resulting from his resignation as principal of the theological faculty had to be offset somehow. But they were often delightful occasions. There was, for instance, the autumn week in 1911 when he went to Munich with Widor to play at the Festival of French Music. A certain wealthy count who had a great champagne plant and sold to all the big hotels went to Widor and said, "I have to eat at these hotels and I cannot eat alone. I must have a little company with me. Do you know one or two French students who would have lunch and dinner with me regularly?" Of course Widor suggested Schweitzer, and of course Schweitzer accepted. For reasons of economy he had been eating in small restaurants, and now to his surprise he found himself for the remaining six days having lunch and dinner in the big hotels. The count naturally had to honor his own product, and always ordered champagne. Other distinguished guests were there. In this way Schweitzer came to know the old French organist and composer, Charles Camille Saint-Saëns, who was also an occasional guest at the table.

Widor and Schweitzer had come particularly to give Widor's Second Symphony for Organ and Orchestra. The day it was to be given both were invited to dinner. Schweitzer declined with thanks. He wanted to be fresh for the symphony, which is very difficult. But Widor went. At eight o'clock, when they were to begin, Widor was not there. At five minutes past he had not arrived. At ten minutes past he appeared, rushed to the rostrum, and began at once to conduct the orchestra with one hand while he searched for his glasses with the other. He was unable to conduct the symphony without the score, and neither he nor the orchestra was thoroughly familiar with it. With his baton first in his right hand and then in his left he searched in his pockets, one after the other. They were a quarter of the way through before he found them. Had not Schweitzer been so sure of himself and supported so well with the organ, the whole thing would have been disastrous. Said Schweitzer afterwards, "You see, I was right in not accepting the invitation."

Towards the end of his medical course Schweitzer began to prepare, in collaboration with Widor, an edition of Bach's organ works.

Five volumes were completed before his departure, and published later. This too meant many days in Paris, and occasional visits of Widor to Gunsbach. It was not an easy enterprise. Bach had left in his organ works no suggestions for registration or changes of manuals. The organs of his day were so constructed that automatically the pieces were rendered as he intended. When, after a long period of oblivion, Bach's organ works again became known in the middle of the nineteenth century, organs had changed, and even those in Germany who knew the old traditions in organ playing were abandoning them. But by a queer paradox the French organists remained loyal to the old German traditions, which they had learned from the Belgium organist Lemmens, who had been a pupil of Adolph Friedrich Hesse of Breslau. And the splendid tone of the great French organs made it possible to render Bach as Bach had intended.

The new edition was intended for those who knew only the modern organs. Schweitzer and Widor tried first to show what the registration and manual changes had to be on Bach's instruments, and second to suggest how the variations in volume and tone possible on the modern organ might be used without injuring the work. All these suggestions, however, were contained in the introduction, and not attached to the pieces themselves. To both men the important thing was the architecture of the piece. Tone was secondary to lines of melody, which must always move along side by side with perfect distinctness. Perfect plasticity in phrasing, loveliness of tone, a moderate tempo—these were the authentic marks of Bach's organ works.

These were all rich years for Albert Schweitzer, rich in the variety of their activity, rich in the many friends who gathered around his brilliant and charming personality. It was at this time that he came to know well Marie-Joseph Erb, the pianist who had so thrilled the small boy at his first concert in Mulhouse. About the same time—perhaps a few years earlier—Schweitzer had journeyed with Ernest Munch, as already related, to Frankfort to hear Siegfried Ochs, the director of the Philharmonic Chorus of Berlin, perform, with the help of the Cecilia Society, Bach's B minor Mass, and he also came to admire greatly this fine musician. His tributes to these men should not be forgotten.

❦

MARIE–JOSEPH ERB [1]

WHEN I first became acquainted with the organist Marie–Joseph Erb, I immediately felt admiration and sympathy for him. That which struck me in him was the flexibility of his playing and his profound acquaintance with all the resources of the sacred instrument. He did not seek to produce effects with his registration, yet his execution, so simple in appearance, brought out the meaning of the work he was interpreting by means of the sonorities he employed. In many respects his playing resembled that of Alexandre Guilmant.

The opportunity to know Erb better came in 1908, when the Silbermann organ in the St. Thomas church in Strassburg was being restored. The church council, on my request, charged Erb, together with myself, with the responsibility of deciding the character of this restoration—which was entrusted to the organ builder Frédéric Härpfer of Boulay—and of supervising the work.

It was the first time, so far as my knowledge goes, that an old organ was restored instead of being replaced. I had secured from the church council approval for my plan of preserving the ancient instrument, while replacing all its defective or worn-out parts, and adding modern diapason pipes. I was greatly relieved when Erb said he was ready to share the responsibility with me. How many hours we passed together at the organ as the work progressed, trying with the builder, Frédéric Härpfer, whom Erb valued as highly as I did, to find the best solution of our problems! In these conferences I was able to appreciate the profundity and extent of the knowledge of organ building that Erb possessed.

When the restored instrument was dedicated, Erb was the first to play on it, using an organ concerto of Bach's. The rendering of this concerto showed the musicians who were present at the dedication that the task of conserving this ancient instrument was fully justified and had been well carried out. For the first time we learned

[1] From *Un Grand Musicien Français: Marie–Joseph Erb*. Strassburg–Paris: Editions F.-X, Le Roux & Cie., 1948, pp. 84–88.

how Bach's music must have sounded when executed by a great
builder of his age; and we were able to imagine the effects which
could be produced with the resources offered by the sonority and
the arrangement of keyboards in these ancient instruments. How
many times since, while playing on the St. Thomas organ, have I
been reminded of the splendid rendering of Bach given us by M.-J.
Erb at this dedication!

Some years afterwards, Erb and I had to do with the construction
by Mr. Härpfer of the organ in the *Salle des Fêtes*, then called the
Sängerhaus. In order that I might judge the sonorities, as we planned
the slight changes necessary for the harmonization of the stops, Erb
improvised while I listened at the back of the hall. But many times
these improvisations were so interesting that as I followed them I
forgot to make the comments and indications which were to help
us secure the perfect harmonization of the various stops in the new
instrument.

The new organ in the *Salle des Fêtes* was first played by Widor.
At the inaugural concert two symphonies for organ and orchestra
were played, one composed by Widor and one by Erb; the second
had been composed expressly for this occasion. I played the organ
for both works.

In studying the Erb composition, I became aware of its worth.
The themes were rich, the structure of the work ingenious, and the
organ and orchestra complemented each other and blended with each
other admirably. Widor also admired the score. All of us who were
friends of Marie-Joseph Erb hoped it would be published, and take
rank among the most beautiful compositions for organ and orchestra.
For various reasons, Erb, in spite of our begging, could not make up
his mind to undertake its publication. I have always regretted it.

His lovely piece for the violin and organ, based on Gregorian
motifs, I have included a number of times in my church concerts
in foreign lands. Each time the violinists have expressed their delight
in making the acquaintance of a work so profoundly inspiring, where
organ and violin are handled with equal mastery.

The compositions written by Erb for the theatre have always surprised me by the quality of their dramatic sentiments. We are all
inclined to class Erb as a composer only of pure music, but in listen-

ing to his works for the theatre I have been struck from the first by the variety and the flexibility of his talent. His dramatic music shows an admirable comprehension of those exigencies of music which must develop in conformity to the events and movements of the stage; and also an elevation of style that is often lacking among those composers who think they are ordained to write for the theatre. The dramatic music of M.-J. Erb is lyrical, and at the same time picturesque in the best sense of the word.

In a conversation with him one day, in the course of which I congratulated him on the remarkable theatrical qualities of his dramatic music, I said to him, "Some day you must find a libretto of distinction which will permit you to express the full measure of your talent. Then you will create a work which will attract attention and place you among the masters of music for the contemporary theatre."

Before my departure for Africa, I tried for several years to find an operatic subject suitable for the quality of Erb's gifts. To no purpose, however; then Erb wrote himself excellent librettos for *The Iron Man* and *Saxophone and Company*.[1] Unfortunately I was not able to be present at the theatrical presentation in Strassburg of these two lyrical works.

I was able, however, in each of my European sojourns, to note the influence Erb exerted on the musicians of the new Alsatian generation. He devoted himself completely to his pupils; they knew what they owed him, and they worshipped him.

A close friendship existed between Erb and myself. He knew the interest I took in his creations. Between 1920 and 1923, when I stayed often in Alsace, I had the pleasure of seeing him many times and of keeping in touch with his activities. I remember particularly some charming afternoons Widor and I passed at the home of Mr. and Mrs. Erb. Widor, when passing through Alsace, always stopped to visit the Strassburg master. I had the opportunity then of listening to some very interesting conversations about music and musicians.

What impressed especially those who had the privilege of coming close to Erb were his simplicity and his modesty. His very nature

[1] *L'Homme de Fer* and *Saxophone et Cie.*

made it impossible for him to assert himself. He interested himself without prejudice in the musical creations of various schools and personalities, trying to judge them only in accordance with their innate worth. His criticism was never harsh. He believed that what was destined to endure would endure, and that the rest would of itself pass quietly into oblivion. He had a calm and wholesome wisdom from which he never swerved.

Such was Marie–Joseph Erb, as I knew him, and admired and loved him. I am sure that his memory and his works will always give him a place in the history of Alsatian art and in the hearts of the Alsatian people. As for me, I consider him the most remarkable of all the composers Alsace has produced.

❦

SIEGFRIED OCHS [1]

A CERTAIN performance of the Bach *B minor Mass* by the Cecilia Society of Frankfort, under the direction of Siegfried Ochs, was for me unforgettable. It was about 1908, I believe. It was the first time I had heard him direct it. The impression I then received remained decisive in my judgment of his reading of Bach, and was only strengthened by everything I heard of him later.

What impressed me again and again in Siegfried Ochs was his profound and unique study of the composition. One could tell from the chorus that he was the master of his subject. He had completely immersed himself in the tone-lines he was rendering, and made them resound as vital wholes. Moreover, the stress he put on enunciation always struck me as exceedingly pleasant.

But he required a technically perfect rendering not only of the chorus but also of the orchestra. And this was something new in those days. Siegfried Ochs was one of the first to understand the meaning of the phrasing and accents in Bach; and he worked accordingly. Heretofore it had not been felt as self-evident that the Bach tone-lines for the strings could be properly rendered only if all the players

[1] From the *Fest–Programm des Berliner Philharmonischen Chors*, Berlin, December 5, 1932, pp. 11–13.

phrased and accented in the same fashion; but for Ochs this was axiomatic. Therefore he made with the greatest care every necessary notation in the parts before he laid them on the music rack. With what conscientiousness he did this work I was able to see for myself, when, about 1911, he placed at my disposal for the *première* in Barcelona his manuscript of the parts of the *B minor Mass*. And the pains he had taken were well repaid by the results. With Siegfried Ochs one was again and again surprised by the plastic and vital way in which the orchestral parts were brought out. How splendidly flowed along the accompaniment of a Bach aria under his leadership, because the tone-line had been fashioned in accordance with a clear and well-considered conception!

If today much more care is given to phrasing and accenting in Bach than one even dreamed of in an earlier day, this is in large measure due to the influence of the standards Siegfried Ochs left behind him for those who undertake to conduct Bach's music.

Furthermore, everyone who values Bach's work must take satisfaction in the great appeal of Ochs' rendering of it. Siegfried Ochs had made a clean sweep of the ideal which had been accepted as classic for the playing of Bach, as only a person as full of feeling as he was could have done. He had attacked the widespread opinion, accepted even in the circle of excellent musicians, that Bach must be played in rigid time and generally in the most objective manner possible—in their words, "played down and sung down." He was conscious of the elementary vitality that makes itself felt in this perfected form. And he tried to do equal justice to the life and the form. Great architecture in colossally vital lines: this hovered before him as his ideal for the rendition. And even when one was not inclined to agree with his tempi (which he liked to make too lively), and his dynamics (which he liked to elaborate too richly), and in general with his inclination to virtuosity, one still found his rendition a genuine experience. For Bach's music as he performed it always took shape before the hearer in its mighty lines and in its rich individuality. This interpreter, who was always striving for the most refined result, possessed at the same time by nature the gift of great simplicity. This has always appeared to me to be the secret of his music.

That Siegfried Ochs accomplished so much in his rendering of

Bach is to be explained in the end not simply by his musical sensitivity and ability, but also by the fact that Bach was for him a spiritual experience. Siegfried Ochs had a nature that drew him to the creator of the Passions and Cantatas. Whoever had the good fortune to get more closely acquainted with him learned that this eminent director was a man of great depths, and lived in the works of the master of St. Thomas not simply as a musician but also as a great soul. To him the piety embedded in the texts meant something.

And this comprehension of the spiritual in Bach's work made itself felt in his renderings. It was imparted during the rehearsals to those who worked with him; in the performance to those hearers who had ears to hear.

Hearing the *B minor Mass* directed by Siegfried Ochs, and *Tristan and Isolde* directed by Felix Mottl, were for me two equally unforgettable experiences.

May the Philharmonic Chorus of Berlin, which gave us under Siegfried Ochs such perfect performances of Bach, and which now under Otto Klemperer celebrates its jubilee with the *B minor Mass*, continue to fulfil its mission of bringing us close to Bach in the spirit of its great and never-to-be-forgotten director.

❧

*T*HE time for Albert Schweitzer's departure to Africa had come very near. To a crowded congregation in St. Nicholas one spring Sunday in 1912 he preached from the high pulpit his last sermon there. "May the peace of God which passeth all understanding keep your hearts and minds in Christ Jesus." He had used those words to end every service at St. Nicholas all through the years. On this closing Sunday the benediction had become his sermon text.

His last course of lectures at the University in the winter of 1911–1912 had been on the reconciliation of religious truth with comparative religion and natural science. In the spring he gave his last lecture, and with a feeling of deep sorrow he stepped down from the platform in that second lecture room at the east of the main entrance of the University building, knowing that the world that had been his was to be his no more.

That spring he spent in Paris studying tropical medicine. He had passed his medical examinations the previous December, paying for them with the fee he received at Munich with Widor, but he did not receive his degree until February, 1913, when he had completed his year as an intern, and had submitted his doctoral thesis. This was his Psychiatric Study of Jesus. Seldom has so small a book resulted from such voluminous reading and research.[1]

On June 18, 1912, he married Helene Bresslau, who had been born in Berlin. Her father was a distinguished professor of history there, later moving to the University of Strassburg. She had been a social worker in Strassburg, and had been of great assistance to Schweitzer in various ways, finally studying nursing that she might be the better equipped to work with him. She, too, had a brilliant mind.

They spent the following months, as much of them as they could, in Gunsbach. But the funds had to be collected for the proposed African hospital, the supplies had to be purchased and packed, and the manuscript for the second edition of the book on Jesus had to be completed.

In February, 1913, seventy packing cases were sent off to Bordeaux, and on March 26, Helene and Albert Schweitzer embarked for Africa.

[1] The Psychiatric Study of Jesus, by Albert Schweitzer. Boston: The Beacon Press, second edition, 1949.

VII

Africa

QUICKLY, by stream and jungle ways, by dugout and river boat, the news spread through the forest that a white doctor had come to the mission station at Andende. The natives and officials carried the word, the beat of the tam-tam spread it abroad. And the sick came in large numbers to be healed. There was no time to prepare for them. The little bungalow on the hillside, surrounded by its broad verandas, was filled with white patients. An old henhouse became the consulting room, and bamboo huts with palm-leaf tiles began to shelter the native patients. In the fall of 1913 a small building of corrugated iron was built, with an operating room, dispensary, and consulting room; and there the ill were treated. There was a surprising amount of lung trouble, and heart trouble, and urinary diseases. And there were of course the tropical maladies: malaria, leprosy, sleeping sickness, dysentery and ulcers. The operations were mostly for hernia and elephantiasis tumors. It was hard to secure good orderlies and interpreters; but Mrs. Schweitzer proved to be a tower of strength. She took care of the dressings and the linen, prepared the operating room, administered the anesthetics, nursed those who were gravely ill, and still somehow found time to look out for the household.

At the end of a few weeks there were at the hospital forty patients and their attendants.

In the late afternoons of those early days, before the sudden coming of the tropical night, Schweitzer used to sit for a few moments on the veranda of his house and look out upon the peaceful scene with a sense of joy and satisfaction in his heart. It was a beautiful country. He could look far up the broad river to the low line of far-off mountains. At the right was the large island where was located the administrative center of Lambarene. At the left was the primeval forest, dipping its roots into the waters of the Ogowe, losing itself in the uncharted distance. River and sky and forest seemed blended in some kind of mystic unity; and as he sat there he could forget the cruel tragedies of the jungle, the strange superstitions that shackled the native mind, and for a brief moment even the sick stretched out on their raffia mats below him there in the bamboo huts.

Soon he found that the sacrifices he had been prepared to make were not demanded of him. At the very outset he realised that he would not have to sacrifice his music. The Paris Missionary Society had given him a zinc-lined piano with pedal attachment, specially designed for the tropics. And now he knew that in the solitude of the forest, against the background of the chanting of crickets and toads and the mysterious noises of the jungle, he had such an opportunity to perfect his technique as he had never had in Europe. He set to work to learn by heart the great music of Bach, Mendelssohn, Mozart, Widor, Max Reger and César Franck. Even though he could find each day but half an hour for this practice, he could still go on with his music. Indeed, during the first three months he got three more volumes of Bach's choral compositions ready for the publisher. They were not to be published, however, for many years to come.

He found, of course, difficulties he had not known in Europe. There was the terrible humidity of the climate; the voracious termites with an appetite for wood and paper; even the petty thieving of the very people he had come to help. One day he found that someone had stolen his edition of Wagner's Meistersinger, and, what was even more serious, Bach's St. Matthew Passion, to which he had added his carefully worked out organ accompaniment.

He had agreed to give up his preaching, but to his great joy the prohibition was quickly removed by the missionaries in Africa, so much broader minded than the mission board in Europe. To preach to the natives of the jungle, most of whom had never heard of Christianity before, became to him a thrilling delight and an inexpressible privilege.

The dry season gave way to the wet season. The second dry season came, with its overcast skies and its cooler temperatures. Then, suddenly, in August 1914, came the ominous word that there was war in Europe. The Schweitzers, by the accident of their birth, were German citizens. A stupid French government ordered the hospital closed. The Schweitzers were to consider themselves prisoners of war. The day after this news had been brought him Schweitzer began work on a new book, The Philosophy of Civilization. The coming of war had made that subject much more important than the completion of his book on Paul. And even when the hospital was reopened after a few months, largely because of Widor's influence back in Paris, he continued to work on this book that was to engross his attention for the next thirty-five years. His writing was another of the possible sacrifices he had not been called on to make.

Civilization was falling to pieces, he thought, because our traditional attitude of ethical affirmation had been weakened. But how can this attitude be demonstrated in thought? For long months Schweitzer vainly sought the answer to this problem. Then, one bright day, in September 1915, while he was making a long river journey, the answer suddenly came to him in the phrase "Reverence for life." Perhaps it was the playful disporting of a herd of hippopotamuses in the water about his boat that brought him this revelation. At any rate, it was a turning point in his intellectual life. Undoubtedly life was as precious to these ugly, vicious creatures in the river as it was to us. If we are life that wills to live in the midst of other life that wills to live, then we must respect this other life, whatever its nature, just as we demand respect for our own life. This became the central thought in the ethical and philosophical system he began at that time to build.

After spending the hot, rainy season of 1916–17 on the coast because of his wife's poor health, Schweitzer returned to his work at the hospital; only to be almost immediately informed that they were to be transferred as prisoners of war to an internment camp in France. Saddened by the forced closing of his hospital, which he was not to see again for seven years, but still reveling in the unexpected leisure that came as a boon to his writing and music, he spent the time on the steamer learning by heart Widor's Sixth Organ Symphony and a number of Bach's fugues.

Their first internment camp was at Garaison, an old monastery

under the shadow of the Pyrenees. The name of the camp, significantly enough, was the Provençal form of the French word for
"healing" (guérison), and soon Schweitzer was permitted to practise
as a doctor among his fellow internees. But he still had plenty of
time for his writing and his music. On a simple wooden table, made
for him by a friend in the camp, he began once more to "play the
organ"—the table-top his manuals, the floor his pedals. Another
prisoner drew an amusing silhouette, showing the doctor practising
at his "organ" with such vehemence that the dishes on the table
went flying into the air.

There were gypsy prisoners at the camp also, who had played
their music in the cafés of Paris, and when they heard that Albert
Schweitzer was also a musician they accepted him as one of themselves and welcomed him to their loft concerts. Mrs. Schweitzer was
awakened on her birthday by a serenade the gypsies played outside
her door, the waltz from Tales of Hoffmann.

Thus passed the winter at Garaison. In the spring they were transferred to St. Rémy de Provence. This institution had belonged to
the Catholic Church, and had been set aside as an asylum for the
insane. Here it was that Van Gogh had been for a time imprisoned.
Schweitzer became once again a doctor, not simply for the camp but
for people living at some distance from it. On Sunday there were
Catholic and Protestant services. Schweitzer played the harmonium
for the Catholic service, and because everyone liked to hear Schweitzer play the whole camp became Catholic. Then came the Protestant
service, when again Schweitzer played the harmonium, and alternated with Pastor G. A. Liebrich, another Protestant clergyman, in
preaching the sermon. His writing continued. Even in these internment camps Schweitzer found it possible to carry on all his activities:
he was still a preacher, a musician, a philosopher, a physician.

At the end of July 1918 he was back again in Gunsbach; an exchange of prisoners had made this possible. Gunsbach was close to
the front. The roads were camouflaged; the people carried gas masks.
But his father was there to greet him, and it was home. In November the war ended.

Then followed six years of uncertainty. At the beginning of that
period his health was bad. Two operations were necessary, the result

of the dysentery from which he had suffered after his return from Africa. He did not know whether he should ever be able to return to Africa; and he knew that his neglected hospital at Lambarene was reverting to the jungle. The immediate problem of his living was solved by the offer of a post as physician at the city hospital in Strassburg. He returned also to his old pulpit at St. Nicholas.

His leisure was spent on Bach's choral preludes, but the publisher had lost interest in the work for the time being; so this chore was put aside for continuing work on the Philosophy of Civilization. There were at this time changes in his family. Towards the end of the war his mother had been killed in a tragic accident at Gunsbach. On January 14, 1919, his own birthday, a daughter Rhena was born to him. "One generation passeth away, and another generation cometh."

His confidence in his musical skill was restored when once again, in October 1919, he played for his friends at the Orféo Català in Barcelona. He knew then that his work on his pedal piano at Lambarene, his wooden table at Garaison, his harmonium at St. Rémy, had been worth while. He had not returned to Europe an amateur. His Christmas that year was gladdened by an unexpected invitation from Archbishop Söderblom of Sweden to deliver the next spring a series of lectures at the University of Upsala. He accepted; and then the kindly archbishop suggested a series of other lectures and recitals in Sweden; these enabled him to pay off the greater part of the hospital debts. He returned to Alsace with health restored and mind at peace. Now again he knew it would be possible to return to Africa.

But not at once. At home once more, he set at work to write an account of his African experiences, in a book that an Upsala publishing house had commissioned him to write. On the Edge of the Primeval Forest was published in 1921. That spring he was back again playing Bach's St. Matthew Passion at the Orféo Català, the first time it had ever been given in Spain. When he returned, he resigned from St. Nicholas in Strassburg, and from his post at the city hospital. He knew now that he could support himself as a writer and organist. He retired with his wife and daughter to Gunsbach, where he could continue to work in quiet on his Philosophy of Civilization.

In the summer of 1921 Professor Archibald T. Davison was again in Europe with the Harvard Glee Club. As already recounted, he had been associated with Widor and Schweitzer earlier in Paris. Now he met Schweitzer again in Strassburg; and many years afterwards wrote an entrancing account of Schweitzer the organist in his middle forties.

"On July fifteenth," he wrote, "Schweitzer took us to St. Thomas Church for organ music and singing. The church was dark except for the necessary lights around the organ, and a single candle in the church itself, so placed as to make my motions visible to the Glee Club, which sang unaccompanied church pieces in the intervals between the organ numbers. Finally Schweitzer invited me to the organ loft to inspect and to try the organ.

"There it was, very much as it was in Bach's day, devoid of all the labor-saving devices of the modern instrument, cumbersome, and, from the point of view of one who had been used to the mechanically effortless instruments of America, calculated to set up for the player almost every conceivable impediment to easy and comfortable manipulation. That was my first experience with the type of organ which had served Bach; and like many another, I found myself soberly pondering the manner in which the average 'concert' organist deals with Bach's music. When Schweitzer sat down to play the G minor Fantasia and Fugue as a crown to a memorable evening, one was literally transported back into another St. Thomas's, and there came vividly to mind all of Widor's admonitions concerning speed, clarity, legato, rhythm, and dissonance in the performance of eighteenth century organ music; admonitions born not of what one might think Bach would have liked had he had at his disposal the instrument of to-day, but born, rather, of a knowledge of the organ for which Bach actually composed, and, of equal importance, the organ on which he played. . . .

"Before Schweitzer began to play, he made sure that all was in readiness for the performance. Two assistants were to draw the stops; one at his right hand, the other directly behind him, posted at that section of the organ located in the rear. Even such stops as Schweitzer could himself reach, were in the care of a helper, as, with proper and characteristic conscientiousness he would not allow himself for any reason to interrupt the contrapuntal lines. The omission of a brief phrase, even of a single note, was unthinkable. The music began. The 'machinery' of the old organ was plainly audible, but it was clear that Schweitzer was not aware of it. Lost in the music, only the eloquence of Bach concerned him; and soon, for his hearers who were standing about the organ, all the mechanical intrusions disappeared in the superb playing of transcendent music. Only once, indeed, after the beginning, did any physical element make itself felt. That was at a climactic point when a considerable dynamic addition became necessary. As the music swelled up towards its peak, the assistants looked hurriedly at the music and placed their hands near the group of stops to be drawn. Suddenly the player threw back his head and shouted 'jetzt!' whereupon, with a sudden and well-synchronized stroke, the assistants pulled forth the required handful of stops with a terrific clatter. Amazingly, these diversions, not to be imagined in the 'organ recital,' were but dimly realized by the listener; so overpowering was the effect of the music and its registration. That was the miracle. One forgot everything for the moment, the awkward manipulation of the stops, the noise of the shrunken mechanism, even the player himself. Only Bach was there. It was the complete relegation of all agencies of performance to a position of total unimportance, with a corresponding glorification of the music itself. Modern virtuosity of every type has too often created a barrier between the composer and the listener. Too often, indeed, is the music no more than a vehicle for the self-expression of the interpreter. Of all that there was nothing on that evening in Strassburg. For once there was the realization of that so-oft-dreamed ideal, the artist at one with the composer." [1]

Doctor Schweitzer adds a little sequel to this lovely evening at St. Thomas. The Glee Club was staying at the Hotel Terminus near the station. It was a hot evening in July, and they walked back from the church together. Doctor Schweitzer said good-night. The others went to their rooms and he started back to his house. Then Doctor Schweitzer realized how warm and tired he was, and decided he would return to the sidewalk café for a refreshing drink. As he sat down at a table he heard familiar voices behind him. There were all the students, with Professor Davison, sitting at the tables having beer. "Well," said Doctor Schweitzer, "it seems that we all had the same idea." Then they passed a delightful hour of relaxation together.

There were many journeys for lectures and concerts during the next two and a half years. In the autumn of 1921 he was in Switzerland. In November he was back again in Sweden. He had made many friends there, and had come to love the country. The Swedish organs pleased him; they were not large, but some of them had very beautiful tone. The next year, 1922, he was lecturing and playing in England; in Sweden and Switzerland again; and in Denmark. In 1923 he went to Czechoslovakia on the invitation of Professor Oscar Kraus of the University of Prague.

So the months passed swiftly away, with music, study, writing, speaking. In the spring of 1923 the years of work on his Philosophy of Civilization came to fruit, and the first two volumes were published. This same year too his book on Christianity and the World Religions was published; and soon after his Memoirs of Childhood and Youth, the vivid memories of his early days in Alsace.

He was now ready to return to Africa. The evening before he was to leave he dedicated a new organ at Mühlbach, an organ which had been planned by him and built by the organ builder Härpfer, a small but remarkably beautiful instrument. Refreshments were served in the parsonage, and a delegation from the historic Münstertalvereins surprised him with an artistic diploma that made him an honorary member. The bells of the new church were rung, and the church was crowded with people from far and near. After a little Schweitzer spoke to the loved people of his severely tried valley. Said he:

"I first played in this church as a nine-year-old boy. My Grandfather Schillinger had built a fine organ under the direction of the organ builder Stier. How happy I was before my first journey to Africa to restore it! Then in the primeval forest I read in a Swiss paper that not merely the organ but the church and the pastor's house, indeed the whole village, had been destroyed in a barrage. It seemed as if my heart would break. The next day I met a Negro king, who lived across the river from me in Lambarene, and he said to me: 'Oganga, why are you so sad?' I said, 'In my homeland they have destroyed things that are beautiful and dear to me. There was an organ among them.' And the king asked, 'What is that, an organ?' I had difficulty in explaining to him what an organ was. (You know I also have frequent trouble in explaining this to Europeans.) Then I asked him, 'King, will you give me the beautiful mahogany tree that stands there on the bank of the river, spreading out in such majesty?' 'Yes,' said he, 'I will give this to you for the organ in your homeland.' How I thanked him, when I thought of you, dear homeless people! I had men come to fell the tree and saw it up into boards by hand—there is no other way of doing this in Lambarene; and had the boards placed under a roof, and planned to sell them for you when they were dry. But soon after that I was made a prisoner. When I came back a few years afterwards the great pile of beautiful boards had rotted, the roof I had put over them along with the rest. Then again I grieved for your organ. But when I was in London after my return, a leading churchman there permitted me to give a concert for you in his church. Then I laid the foundation for your instrument. Now it is finished. It has a lovely tone, and you should learn from it of that world where there is no more war, a world which is stronger than all wars. Gott mit Euch!"

Then Schweitzer played on the organ, an hour of lovely music: Bach's overtures and preludes, Mendelssohn's choral sonatas, Widor's Christmas Music, and Luther's Ein feste Burg. It was as if a great cathedral organ were unfolding its fullness and splendor. Here was the model for all village organs—seventeen registers, rich enough to play all worthwhile compositions.

Late that evening he drove in a car to Colmar, and his friends of Mühlbach bade him a last farewell. The next day he left Strassburg, and a few days later he was at sea, bound for Africa.

VIII

The Revolution in Organ Building

IT was at dawn on the day before Easter that Doctor Schweitzer arrived once more at Lambarene, after an absence of almost seven years. The hospital buildings were in a sorry state of neglect. It was symbolic, perhaps, that he had arrived at the Christian season of resurrection, for the hospital had died and the time was come for its resurrection. For more than a year he labored to reconstruct it. Everything was sacrificed to it except his music. At evening time his tired body found relaxation and his weary mind found refreshment at his piano. Even in the heart of the jungle his reputation as a musician spread, though sometimes a bit distorted. A certain timber merchant, passing by the hospital, said to him, "Doctor, I am told that you play the harmonium beautifully. I wish I did not have to hurry to get home before the tornado strikes, for I like music too, and I should like to have you play one of Goethe's fugues for me."

Hardly had the hospital been rebuilt, when famine and dysentery struck simultaneously, and it was immediately evident that the hospital would have to be enlarged. That meant moving the whole institution, for there was no room for expansion at Andende, shut in as it was by the river in front, the hill at the back, and the swamps on either side. A new site was found a little way upstream, and immediately began the laborious work of clearing the virgin growth of the forest, bringing land into cultivation, and erecting a whole set of new buildings. Again Doctor Schweitzer found himself a lumberman, a mason, and a carpenter, as well as a physician; but by the summer of 1927 the "doctor's village" at Adolinanongo had been established, and the doctor felt free to return again to Europe, though a year and a half later than he had planned.

His return, in July 1927, was preceded by two more articles on organ construction. It was now twenty-one years since he had written The Art of Organ Building and Organ Playing in Germany and France. It was time to pause and take stock, to see what had happened in these two decades since he had challenged the organists and organ builders of that day to halt and see where they were going, and to return to the lovely organs of the years between 1860 and 1880. So he wrote an epilogue to the 1906 book, in which, while modifying two or three of his earlier recommendations, he nonetheless reëmphasized his central conviction and rejoiced in the victories already won. In addition to the epilogue, an article upon reform in organ building appeared in the Monatschrift für Gottesdienst und kirchliche Kunst. The revolution in organ building, for which he had labored so hard, had begun.

❧

THE 1927 EPILOGUE [1]

A LITTLE more than twenty years ago the cry was raised in this book: Back from the modern factory organ, produced by the devil of invention, to the true organ with its beautiful tone! Strangely enough, until then there had been no one to ask organists and organ builders where organ building and organ playing were really going. It was accepted as self-evident that the booming factory organ was the instrument of the future, and that as soon as possible all earlier organs would fall to the axe and the furnace.

That I myself was not deluded by the modern factory organ, I owe to the circumstance that I grew up among beautifully toned organs. As a boy I played on the Walcker organ, which had been built in the best days of this concern, in the sixties and seventies of the past century. One of these, with sixty-two stops, stood in the evangelical church of St. Stephen at Mulhouse in Alsace. Towards the end of the century it was so renovated and modernized by the house that had installed it that nothing was left of the old, lovely tone. The

---

[1] From *Deutsche und Französische Orgelbaukunst und Orgelkunst*, by Albert Schweitzer, Leipzig: Breitkopf & Härtel, 1927, pp. 49–70.

other, with about forty stops, in the evangelical church at Munster in Alsace, I was able to save from that fate. But it later fell a victim to the war. As an eighteen-year-old lad I came to know the Paris organs of Cavaillé–Coll, with their wonderful foundation stops and mixtures. As a student in Strassburg I was intoxicated with the sound of the Silbermann organs in St. William and St. Thomas, and with their delightful sister in the Evangelical state church in Colmar. The St. William organ had to give way towards the end of the century to a modern factory organ; both the others were saved.

For long years I ventured to bring my heretical belief in the beauty of the old organs and the inferiority of the modern factory organs, with their consoles studded with push buttons, to the ears of friendly organists. What I heard from them on the subject did not encourage me to carry my old-fashioned ideas any farther. When, however, the praise of the factory organs that had taken the place of the older, more beautiful ones became ever more exuberant in the newspapers as they were dedicated, I overcame all my scruples, and in 1906 came out publicly with my heresies. I owe it to the intelligent reception of the editorial staff of *Musik* that I found a publication that would print such foolishness. The friendship of the house of Breitkopf & Härtel made it possible for my treatise to live on as an independent book.

At first the only result was that many organists gave up their former friendly associations with me. There was no lack of sarcastic letters. A well-known Berlin organ *virtuoso* said that I was ready for the insane asylum.

The slaughter of the old organs went on. With great difficulty I was able to save the organ at St. Thomas in Strassburg; its death sentence had been already drawn up in the form of a cost estimate from a powerful organ factory. That the necessary number of votes in the chapter of St. Thomas was found to preserve it was due to two intelligent pastors and to the teacher of constitutional law, Laband, who as legal counsellor had in this corporation a place and a voice.

This first victory came in 1909. Guido Adler, who was responsible for the preparation of the third congress of the International Music Society, which had been invited to Vienna, got in touch with me, and requested that I should give an address at the congress about organ construction. In preparing for this address I sent a questionnaire in German or French about the problem of organ construction to organ builders and organists in all European countries; principally, however, to the German, Austrian, Swedish, and French, because with these I had the closest relations. The answers that came in were to provide the material for the work of the organ section of the Vienna Congress. This effort revealed how little sympathy there was for raising the question of organ construction at all. Instead of answering to the point, many of those addressed came out with threats against those who would encroach upon the freedom of the organ builder, and, as one man wrote, "would like to make all organs on one last." Worst of all were the answers of many organ builders and many organ inspectors. There were organ builders who did not understand what it would mean to them to have minimum prices set which would permit them to do artistic work. They saw only that a movement was on foot that would make it impossible for them to drive their rivals from the field by underbidding or by means of the newest inventions. Very many of them had at that time not the slightest comprehension of the whole matter.

Many official organ inspectors were unsympathetic to the enterprise, because many unofficial persons were presuming to meddle in these organ matters, and wished to leave the responsibility for ordering and examining organs in a particular region not to the discretion of a single expert, always one and the same, but to the consensus of opinion of several experts.

Along with the uncoöperative and suspicious answers there arrived, however, an imposing number of others that went to the heart of the matter, and expressed the opinion that a discussion of organ building was to be desired.

This congress of the International Music Society in Vienna, from May 25 to 29, 1909, elaborated the *International Regulations for Organ Building*.

In the very first hours of the assembly the members of the section on organ building found themselves of the opinion that something should be undertaken to restore the organ builders to the position where they could build in accordance with artistic principles, without destroying themselves in the effort. To us it seemed most urgent to work to this end. Therefore we formed a plan for drawing up regulations for organ building to which every organ builder could refer when confronted by purchasers and experts, in order not to be underbidden or eliminated by competitors peddling the most modern inventions.

The material for such regulations lay in my lecture about the state of organ building at that time, printed in the annals of the congress, and in my report on the answers received from the questionnaire.

In four days these regulations for organ building were drawn up and issued! We renounced the congress festivities; our section sat, so to speak, permanently; we took hardly time to eat or sleep.

Dr. Xavier Matthias, the representative of church music on the Catholic theological faculty at Strassburg, and I presided alternately over the sessions. The Austrian organ builders Rieger and Ullmann, the organ builder Härpfer from Boulay in Alsace, the Viennese organ inspector Walter Ehrenhofer, and the Viennese engineer Friedrich Drechsler, were specially helpful with their technical knowledge. The last two named deserve great credit in the fulfilment of our task.

The *Regulations*, about fifty pages long, were issued, at the expense of the International Society of Music, in German and French; and were sent without charge to the experts in organ construction, the organ builders and the organists, to whom the questionnaire had previously gone. An Italian edition was later added, which the organist Carmelo Songiorgio (Mazara de Valle, Sicily) took charge of.

Thus for the first time were set forth the conclusions emerging from a thorough discussion of the ideal to be sought in organ building. The *Regulations* offered standards for keyboards and pedals, and specified in what way the pedals should lie under the manuals, and what distance was to be kept between the manuals. Size, form, free play, depth, strength of resistance, elasticity of the keys for the best playing—all these were determined.

It was set forth as a necessity that every organ, no matter what the number of its stops, had to be complete in external arrangements, that is, it must have at least two keyboards, stretching from G to g³, pedals stretching from C to f¹, and a swell box.

The complicated console, with its many blind and fixed installations, was stripped of its repute, and the utmost simplicity was suggested as the solution. Instead of many different kinds of registration helps, it should have that one in particular which the artistic logic of organ playing demands, but which is not found in the consoles of the factory organs because it is more difficult to build and more expensive than many of the impractical inventions. This significant and valuable registration help is the one that makes it possible, on each separate manual and on the pedal, to add as desired to the stops drawn other stops prepared in advance, or to substitute these stops for the stops drawn and then retire them again. In addition, a *sforzando* and a register *crescendo*, which by means of a balance lever bring all the stops of the organ into play or silence them, and in such a way that the successively introduced stops, at the discretion of the musician, permit the drawn registration to remain or to be retired.

A three-manual organ with hardly more than a half-dozen registration helps, in place of the fantastic console of the modern factory organ provided with some dozens of them! A two-manual organ with fewer than a half-dozen!

And on every organ about the same registration helps and the same arrangement of the console. On the left side, the couplers of the pedals to the manuals and those that couple the manuals together; on the right side, registration helps arranged as stops and pistons for the hands as well as pedals for the feet, with the pistons and pedals working together or independently of one another.

In respect to the stops, the *Regulations* expressed the opinion unheard of at that time, that it was not a matter of their number but of their quality. What a feat the reëstablishment of this self-evident truth was, the present generation can no longer appreciate. How often did I have the experience of seeing in those days construction estimates offering many cheap little stops gain a victory over those that dared to offer excellent stops in smaller number! And whenever the organ expert had the exceptional wisdom to recommend the more excellent proposal, the congregation opposed it and ordered the organ with the greater number of stops! The organ builders, if they wished to receive any orders, had to submit to this stupid tyranny! The opposition to this madness took final form in these regulations for organ construction.

By what means, however, were the artistic fullness and beauty of tone produced in the pipes? On this there was excited discussion in the section on organ construction. Everyone agreed that the increased wind pressure was to a large extent responsible for the unpleasant sound of the modern factory organ. But long deliberations were necessary before we dared to draw up in the *Regulations* the statement that the foundation stops and the mixtures should be fed with wind of only 70 to 85 mm. [2.76 to 3.35 inches] pressure. It was readily agreed that generous dimensions and thick walls in the pipes had great influence on the beauty and fullness of the tone. But to many it seemed too bold to state that the modern technically perfect wind chest was equally responsible for the unpleasant sound of the factory organ. The defenders of the old chest did not at that time know how to prove this from a physical point of view. On the other hand, it had to be admitted that when, in rebuilding, old pipes were set on new chests they fell far short of giving forth the same full, round tones as before. On this subject we extremists in the section on organ building were able to get approval for a sentence in the *Regulations*, very carefully framed, which laid down the advantages in tone production of the slider wind chest. After we had accomplished this we breathed easily again.

It was also difficult to push through the opinion that mechanical action from the keys to the wind chest was artistically the most perfect; and that in smaller and middle-sized instruments, where there were no technical objections, it had an unquestionable advantage.

So in the 1909 *Regulations for Organ Building* we favoured the old, simple, tone-beautiful organ. The timid ones were carried along by the courageous.

By its thoroughly unbiassed declarations the *Regulations for Organ Building* made an impression even on those who at first were not receptive to this idea of "Back to the old organ." In the following years there began to appear a critical attitude towards the modern factory organ, even though the murder of old organs went on almost without slackening. People began to concern themselves scientifically and experimentally with the problem of the wind chests and the dimensions and tones of the pipes. All this led one to anticipate that the problem of getting the true organ might be nearer solution at coming congresses of the International Music Society, where greater participation and more valuable material might be expected.

The World War put an end to such congresses for the time being. But the idea went on its way even without congresses, and even in the midst of the anguish of the time. On concert trips, which after the war took me into almost every country in Europe, I was able to see that the idea was making headway. Everywhere organists gave their support to it. The science of organ building was once again honored. Where the old organs still remained they were genuinely valued. News was bruited about of astounding conversions: organ manufacturers and organ *virtuosi* began to idolize what they had formerly burned.

But recently the depreciated currency of Middle Europe almost proved disastrous to the old organs of the north. I passed through this crisis in Sweden and Denmark. Because the factory organs of Middle Europe could be had very cheaply in these lands with hard *valuta*, and because up there they still had their former attraction, people began to do away with the old organs in order to provide themselves at the favorable moment with modern wares. I was able to coöperate with Bangert, the cathedral cantor from Roskilde (Denmark), and with other northern experts, in the saving of a few specially threatened old masterpieces.

Today the fight is won. Scientific experts in organ building and old organs, like Ernst Schiess of Solothurn and Hans Henny Jahnn of Hamburg, are actively rebuilding old organs. In the Institute of Musical Knowledge at the University of Freiburg in Baden, Professor Willibald Gurlitt and his pupils are engaged in research into old music and old organs. Societies have arisen for the preservation of old organs.

We had not dared to hope that a young generation would carry on so soon and so strongly what we had undertaken in Vienna against the spirit of the time. With deep emotion I think of those who shared with us the work of those wonderful days but were not permitted to see the triumph of the idea.

At the wish of the publishers, the book about *The Art of Organ Building and Organ Playing in Germany and France* was republished in its 1906 form, as a kind of document from the beginning of the fight for the true organ. Only a mistake on page 20 concerning the Mecklin organ in the *Oratoire* at Paris was corrected.

To the ideal that I set forth in that book I am still loyal today; only in details have I departed from my views of that time, or gone beyond them. For instance, I have become convinced that the divided wind chest with different pressures, advocated by the successors of Cavaillé–Coll, does not in reality fulfil what it promised in theory. The organs provided with it have a less rounded tone than the old organs of Cavaillé–Coll with their simple slider wind chests; hence I consider the slider wind chest to be the one that produces the more beautiful tone. Here I leave the question open; whether for acoustical reasons we must go back to the slider wind chest, or whether in the end the inventive spirit of our organ builders, working on the relevant problems, will succeed in building modern wind chests that will equal in acoustical merit the slider wind chest.

I have become ever more certain that the mechanical tracker is from an artistic point of view the ideal action between keys and wind chest, as more organs with pneumatic and electric action have come under my hands in different lands since that time. I plead, then, that all the smaller and middle-sized organs should be furnished with good mechanical trackers. In the larger instruments, where pneumatic or electric action seems to be technically required, a mechanical tracker, however short, should be added to the pneumatic or electric action, in order that the keys may retain the ideal elasticity indispensable for good blending and good phrasing.

In one important respect I go beyond the 1906 book and the *Regulations* for organ building. More and more there is borne in upon me the artistic significance of the *rückpositiv*. That a group of stops is not contained in the main case, but sings out freely in the church, has an influence on the total sound of the organ. The complete instrument consists of three personalities: the main organ, with its round, full tones; the *rückpositiv*, with its bright, free tones; and the swell organ, with its intense and sustained tones. The character of the perfect organ depends upon this trinity. The old instrument had only two tone individualities: the main organ and the *rückpositiv*. The third organ, housed in the main case, was so undeveloped and so set up that it played no individual rôle in the total harmony. The modern instrument, which has no *rückpositiv* organ, has again therefore only two tone qualities: the main organ and the swell. The second organ (the *rückpositiv*), spoiled by being placed within the main case, has no tone individuality of its own, but is only an addition to the first. It is not the number of manuals that determines the quality of the organ, but the number of tone individualities. Since Cavaillé–Coll took the *rückpositiv* away from the five-manual instruments at St. Sulpice, Widor plays—as I am accustomed to charge him—on a two-manual organ with five keyboards. In spite of its hundred stops, the St. Sulpice instrument has only two tone individualities: the main organ divided among four keyboards and the swell organ. The organ at Notre Dame is the same. We must once more build instruments with *rückpositivs*.

That will be hard, of course. The arrangement of a *rückpositiv* involves a heavy additional expense. But it is better to have fewer stops and a *rückpositiv* than more stops and only two tone individualities. Without a *rückpositiv* there is no ideal, complete instrument. A second organ of eight stops, arranged as a *rückpositiv*, is superior to one of fifteen stops that stands in the main case.

Artistically it is not sensible to build organs with more than two manuals, unless it be for very large rooms which demand an exceedingly great number of stops. In this case one may separate the main organ into two manuals. One gets along well, however, with three manuals up to eighty stops.

On the other hand, three manuals should be provided wherever possible for even thirty stops, in order that the instrument may have a *rückpositiv*. No one should be influenced by the consideration that the instrument could have, with the money spent for the *rückpositiv*, many more stops. The instrument with the *rückpositiv* is always better, regardless of the number of stops.

The bigger the room, the more necessary is the *rückpositiv*. In small churches an organ with two tone qualities is pleasing, because here the instrument is not far away and is not placed high, and the great organ itself sounds out directly in the church. The farther and the higher the instrument is moved away, the more necessary it is that a group of stops should be moved out below.

An objection to the *rückpositiv* besides its cost is usually advanced; namely, that the accurate pitch of the instrument becomes impossible, especially in heated churches, since the *rückpositiv* stands in cooler air than the parts higher up. I have never found such a disadvantage really noticeable, except for a few Sundays and in relatively small, overheated churches. The larger the room, of course, the more equable the temperature in the region of the organ loft.

To equip an instrument with two swell organs is not reasonable. The large quantity of wood in the organ casing injures the production of the tone.

Echo organs continue to be sentimental toys which have nothing to do with the true organ.

In many places the solution "Back to the old, tone-beautiful organ" has been misunderstood to mean that the organ of the eighteenth century should be exalted as an ideal. This is not the case. By "old" organs is meant those organs made before the era of the modern factory organ, at a time when the masters of organ building were still free to work as artists; that is, the organs of the seventeenth century and those of the eighteenth century into the seventh decade.

Certainly we must preserve the still existing old organs of the seventeenth and eighteenth centuries as historic treasures; and as far as possible restore them reverently even with their failures and weaknesses, in accordance with their nature. Certainly we must learn to know the organs of that time much better than we know them now. What precious things, still unrecognized, may be the old organs of Spain, and particularly of Catalonia! We will once more take over many of the manifold pipes of the earlier organs, as we are beginning again to honor the slider wind chest for its acoustical qualities.

Our ideal for the organ has also been shaped by the achievements of the great masters of organ building in the first seven decades of the nineteenth century. Moreover, we must make allowances for the demands which the leading organ composers—César Franck, Widor, Reger, and the others—make of the organ in their writings.

All these were responsible for the enrichment of the organ in the nineteenth century through the development of the swell. Out of the meagre echo organ with its small Venetian blind swell came the well-furnished, intensively working modern swell organ, which enriches the sound of the instrument with a new tone personality, and at the same time endows it with a hitherto unsuspected flexibility.

In the arrangement of the instrument a swell must be provided that is suited to it. It should have the most stops of all the manuals. In a two-manual instrument of fifteen stops I would allot five to the first organ, seven to the second, and three to the pedal. With a two-manual organ of twenty, twenty-five, or thirty stops, I would dispose them about like this: 7, 9, 4; 8, 12, 5; 10, 14, 6.

In a three-manual instrument with a *rückpositiv*, of thirty stops about nine would be placed in the great organ, five in the *rückpositiv*, eleven in the swell, and five in the pedal. With forty stops the arrangement would be: 12, 7, 14, 7; with fifty stops: 15, 8, 18, 9; with sixty stops: 20, 11, 25, 14.

The *rückpositiv* can remain rudimentary, for its stops are most expressive. If it is set opposite the great organ as a second organ, it is in a position to be coupled with the swell chest. In the older organs, where its keyboard lay under that of the great organ, and with the coupling technique of the time could not be connected directly with the third organ, this did not work. Therefore the *rückpositiv* had to be at that time as complete as possible; today it can remain incomplete.

The difficulty of getting enough stops within the case of the *rückpositiv*, and the impossibility of connecting the *rückpositiv* directly with the third organ by the couplers of that day, led builders to neglect the acoustical and artistic significance of the *rückpositiv*, and to spoil it by placing it as a second organ within the casing of the great organ.

If the second organ in the three-manual instrument is not constructed as a *rückpositiv*, but is placed within the great organ case, it can remain, in spite of this, incomplete. It is then of course not an independent sound personality, but only an addition to the great organ.

Under all circumstances, we must hold fast to the principle that the swell must be the most complete. If the number of stops in the organ permit only one mixture and one reed, these should then be placed in the swell.

It is important in the disposition to take into consideration the registration plans of the leading organ composers. César Franck, Widor, and the other Romantic masters, assume that the swell organ is supplied with an intense gamba stop; a *voix celeste*, no less intense and of not too narrow scale; an oboe 8'; and a trumpet (*clarion*) 4'. They expect to find a clarinet 8' in the *rückpositiv*. If through some whim of the builder these stops are not found in their places on an organ, then in order to render the works of these masters and all the composers influenced by them the entire registration must be upset.

Moreover, the arrangement must take into consideration the demands made on the organ for the accompaniment of Bach cantatas and Passions. Besides a soft, open flute the swell should contain a soft and not too narrow salicional and a pleasant principal-flute. If these three stops in this quality are not available, the proper accompaniment of the recitatives and arias is not achievable.

If a *rückpositiv* is constructed, it has the immediate advantage that the solos in Bach's works may be accompanied by stops which are near the singers and the instruments. This is in the tradition of Bach's time. In this case the bright, mild *musikgedackt*, which played the principal rôle in accompaniments of that age, should not be forgotten. An 8' gemshorn should be provided for accompaniments on the *rückpositiv*. Wherever possible a mild bourdon 16' should also be provided for it. If there is a bourdon 16' in the second organ, one can use this with the left hand for the playing of the bass in the recitatives and the arias, while the right hand plays the chords in the swell organ.

Under all circumstances a beautiful, broad salicional 8' must be had along with a bourdon 8' and a flauto major 8' in the great organ. It makes no sense to forsake these old traditions. Salicional 8' cannot be replaced here by any other stop. A gamba 8' also belongs traditionally to the first organ. One should not be afraid of having the gamba 8′ and the salicional 8′ in different dimensions in the great organ and the swell organ at the same time.

The English custom of giving two or three different principals to the great organ on the larger instruments has much to say for itself.

In the swell organ of Swedish instruments built between 1850 and 1890 there is usually a waldflute 2′. This broad-dimensioned open flute is much more expressive than all other 2′ stops in the swell, and is of supreme importance.

The question of the reeds is still unsolved. The most beautiful reed stops are found on the organs of the great German organ builders of the sixties and seventies of the past century, and on English organs of that same time. They speak with a wind pressure of 80 mm. [3.15 inches]. Their tone blends most beautifully with the foundation stops and mixtures, and with them builds up to a splendid *fortissimo*. When will these reeds, which have the advantages without the imperfections of those of the eighteenth century, be built again?

They fell into disuse because they did not speak so promptly as those of Cavaillé–Coll, and had less brilliancy, and because reeds with high wind pressures did not cause the same trouble in voicing as the others. If the choice lies between a prompt entrance and tone, one should always choose tone. The time is gone when uneducated experts in organ construction could terrorize the organ builders by finding fault with every slow onset of tone as a failure. A beautifully toned reed stop will never speak promptly. A beautiful salicional and a gamba also need some time before they speak. But this makes no difference in playing. In the full organ the delayed speaking of the reeds does not disturb; hardly, even, with the lazy reeds of the eighteenth century. The speaking is improved to the degree that other stops sound at the same time. The reeds are carried along by the others. Not the most precise speaking, but the utmost beauty, is to be sought; not only in the reeds, but in all other stops.

The intensive reeds of the French organ, speaking under high wind pressure, do not blend with the other stops, but kill them. Moreover, they make impossible the *legato*. In the full French organ the tone line emerges hacked into pieces. Cavaillé–Coll's reeds cannot be used, therefore, for a Bach *fortissimo*. Hence there arose among French organists the extraordinary opinion that Bach himself, in his preludes and fugues, had disregarded the reeds. In the Paris Conservatory this was accepted in his day as dogma.

One of the chief tasks for modern organ construction, therefore, is to build again the beautiful reeds of the time of 1860.

There is no reason to take exception to the single reed stop with high wind pressure which is found in English organs as a solo tuba beside the usual reed stops, or to several of them. The mistake is only in furnishing an organ exclusively with intense reed stops.

Concerning the problem of the console, I stand on the ground of the *Regulations for organ construction*. Cavaillé–Coll, with his ventil for mixtures and reeds, offered as registration aids the device by which mixtures and reeds chosen in advance could be brought in or retired on every manual and on the pedal. In this way he in principle blazed the right trail. But he limited the introduction of the previously prepared stops to the two ranks of pipes named.

Yet, even when extended to all stops, the device for introducing the chosen stops gets its full value only when it is so laid out that the previously drawn stops may be retained or retired at will. To add new stops to those already drawn and to retire them again, to bring in new stops in place of those already drawn, and when the latter are introduced again, to retire them: this, as you know, is the twofold action—which is what all registration amounts to. The ideal is to accomplish both with a single device. Then a pedal or a draw-stop (piston), at a selected time in advance, has to secure or release the drawn stops at the moment when the prepared stops are introduced. This may be accomplished technically without difficulty.

When in 1909 the doubly available introduction of stops chosen in advance was demanded by the *Regulations for Organ Construction*, it was already realised on several Alsatian organs, as well as the similar doubly available stop *crescendo*.

Many organists and organ builders find it at first difficult to believe that with this simplified console the introduction of the stops already chosen for each separate manual should be more advantageous than the usual blind combination by which a piston or a pedal changes the registration for the whole instrument. They think they can accomplish more with half a dozen such general blind combinations than with the arrangement suggested by the *Regulations* for

organ construction. But the advantage of a series of such general
blind combinations, working on the whole organ, and each time retiring the entire drawn registration, is only apparent. These combinations would be useful if their registration remained, continuing to
alter the whole registration and to carry over from one tone color
into the other. But usually the logic of the composition requires that
stops should be added to those already drawn, now on this manual
and now on that, or should replace them, only to be withdrawn at a
later moment and leave the former alone speaking. It is also more to
the purpose that the console should make possible the introduction
of selected stops on each separate manual. For three-manual instruments the *Regulations* for organ construction provide in addition
another pedal or piston, which adds or takes away together all the
prepared stops of the organ.

In time the normal console will win the day because of its simple
utility. The important thing is that in the future every console should
be equipped with the doubly available introduction of prepared stops
for the separate manuals. Over and above that, the organ makers
may offer us whatever they wish in the way of registration helps from
the console of the old factory organ, in order to modulate in economical fashion from the earlier complexity to the coming simplicity.

It should be accepted as self-evident today that the couplers and
registration helps should be arranged both as draw stops and pistons
for the hand and as pedals for the foot. It may remain a question
whether there is any real need to tie the two together so that they
operate every time as a unit and permit the musician to release with
either the foot or the hand, at his pleasure, the stops brought into
play by the foot, and to release with the hand or the foot, at his
pleasure, the stops brought into play by the hand. Formerly I was
for this tie, since it offered great advantages. My observation has
taught me, however, that most musicians, in accordance with their
custom, use exclusively either hand or foot for these playing aids.
In the face of this fact the work and the significant costs involved
in installing this connection of draw-stop (piston) and pedal do not
any longer seem to me justified.

The principal thing is that the playing helps should no longer be
arranged exclusively for the hand, but also for the foot. Before the

coming of the factory organ console they were invariably built, even in Central Europe, as pedals. For the operation of the playing helps it is easier to free a foot than a hand.

It is a very practical thing on the English organ that the manual and pedal couplers should stand together on the left as draw-stops for the hand, next to the lowest keyboard and under the lowest row of stops. There they are actually more easily and more securely reached than farther to the right under the left half of the front board of the lowest keyboard, to which the *Regulations* for organ construction assigned them. On the basis of this experience I should now be in favor of the English arrangement of the draw-stops or pistons for the couplers. On the place left free below the left half of the key strip of the lowest keyboard would then be found space for draw-stops or pistons for the introduction of the selected registers; they would be better situated there than at the left above the top keyboard.

We Central Europeans, too much occupied with registration helps, have neglected many things in the arrangement of our consoles which would make direct hand registration easier. Formerly the registration stops were on both sides of the keyboards and over the upper keyboard. With the left hand—which one can free incomparably more often than the right—the player could not only manipulate the stops placed at the left but also the stops above the top keyboard. Since the stops are no longer placed above the upper keyboard, the very valuable hand registration can stretch over only one-third of the stops instead of two-thirds. This is a great disadvantage.

On the old Walcker instrument at Mulhouse, where the draw-stops were still arranged in the earlier manner, I was able to manipulate all the stops of the great organ and of the second organ—and the couplers too, which lay at the left next to the lowest keyboard—with the left hand; and also even some of the stops for the third organ which lay at the right of the manuals, but so high that the left hand could reach them comfortably. Only the pedal registers, whose stops lay at the very bottom at the right of the manuals, could not be operated by hand registration.

Compelling reasons for abandoning this comfortable arrangement cannot be adduced. In England it has been retained. One should see what the English organists accomplish entirely by direct hand registration!

Therefore one should not forget the most important matter in relation to playing helps: the most comfortable arrangement possible of draw-stops for hand operation. Away with all considerations of symmetry. The supreme law in the arrangement of the stops must be that the largest possible number of them should be made accessible to the left hand in the most comfortable way possible. So let them be placed at the left next to the manuals and above the top keyboard. The space at the right next to the keyboards, which can be reached only with such difficulty, may be left entirely free, circumstances permitting, or may hold the pedal stops, if these cannot be arranged anywhere else—or even the name plate of the firm of organ builders, which usually claims the best place of all above the highest manual. As many as forty draw-stops can easily be arranged next the manuals at the left and above the top one.

I firmly believe that draw-stops are more comfortable than pistons or keys; the hand can seize them better. Moreover, it is a much more natural motion to pull or to push with the whole hand than to manipulate a key or a piston with one finger.

The idea for which I prepared the way twenty years ago has conquered. In my rejoicing over it there is mingled sadness. The victory came unexpectedly early, yet still too late. When we lived in prosperity and disposed of great wealth for the purposes of art, we built commonplace organs. Today, when the ideal of the organ has advanced, we are so impoverished that we can spend very little for organ construction. For a long time to come we may not think of replacing the common organ. Every Sunday the sins committed in the past shriek in our ears.

Who will bring back again the old, beautiful organs, which in our blindness we destroyed?

Who will again produce for us the masters of organ construction, who in that senseless period when the manufacturers were industrializing organ building were ruined by the dozens and had to give up their calling?

Lao–tse's word is fitting here, "He who conquers should demean himself as at a funeral."

Therefore we must carry on in little ways what then we could have accomplished in big ways. Only a future generation will richly benefit by the knowledge to which we have returned.

We work for the future. We pray that it may come to pass.

❦

REFORM IN ORGAN BUILDING [1]

IN a valuable treatise, "The Organ as an Artistic Memorial," in the *Monthly for Divine Worship and Ecclesiastical Art*," [2] Peter Epstein of Breslau pleads for the preservation of the old organs. In it he names me as one of the first to call attention to the significance of the older instruments. It is somewhat misleading that in his exposition he makes me demand a return to the organ of the eighteenth century for the proper rendering of Bach's organ works, inasmuch as others demand the harpsichord for the piano works of the master. To avoid misunderstandings I should like to set forth briefly the case against the modern organ.

Neither in my treatise on the art of organ building in Germany and France (1906), nor in my book about Bach (1906), nor in the deliberations on organ building at the Vienna Congress of the International Society of Music (1909), which led to the setting up of *The International Regulations for Organ Building* (Leipzig, Breitkopf & Härtel, 1909), nor in the American edition of Bach's organ works (Schirmer, New York, 1913), have I advocated such archaic ideas. Those who know the old organs are aware that, along with their tone excellence, they have defects that make a simple return to them impossible. It would never occur to us, I hope, to propose as ideal the primitive bellows, the too narrow wind chests, and the generally scant pedal organs of the eighteenth century!

The solution proposed in my 1906 book was: back from the booming factory organ to the organs of the master builders so rich and beautiful in tone.

[1] "*Zur Reform des Orgelbaues,*" in *Monatschrift für Gottesdienst und kirchliche Kunst*, Vol. XXXII, No. 6 (June 1927), pp. 148–54.
[2] *Monatschrift für Gottesdienst und kirchliche Kunst*, No. 12, 1926.

The most perfect organs were built between 1860 and 1880 approximately. At that time the master organ builders created instruments which had in perfection the tonal excellence of Bach's age but without its technical defects.

Why was this skill in building abandoned later? Because the trend of the time was to factories and manufactured goods. The man who was producing organs of the fine old quality failed; he delivered too slowly and was too expensive. When he came with his cost estimate for thirty stops, the builder of the factory organ offered thirty-five stops or even more for the same price. On paper the second organ was superior to the first; that it was inferior to the other and would not equal it in tone production, in spite of the larger number of registers, could not be made clear to the customer. So the producer of the factory organs received the order.

Why could the latter deliver more stops than the organ builder for the same price? He economised in wood, by making the pipes as narrow as possible and giving them the thinnest possible walls. Moreover, he limited the variety of pipes. He standardised and tried to get along with the smallest possible number of pipe types, in order to simplify the manufacture of the organ. Instead of every register having its special pipes, of well-considered dimensions, the same kind of pipes had to serve for several registers. In this way handwork was displaced by factory work. These pipes, made to scale, too narrow and thin-walled, were much cheaper than the others, but could not produce the same tone.

Moreover, the tone of the factory organ was injured by increased wind pressure, in order to extort a tone from these unnatural pipes. Instead of the pipe speaking, the tone blustered through it. And thus, because artistic traditions were abandoned, came the organ with the roaring basses, the shrill treble, and the subdued middle tones—the overvoiced organ.

In order to manufacture as much and as cheaply as possible, the organ builders went on to make other inventions. They sought to substitute pneumatic or electric devices for the mechanical connection between the keys and the wind chest. This had a certain justification for the bigger organs, since their keys were too stiff with mechanical leverage. But with the usual two-manual church organ, this was not a problem, since it could also be played without exertion by mechanical leverage. Yet for the sake of cheapness all church organs were equipped with pneumatic or electric actions. Again the unnatural displaced the natural: a good mechanical action is much more durable than a pneumatic or electric one. Above all else, however, it is much easier to play precisely, to blend properly, and to phrase well on a mechanical organ than on the other. But such professional and artistic qualities could not be considered, because the times called for the cheapest possible manufactured work.

The pneumatic action was fatal for the poor organs also because of the higher wind pressure necessary. Since it had now become too dear, especially in the smaller organs, to construct the bellows in such a way that it could produce wind of different pressures—strong to supply the pneumatic action, somewhat weaker for the pipes—the strong wind necessary for the pneumatic action was also forced through the pipes. In this way the already booming, shrill, and overvoiced organ became still more booming, shrill, and overvoiced.

The wind chest, which so greatly determines the quality of the tone, was also "improved." The slider wind chest used by the earlier organ builders was abandoned and others were built. But none of these modern wind chests is acoustically equal to the old. When in the reconstruction of an organ the old pipes are kept and set in a modern wind box, they no longer have the beautiful tone they had before; the tone becomes dry, loses its roundness, and no longer carries.

In just what the acoustical quality of the slider wind chest consists cannot yet be surely proved—as indeed so much else in the speaking of the pipes remains still acoustically unexplained. For the time being we must be satisfied with knowing that the pipes and wind boxes formerly built produced a more beautiful tone than the present ones. Next to the slider wind chest comes the cone chest (ventil wind chest).

The many registration devices in the console helped very much to carry the factory organ on to victory. Towards the end of the century there appeared an orchestral conception of the organ. It was believed that one could not do enough in varying the tone color. Hence organs were called for with many contrivances for changing the stops. Three-quarters of these registration devices were unnecessary and served no purpose. In order to obtain these modern consoles organists sacrificed their beautiful organs, and exchanged them for instruments with mediocre tones. They valued the cow for the horns rather than for the milk.

Towards the end of the century, twenty years after this unwholesome development in organ building had set in, matters had already progressed to such a point that the builders of the factory organs could no longer produce worthy organs even if they wanted to. They no longer had the facilities to build in the former manner; moreover, they no longer had the workmen who knew how to install the mechanical action and make pipes artistically. In general, their workers were so specialized that they were no longer accomplished craftsmen in the whole field of organ handcraft.

Therefore the process of replacing the beautiful old works with ugly and unstable factory organs continued. This instability was even exalted into a principle. Organists and organ builders persuaded each other that the organs installed would have to be rebuilt every twenty or twenty-five years: first, because they would no longer be functioning well, and second, in order that in the modernised form they might benefit by all the discoveries that had meanwhile appeared.

How did it happen that the organists paid so little attention to the tonal qualities of these organs? They had lost their sensitivity to tonal beauty and tonal richness. A great deal in the history of mankind is to be explained in the end only by the inexplicable—that a generation has lost its comprehension of something.

Today has come the desire to work our way out of this decline. Those who have so long been considered backward because they were prejudiced against the modern factory organ, now find listeners. The old, beautiful organs that remain are again valued; though, unfortunately, there are now left only poor remnants of the splendor that was still there a generation ago.

The program for the future is simple: that we should again build with artistic principles, starting once more with the fine traditions of the earlier organists.

A prerequisite for this is that when an order is given for an organ, our concern should be not just for the number of its stops, but for its quality. This basic principle must become axiomatic to congregations and church authorities. Until this happens organ building will not improve.

But when we shall have accomplished this, everything else will come of itself. No witchcraft is required to build a good organ. When we cease demanding of our organ builders more stops than excellent and artistic workmanship can furnish for the designated sum, and when we allow them the necessary time to build, they will again become genuine organ builders. An outstanding musician, a conservatory director, some years ago wanted an organ ordered for a concert hall at the end of July to be ready for the opening of the fall concerts!

In studying an estimate, one should see that it is not the largest number of stops cheapest in material and work that are advocated, but rather those necessary for the perfected quality of the organ. A good sixteen-foot violone in the pedal is much more expensive than two or three other stops, but it is essential. Twenty excellent stops are more expressive than thirty mediocre ones.

For the form, the dimensions, and the mouths of the pipes, we shall once more be guided by the treasured models of the old organ builders. Naturally we shall strive to improve upon them; but our efforts must be genuinely artistic, and not efforts to serve the factory business.

The return to normal pipes carries with it the return to normal wind pressure. In this way we shall get pipes that speak in a natural way, that is, pipes that let the tone take shape instead of forcing it out.

The question of the wind chest will bring difficulties. We can get tones that carry in their perfect beauty only from the slider wind chest. But the organ builders will be on the defensive against it; they will have to sacrifice many technical advantages offered by the modern chests. It is to be hoped that they will try to build modern boxes which are equal to the slider wind chest in tone production. If they succeed, much will be gained; if they fail, there is nothing for them to do but to return to the slider wind chest, which the *International Regulations for Organ Building* (1909) declared to be acoustically more advantageous.

In the smaller and medium-sized organs we shall surely come in time, if the striving for the artistic organ continues, to the mechanical trackers from the keys to the wind chest. That the keys in this method of organ construction work a little harder than in the usual keyboard is of little consequence, compared with the great advantages this method offers in precision and clarity of playing, and in the durability of the organ. Perfected mechanical trackers are now offered that function noiselessly and that load the keys as little as possible.

It is true that mechanical action costs a good deal more than pneumatic. But it is better to dispense with one or two stops and have the mechanical action.

With the larger organs, where significant distances between the keys and the wind chest must be overcome, we shall have to enlist the aid of pneumatics and electricity in such a way as to keep as far as possible the mechanical action. In this manner the keys will retain the qualities of mechanical action.

In the console we can dispense with a good part of what is supposed to be necessary for good playing. The generally complicated and sensitive consoles with their innumerable registration devices belong to a time already past. A pedal that brings in all the stops one after the other, a register *crescendo*, a *mezzoforte*, a *forte*, a *tutti* (*sforzando*)—a pedal that permits the stops pulled out in advance to reinforce the registration already drawn or to retire it, available for each separate manual or for the whole organ (the doubly available blind combination of the *International Regulations for Organ Building*): these are the playing aids that make possible all the registration required for classical or modern organ music, as far as the player himself can undertake it. If one permits the organ builders some day to build the simplified console recommended for all organs in the *Regulations*, a great deal of money will be saved which can be used to good purpose on the stops!

In church instruments of three divisions we should try wherever possible to have the second organ project out into the church from the gallery as a *rückpositiv*; this is what the older builders did. It was a serious mistake to house the three divisions together in the main case, as they did from 1850 on. The stops in the *rückpositiv*, sounding out freely and directly in the body of the church, produce an effect not otherwise possible—to say nothing of the fact that the *rückpositiv* belongs to the architecture of the instrument.

Of course the *rückpositiv* costs a good deal more than a second organ placed within the main casing; but a *rückpositiv* of seven stops produces a better effect than a second organ of twelve stops enclosed in the main case.

In all this harking back to the prized, artistic traditions of earlier organ building we shall still, however, build modern organs, in so far as we equip them with strong swell boxes. The Venetian swell, as it was developed by Cavaillé–Coll in the sixties of the last century, is the only revolutionary advance over the older masters.

With Cavaillé–Coll the meagre echo organ, enclosed in wooden shutters, became the well-furnished swell organ, which gave to the tone of the entire instrument an expressiveness and a flexibility it had not previously possessed. Every instrument, therefore, should have a good swell organ. To accomplish this, the shutters must leave enough space for the required number of stops, they should be made of thick boards, and they should be so constructed that they close tightly. How far the factory organs fall short of these requirements, because they economize on their swell boxes!

The swell organ should have at least as many stops as the great organ. In the smaller instruments with only one reed stop and one mixture it is well to put these in the swell organ.

The organ of the future is, then, an organ which has all the excellent and precious tone quality of the organs of earlier generations, which preserves as far as possible the *rückpositiv*, and which is enriched by the possibilities for expression to be had from a well-furnished swell.

We shall then of ourselves go back to the practice of supplying the organs in the earlier manner with mixtures, that is, with stops with harmonic ranks of pipes. The unified stops are intolerable in the modern harmonic organ; they enhance only the shrillness, which the tone already has to a certain extent. Even a fifth will not blend with the foundation stops in a way pleasing to the ear. But if we once again have normal pipes, speaking under normal pressure—which means an organ poor in harmonics—then beautiful mixtures will be necessary to add artistic overtones.

In order to judge the tone of an organ, one first pulls out all the eight-foot stops and plays a polyphonic movement. In the midst of the web of tone the alto and the tenor must come through well; and the tone, even when the stops are played in the upper register, should never be unpleasant. Thereupon one lets the four-foot and two-foot stops enter, and repeats the test. Finally, one plays Bach fugues for a half-hour without interruption on the full organ. If the hearer is able to follow the voices clearly, and if he finds the sustained fullness of tone is not exhausting, then the organ is good. The full organ from a modern factory, in this test with Bach fugues, produces a chaotic uproar which cannot be endured for five minutes.

This, for our time, is the way back to an organ that is rich and beautiful in tone. It is a matter of getting for the available money that organ which sounds best, instead of that one which in the bid makes the most grandiose appearance. When artistic competition shall have taken the place of commercial rivalry, organ building will of itself find the right path, because organ builders will arise who will build in the excellent and artistic manner of the old masters, and produce organs on which not only Bach but the moderns will sound as they ought to sound.

❦

*B*Y 1927 the pendulum in organ building had already begun to swing to the other extreme; and again Albert Schweitzer quickly saw the danger. The rapid development of the organ made possible by the introduction of electricity at the beginning of the century produced its own reaction. In the effort to imitate the orchestra a huge variety of new stops had been added. The passion for size, against which Schweitzer had raised his cry of warning, had gone to an absurd degree; people began to talk about the world's biggest organ. For a time it was the one set up at the World's Fair at St. Louis in 1904. Then the distinction—if it were that—went to Philadelphia, where a five-manual organ with 232 stops and 18,000 pipes was installed at Wanamaker's. But in 1932 the giant of them all was built for the convention hall at Atlantic City; incredible as it may be, this organ had seven manuals, 1,233 stops, and 32,882 pipes!

It is to be hoped that no further efforts will be made to build "organ skyscrapers." These organs were marvels of technical ingenuity, with a multiplicity of gadgets and devices; the stops ranged from the merest whisper to the most frightful roar; there were often fine solo voices, and an appeal to sentimentality. But most of these organs were overpowering and dull, lacking the pure, clear, transparent tones of the organs for which Schweitzer was contending.

Hence the reaction began, and organs of the Bach type began to be favored. But compositions of the romantic and modern periods could not be satisfactorily rendered on these organs; Schweitzer himself had not considered the organs of the seventeenth century as ideal, but only as the predecessors of the ideal organ. Today, however, some of our modern organs have successfully combined the tonal beauty of the older organs with the register riches and mechanical excellence of the modern period. This was exactly what Schweitzer had hoped for and worked for. In some unimportant respects the evolution of the organ had proved him unduly pessimistic about the future; but in the main he was right, and the better organs of today are in considerable measure the gift to the world of Albert Schweitzer. Even in 1927 he believed that in all essential matters the fight had been won.

The two and a half years he was now to spend in Europe were filled once more with his manifold activities and interests. Lectures and concerts in Sweden, Denmark, Holland, Germany, Czechoslovakia, Switzerland, and England; in his spare time constant work on his book The Mysticism of Paul the Apostle. In 1923 he had built a house at Königsfeld in the Black Forest, and there during this period he did much of his writing.

On August 28, 1928, on the invitation of the city of Frankfort, he delivered his famous address on Goethe, and in recognition of his service to humanity in the spirit of Goethe, received the Goethe Prize.[1] The money he received was used to build his present house

---

[1] See "The Goethe Prize Address," in Goethe, Four Studies, by Albert Schweitzer. Boston: The Beacon Press, 1949, pp. 103–113.

at Gunsbach in the Munster Valley of Alsace, but it is characteristic of Schweitzer that in the next few years he gave to German charities an equivalent sum which he had earned from concerts and lectures.

We have from this period of his life four fascinating glimpses of Schweitzer the musician. In December 1928 he was in Prague for lectures and recitals. One day he lunched with President Masaryk, practised on the organ at the Smetana Saal until 7.30 P.M., listened to a concert, ate a few sandwiches, returned to the organ until almost midnight, and then went off for a pleasant supper with some friends until 2 A.M. The next day he gave an organ concert in the afternoon, and then played on the organ of the Evangelical Church until almost midnight; when, to his great amusement, the police informed him that he was disturbing the peace and keeping the citizens of the neighborhood awake.

Doctor Alice Ehlers, now professor of music in the University of Southern California, first met Doctor Schweitzer in 1928, when she was giving a series of harpsichord recitals in Europe. After one of Schweitzer's lectures he had invited any who wished to join him to a nearby restaurant. Doctor Ehlers was sitting quietly at one table with some friends, when one of Doctor Schweitzer's assistants came over and asked, "Are you Doctor Ehlers?" Too surprised to answer, she only nodded. The assistant said, "Doctor Schweitzer would like to meet you."

"It is hard to describe my feelings," writes Doctor Ehlers, "as I approached Doctor Schweitzer. I remember that I felt like a little schoolgirl, and I am afraid that I behaved like one. Doctor Schweitzer must have understood my puzzled expression. He took out his African diary, a most interesting book he always carries with him; it contains hundreds of pages of very thin paper, unbound, but held together in such a manner that new pages may at any time be added. In this diary he showed me a remark he had written while in Africa: 'When in Europe, I want to meet Alice Ehlers; interesting programs; unusual.'

"Then he explained that his friends kept him informed of what was going on in Europe by sending him magazines and programs. In this way he had followed my concerts, and, as he expressed it, the quality and the outspoken tendency of my programs had awakened his interest. No great applause or enthusiastic critic could have given me such happiness as did these words coming from Doctor Schweitzer. I told him that it was his book on Bach which had been my main guide. Amidst all his many friends and admirers, we were able to exchange a few thoughts on Bach; and when he said he should very much like to hear me play, I enthusiastically thanked him. The very next day one of my harpsichords was sent to his residence, where I played for him and Mrs. Schweitzer for a full hour. I started with the C minor Fantasy by Bach, one of the Doctor's favorite pieces, and also one of mine. His encouraging remarks helped me to overcome my first shyness, and I played on and on.

"When I left the Schweitzers, he thanked me, and said: 'Go on the way you started out, and never allow virtuosity to guide you. Always listen to the inner voices in Bach's music; each voice lives its own life, dependently and independently at the same time. If you will look at Bach's music that way, if each voice is allowed to sing out its own beauty, I am sure you cannot fail.' Those words I have remembered all my life."

From that time on Doctor Ehlers used to spend a little time at Gunsbach each summer. "When there were no visitors," she reports, "Doctor Schweitzer would very seldom come out of his study—usually only for meals; after meals he loved to sit with us for a while. He did not speak much, yet we went on talking without making conversation with him; we all knew that these were his hours of relaxation. Doctor Schweitzer is not a voluble talker; he is a great thinker, possessing the magnificent gift of complete concentration. Though the room in which I used to practise was next to his study, it never disturbed the Doctor to hear me practise; he admitted he missed it when I stopped. Often he would come in, sit down, listen to my playing, make his remarks about the music, and sometimes ask for one of his favorite pieces. When I played the piano, he almost always asked for Mozart; he loves Mozart.

"After dinner, when his day's work was done, Doctor Schweitzer would go to the church to practise on the organ. This organ was built after his own design and wishes, resembling the old organs as much as possible. Those hours with him at the organ are unforgettable. I would sit with him on the organ bench listening, and he would ask my opinion, and we would discuss phrasing, tempo, dynamics. It was in those hours that I received my best musical education. The Doctor also loved these evenings; for he was always in his happiest mood when playing the organ. All responsibilities, the whole world, disappeared for him; there was only music—the organ, nothing else. He loves music and needs it. Even in Africa, when working very hard, the day is not ended before he has his one hour of practice on his piano with organ pedals." [1]

Doctor J. S. Bixler, President of Colby College, recalls his visit at this time to Doctor Schweitzer's home in the Black Forest. He was very much puzzled when Doctor Schweitzer smilingly asked him if he would not like to hear a little "Yotz." This was a German word which Doctor Bixler did not understand until Doctor Schweitzer sat down at the piano to play in syncopated time; then he knew that the good Doctor was speaking not German but English—he was talking about jazz.

There is a fine old organ in Ottobeuren in southern Germany, built in the eighteenth century by Master Karl Riepp in Dijon, and restored in 1914 by Steinmeyer of Oettingen. One lovely day in Whitsuntide Schweitzer found himself in that vicinity, and visited the church with a few of his friends. On this instrument he played Bach toccatas, preludes, and fugues; Mendelssohn, Franck, Widor. He ended with the choral prelude "Wenn ich einmal soll scheiden" [When some day I must part]. The prior of the Benedictine cloister came in the exquisitely beautiful baroque church to shake hands with this evangelical pastor and organist; and Schweitzer was very happy to meet him. He knew of the prior's efforts to save the old organ from destruction. Schweitzer said, "Whoever does that is my brother or my sister."

[1] The Albert Schweitzer Jubilee Book. Edited by A. A. Roback. Cambridge, Mass.: Sci-Art Publishers, 1945, pp. 230 f., 234.

IX

The Round Violin Bow

*S*CHWEITZER'S third sojourn in Africa began at the end of 1929 and lasted two years. *This was the period when he published* The Mysticism of Paul the Apostle; *wrote his autobiography* Out of My Life and Thought; *the sequel to his book,* On the Edge of the Primeval Forest, *which bore in English the title,* More from the Primeval Forest; [1] *and his address for the one hundredth anniversary of Goethe's death, which was delivered in March 1932, after his return to Europe.* [2] *He worked also on the third volume of his* Philosophy of Civilization.

Miss Margaret Deneke, the choir master of Lady Margaret Hall in Oxford, who spent a few months at Lambarene towards the end of 1931, tells of Schweitzer's half hour with Bach every evening when the pressure of his enormous correspondence and his hospital work made it possible. She tells also of the voyage back to Bordeaux, of the marvelous improvisations on the boat, and of the organ recital in the Bordeaux church, given for the four nurses who accompanied him, when he played from memory Bach's Passacaglia and the Little E minor Prelude and Fugue. How happy he was to have again, after more than two years, a real organ under his fingers! [3]

In February 1932 he was back in Europe, for a little more than a year of lectures and concerts in Holland, England, Sweden, Germany, and Switzerland. His energy was inexhaustible. He rose early

[1] On the Edge of the Primeval Forest & More from the Primeval Forest, by Albert Schweitzer. Recently republished in America as a single volume. New York: The Macmillan Company, 1948.
[2] See Goethe: Four Studies, by Albert Schweitzer, Boston: The Beacon Press, 1949, pp. 29–60.
[3] Seaver, pp. 125–127.

and worked late, and rushed from place to place to fill his heavy schedule of engagements. He somehow found time to see all the organs worth seeing, but he saw almost nothing else. He said with a grin, "I shall not begin sightseeing until I am seventy-five!" While in England and Scotland he received four honorary degrees: an LL.D. from St. Andrews, a D.D. from Oxford, a D.D. and a Mus.D. from the University of Edinburgh. He greatly valued this recognition from these institutions of learning; yet the honors themselves meant so little to him that later in writing an autobiographical record of this period of his life, he forgot to mention them.[1]

Pierre van Paassen gives a characteristic glimpse of his activities. "I recall," he says, "how Doctor Schweitzer once came to Zutphen (Holland) to preach the Christmas sermon when I was a guest at the manse. He arrived on a Monday, and Christmas fell on a Saturday. We did not see the great man all week, until finally, passing by the cathedral and hearing the organ, we found Dr. Schweitzer covered with dust and sweat, up in the loft busy cleaning the pipes. On Christmas he not only preached the sermon, but also played the organ to the astonishment of the churchgoers, who upon entering the cathedral, looked up in amazement when they heard the prelude and said: 'Is that our old organ?' Archbishop Söderblom told me that Schweitzer did the same thing once in Upsala. But there he worked for two months before he had the organ back to what it should have been." [2]

On January 24, 1933, Concert Master Rolph Schroeder gave a memorable Bach recital for the Strassburg Association of Professional Musicians, and Schweitzer published in the Schweizerische Musikzeitung an essay on the round violin bow which Schroeder had invented, and with which he played. This was the kind of bow that Bach himself had used. With it he had been able to play as chords what with our customary bow can be played only as arpeggios. Schweitzer had seen pictures of this bow in his early boyhood; the angels in the

---

[1] For most interesting accounts of Dr. Schweitzer's journeys see Seaver, chapters VI, VIII, and XI.

[2] From That Day Alone, by Pierre van Paassen. New York: The Dial Press, Inc., 1941.

*Grünewald paintings in the museum at Colmar all have these round
bows.*

❦

THE ROUND VIOLIN BOW [1]

EVERY ONE of us has already suffered from the fact that we
never hear the splendid polyphonic parts from Bach's *Chaconne*,
or from his other works for the violin alone, as they stand on paper
and as we hear them in our minds. They are executed for us in such
a way that the chords do not sound as such but are rendered as arpeggios. Since the bass notes are not prolonged, the harmony has no
foundation. And whenever the polyphonic parts appear, the violinist
must always play *forte* even when the logic of the piece demands
piano for that particular place. For he can play the polyphonic parts,
as far as he can play them at all, only by pressing the bow sideways
on the strings. The sounds that necessarily accompany these arpeggios played *forte* are disagreeable. Great violin *virtuosi* by their
technical skill can make this imperfect rendering somewhat less
imperfect; but they fall far short of executing the Bach works for the
solo violin in such a way as to give the hearer unalloyed enjoyment.

The question now arises whether Bach, that great connoisseur of
string instruments, really wrote something for the violin which can
be rendered on it only very imperfectly. As a matter of fact, he did
not do that. How then? Were he and the players of his time more
skillful than our greatest *virtuosi?* No. But they used a bow different
from ours.

The difficulty with the playing of several parts lies only in the
modern bow, with its straight stick and its hair tightly stretched by
the screw. With this bow it is simply impossible to play all four
strings at the same time; the straight violin stick and the narrow distance between the hair and the stick (the stick of the modern bow
is even bent inward towards the hair in order to secure the desired
tautness) do not permit. The stick, along with the hair, would of
course touch the strings.

[1] *Der runde Violinbogen. Schweitzerische Musikzeitung,* No. 6, 1933.

These difficulties do not exist for the round violin bow—which, of course, is really a *bow*. All of us are acquainted with this bow; it is the one the angels hold in their hands in the old paintings. By slackening the tension sufficiently, one can draw the hair of the round bow over all four strings at the same time without the slightest hindrance from the stick, which is arched outward. Under these conditions nothing stands in the way of polyphonic playing.

The masters of the Bach era and of the era that preceded Bach— not alone the German masters but the Italian and others—wrote in polyphonic style for the violin alone, because they were accustomed to play polyphonic pieces on this instrument with the round bow, and had brought to perfection the technique of this method of playing.

We learn from Nicolaus Bruhns, one of the most gifted musicians of the generation that preceded Bach (he was an organist at Husum in Schleswig, and died at the end of the 17th century before he was thirty), that he was accustomed to sit on the organ bench and improvise polyphonically upon the violin, while playing at the same time one or two parts on the organ pedals.

Whether the round violin was in common use in Bach's days we do not know. It is, of course, exceedingly difficult to reach any definite conclusion on this—as on other questions that have to do with the technique of playing.

Arnold Schering, in a study which dated from the year 1904, is the first to deal with the problem of the violin bow in Bach's time.

The "modern" bow, with its more or less straight stick and its mechanical contrivance to secure tension, originated in Italy and appeared in Germany at the end of the 17th century. In Bach's days —that is, in the first half of the 18th century—it must already have been generally used. But the old round bow, the hair of which was kept taut only by the natural elasticity of the bent stick, was still known, and still used for polyphonic playing.

In the older models of the "modern" bow the mechanical tension was secured by a movable handle with a wire ring hooked to teeth on the back of the stick. Such a bow is found, for example, in the Bach House at Eisenach. In Bach's time, however, bows with the present screw tension were already common.

Until the end of the 18th century these modern bows still had a stick arched slightly outward, which can be seen in the illustrations Leopold Mozart furnished for his book *Die grundliche Violinschule* [The Fundamental Violin School] that appeared in 1770. It was not until the 19th century that a stick perfectly straight or arched inward toward the hair was constructed to offer the greatest possible resistance and to provide a correspondingly greater tension.

The advantages of the straight, mechanically tightened bow are that it is easier to manipulate than the round one, since it is not so high; that its greater tension permits spring bowing and staccato technique; and especially that the tone produced by the stroke with the tauter hair is more intense than that produced by the slackened hair.

Because of these advantages for one-part playing, the straight bow gradually prevailed over the round one during the course of the 18th century. Indeed, it supplanted the round bow so completely that very few round ones have been preserved for us, as anyone who searches the museums will find to his regret.

But in the 19th century Ole Bull, the Norwegian violinist, brought the round bow back into esteem—though only temporarily. Ole Bull's life was like a romance. He was born in the vicinity of Bergen, and got his first instruction from Spohr, whom he then left for Paganini,—then residing in Paris. In Paris all his belongings, including his precious violin, were stolen. In despair he threw himself into the Seine; but he was fished out. A wealthy woman took him under her protection, and gave him a Guarneri violin. The money he earned in his concert journeys in Europe and America he lost in founding a theatre in Bergen and in land speculation in Pennsylvania for the benefit of Norwegian emigrants. He died in Norway in 1880.

As an artist he was a very controversial figure. To some he was a magician with the violin, to others only a clown. But most were fascinated by his playing, because it was different from anything they had heard. In what was it different? In this: that Ole Bull played polyphonically.

How did this happen? He used a bow, like the old round one. For his knowledge of the round bow he was indebted to the circumstance that in the conservative lands of the north it had remained in use well into the 19th century. And this artist whose aim was mastery of his instrument took note of the possibilities this old bow offered him and went to work to realize them. In this he succeeded. Ole Bull's bow was not arched quite like the old one; it had an almost straight stick, but at the point it was bent sharply downwards, and thus achieved the separation of the hair from the stick that was necessary for polyphonic playing.

It is interesting to note that Ole Bull always maintained that he had not introduced anything new with his polyphonic playing, but was pleading only for the true old violin art.

It would have been quite natural for Ole Bull to devote himself to the Bach compositions for violin alone, which offered him such a splendid opportunity for the development of his polyphonic playing. He did not do this, however, but expressed himself mainly in his own works, so far as he did not improvise—which he knew how to do in a masterly fashion. Bach's creations were first becoming really known when Ole Bull's life span ended.

But though Ole Bull did not dedicate himself to the works of Bach which required polyphonic playing, others could have done this, after he had reintroduced the technique of the round bow.

This, however, they failed to do.

How was that possible? There on paper, in their unique splendor, were Bach's works for the violin alone. They could be rendered properly only with the round bow. But the violinists continued to maltreat them with the straight bow: simply because no one wished to undertake—a very simple matter—to have a bow constructed like the old pictures, and with this bow to undertake this interpretation.

I had been long convinced of the need of going back to the old bow for Bach's solo violin works. While I was studying Bach's compositions at the beginning of this century, I begged my friend, the Alsatian violinist Ernst Hahnemann, an excellent Bach player, to let me hear at any price the polyphonic parts of the *Chaconne* with a bow that would make possible polyphonic playing. We took an old bow and altered it as well as we could, to make the distance between the stick and the hairs enough to permit the playing of the four strings at the same time without too much difficulty from the stick. Naturally we lessened in the required manner the tension of the hairs.

What I then heard from the playing with this very imperfect Bach bow was enough to produce in me complete conviction that the Bach works for the violin alone, as well as the works of the other old masters, required the round bow. Thereupon in my book about Bach I demanded that the instrument makers should again furnish us with round bows for the proper rendition of these works, and that the *virtuosi* should again learn the technique of the round bow.

Wherever I could, after the appearance of my Bach book, I talked about this matter with violinists of reputation and sought to win them to this project. But they were all averse to it. Why? They were all convinced that the tone that would be produced by the moderately stretched bow would not please our ears, accustomed as they are to the intensive tone of the violin. To justify this conviction they usually referred to the tone that one gets if one loosens the hairs on an ordinary straight bow, puts the stick under the violin, lays the hairs on the strings, and holding them and the stick with the right hand draws the hairs over the strings with the reversed and completely relaxed bow. They forget that the hairs of the round bow are never as completely relaxed as they are in this violinist's trick.

They also added that Ole Bull, in playing with the round, imperfectly stretched bow, was able to produce only a small tone, which those who criticised his playing always reproached him for. Granted; yet in spite of this smaller tone he delighted his hearers.

Often I heard also from the masters of the violin that a great deal in Bach's polyphonic passages for the solo violin cannot be played as it stands on paper—that is, in sustained chords. Those who expressed this opinion forgot to take into consideration that Bach's fingering, and especially that of the old masters who were accustomed to play polyphonically and were at the same time masters of the fingering technique of the lute (something that one must indeed remember), was probably much more perfect than ours, accustomed as we are to the playing of only one or two parts.

More than anything else, however, it was the fear of not being able to play the single part with a bow inadequately stretched which kept the great violinists of the 19th century and of recent times from venturing to try the round bow. But unknown violinists began to interest themselves in the problem, and went courageously to work on it.

The problem is not simply a matter of returning to the old round bow. The player stretched the old bow by pressing the hair towards the stick from below with the thumb; and held it in this way when he played monophonically. When the polyphonic passages came he relaxed his thumb, so that the set of hairs could be loosened and drawn over all four strings at the same time; for the pieces in which the polyphonic parts appeared the players used specially slack bows.

When in this or that study of the old bows it is maintained that the player also relaxed the bow in order to play a single part *piano*, that is not true. The moment he relaxed with a specially slack bow he could no longer play a single part, since the slack hair played other strings as well. Therefore he relaxed only for the polyphonic playing.

The tightening of the hairs with the thumb was of course limited by the strength of the thumb; therefore this method always remained unsatisfactory. But why not build into the bow a mechanical device, to be manipulated by the thumb, which would make possible a much greater tension or a much greater loosening than the thumb alone could provide? In this way might be created a bow which would unite the advantages of both old and new.

This, then, quite properly became the objective of those who worked on the problem of the Bach bow as it confronts us today.

The first bow equipped with such a mechanism was brought to me by Dr. Hans Baumgart of Rastatt, who had conceived it, and had had it constructed for him by a bow maker at the beginning of the year 1929. It was satisfactory in many respects except that it was rather heavy, and that the tightening and loosening mechanism made much demand on the thumb. What could actually be accomplished with it, I was unable to imagine rightly, since no outstanding violinist was at hand to go to the trouble of making himself familiar with its technique.

Let us not forget also the bow of Berkowski in Berlin.

Now someone has appeared, in the person of Concert Master Rolph Schroeder of Kassel, who has improved the round bow and at the same time is an eminent violinist. His bow and the perfection with which he uses it permit us to say that the problem is in the main solved.

In Rolph Schroeder's bow the loosening and tightening of the hair is accomplished by a lever that takes the place of the handle. The tension possible with this bow is almost as much as that we are accustomed to; in monophonic playing, then, the performer is hardly hindered with this bow. Moreover, the tone produced in single-part playing is almost as great in intensity as that to which we are accustomed with the straight bow. On the other hand, a much greater slackening of tension is possible with the bow of Rolph Schroeder than with the old round bow. Without any noticeable pressure by the hand the hair stretches over the four strings at the same time. Polyphonic playing is therefore even significantly easier than it was for Bach and the old masters.

In order that the stick may not be in the way when the hair is most relaxed for polyphonic playing, it has a very marked arch. Though rather high, this bow is nonetheless not unwieldy, and it is as light as the modern one.

With the fully loosened bow, then, the performer can play in the polyphonic passages as loudly as is generally possible on the violin; he has only to put necessary pressure on the bow.

Its manipulation is the simplest imaginable. During the single-part playing the thumb is pressed against the lever from below, and without any great exertion produces a strong tension. During the polyphonic playing the thumb rests only very lightly against the lever, which, yielding to the resistance of the hair on the strings, gives of itself, as far as the thumb (which always remains on it) will permit. Therefore the bow is not like the old round one, either taut or loose; but instead the player can use a whole series of degrees of tension and relaxation lying in between.

On Tuesday, January 24, of this year (1933), Concert Master Rolph Schroeder played with this bow, after two years of practice with it, the G minor Sonata, which contains the famous fugue, and the Partita, which has the Chaconne for a finale, before the members of the Association of Professional Musicians (Society of the Friends of the Conservatory) in the great hall of the Strassburg Conservatory. At last, chords whose bass notes resounded—chords not only in *fortissimo* and *forte* but also in *piano* and *pianissimo!* And what marvelous *crescendo* and *diminuendo* in the sequence of the chords!

Everything that had been adduced to characterize the experiments with the round bow as hopeless was demonstrated in five minutes of this performance to be untenable! The tone produced with this round bow is a bit less intense than with the modern bow, but nonetheless is always full and wonderfully beautiful; in fact it seems even better. In any case, it meets a great need. It is remarkable that with this bow overtones are far less noticeable than with the ordinary one; this is particularly evident in *pianissimo* playing.

And what has also been said about impossible fingering was contradicted by Rolph Schroeder's playing. It is true that the difficulties of mastering the fingering technique required for sustained polyphonic playing are great, greater than those of the round bow and the thumb lever; but they are not unconquerable. Bach asks nothing really impossible of the violin or of the organ—however great his demands on the performer.

Since the bow of the old masters could be relaxed only to a limited degree, they may have used for their polyphonic playing a somewhat flattened bridge. It is certain that Ole Bull did this.

When the round bow is provided with a lever, however, the slackening is possible to such a degree that without the slightest difficulty the hairs can bend over the four strings of the usual rounded bridge. The flattened bridge, which constitutes a difficulty for one-part playing, is therefore not needed.

Henry Joachim, in an article in the *Musical Times* devoted to the question of the bow for Bach violin solo pieces, expressed the hope that some day a gifted violinist may appear who would play Bach's music with courage and idealism in Bach's spirit and mood, and thus force all concert violinists to do the same.[1]

We who heard Rolph Schroeder know that this hope has been fulfilled. The time has passed when the lovers of Bach had to be satisfied with a wholly inadequate rendition of the polyphonic parts of the violin pieces of Bach and the other old masters because violinists stubbornly insisted on using only the straight modern bow.

[1] This article in German translation has also appeared in the *Schweizerische Musikzeitung*, March 1, 1932.

Henceforth those who would play these works for us must use the round bow which they demand.

❧

IN 1950, in connection with the Strassburg Music Festival, Dr. Schweitzer republished the foregoing article on "The Round Violin Bow" in the official program of the festival and simultaneously in the Strassburg monthly Saisons d'Alsace. This article was subsequently published in English translation in Musical America. It is identical with the 1933 article with the exception of the concluding paragraphs, which are added here.

❧

IT looked for a time after 1934 as if the round violin bow had conquered. Guests from Paris who heard Rolf Schroeder play in Strassburg invited him to perform in Paris, where he had a great success. Thibaud became interested in the bow. In Brussels and Berlin this manner of polyphonic playing evoked a great deal of enthusiasm. In 1939, on the invitation of Professor Stein, Rolf Schroeder was asked to give a course in Berlin on playing with the round bow. But then the war broke out.

Impressed by Rolf Schroeder's playing at Strassburg, Georges Frey, violinist at Mulhouse, decided to devote himself to the round bow. With the help of a Swiss bowmaker he had a round bow built, somewhat like Schroeder's bow, and began to perform Bach's violin solo works in Alsace and elsewhere in France. In this way Mr. Frey initiated many a musician into the correct way of rendering Bach's violin solos.

After the war I heard nothing of Rolf Schroeder for some time. Not until June 1949 did I have any news about him. Then I learned that for some time after the war he had been concertmaster with the Dresden Philharmonic Orchestra, and then had gone back to Kassel, where he had lost all his property, to build himself a new bow, which he considers better than the former one.

During 1949 I became acquainted with the attempts made by Rudolf Gutman of Constance to make a straight bow, the hair of which is at a greater distance from the stick than usual. A continuous row of celluloid rings between hair and stick made the tightening or slackening of the hair possible. Mr. Gutman is not only an excellent instrument maker but also a genuine musician, and has himself demonstrated this bow on the gamba. He told me he thought it possible to perfect this bow by replacing the celluloid rings with a flat sack between hair and stick, filled with air under a certain pressure.[1]

For the time being we have no opinion about the possibility of a future straight bow superior to the perfect round bow of Bach's time. The latter is adequate for the rendering of Bach's violin works as he conceived them and as they should sound, and we do have artists who know how to perform them correctly for us with this bow.

May the coming months, dedicated particularly to the memory of Bach and his works, bring us on the programs of Bach festivals such performances of his violin solo compositions. Thus the correct manner of rendering them will become known, and an increasing number of violinists may be influenced to familiarize themselves with the perfected round bow and the technique of sustained polyphonic playing. Once such a bow for polyphonic playing comes again into use, modern composers will doubtless be stimulated to write once more solos for violin, cello and gamba, and to give new life to a kind of musical composition which has seemed to belong wholly to the past.

[1] In America the violinst Roman Totenberg and the California bowmaker John Bolander have together constructed and demonstrated a bow suitable for the playing of Bach's violin solos. The Bolander bow is convex, and has the screw and head and some of the other structural peculiarities of the Tourte bow.

❧

*I*N 1940 Mr. Georges Frey, who had already begun to give concerts with the round violin bow, was driven out of Mulhouse by the German army. He was afraid he would have to leave his bow behind, but at the last minute he managed to put it into a case with two violins. He escaped to the unoccupied zone in southern France, and continued to give his concerts, at Vichy, Lyons and elsewhere. The conventional musicians were all opposed to the round bow, but he persisted. He found it wonderful on three or four strings, satisfactory on two strings, but not so good on one.

In May 1949 Mr. Frey came to Gunsbach on Dr. Schweitzer's invitation to play for him. It was the writer's great privilege to be there when Mr. Frey arrived. It was an unforgettable occasion. Again there were distinguished guests in the house—A. Haedrich from Guebwiller, deputy Joseph Wasmer from Mulhouse, Auguste Dubois, the famous Alsatian artist. Monsieur Frey began to play in the upstairs study. Miss Gloria Coolidge, the American nurse from Lambarene, came into the room, and Monsieur Frey began to clear the music from a chair he was using as a kind of music rack so that she might sit there. Dr Schweitzer playfully protested, "An artist should not trouble himself about anyone else," he said. Miss Coolidge sat on a stool beside the stove.

Monsieur Frey began to play a Bach fugue. He had not practised it, and did not know it by heart. He tried to follow the score lying on the seat of the chair. He could not see it very well, and in the middle of the piece lost his place and stopped. Dr. Schweitzer jumped up and made a music rack of himself, sitting on the chair and holding the music in front of his face. After a few moments Monsieur Frey said, "It is necessary to turn the page." Someone tried to help, but Dr. Schweitzer turned the page himself, and continued to hold his exhausting pose until the fugue ended. The fingering was very difficult; at times the player had to use his thumb as well as his fingers, and not only the tip of his little finger but the base of it as well.

The picture is etched deeply on my memory: Madame Martin in

front of Dr. Schweitzer's table, Monsieur Dubois on a chair with closed eyes and folded hands, Miss Coolidge on the stool by the stove, the other guests on the sofa in rapt attention; and Albert Schweitzer sitting with bowed head and holding the music in front of him with both hands.

So Bach came to life again at Gunsbach.

X

Records for the World

ALBERT Schweitzer has spent most of the time from 1933 to 1959 in Africa but he has often made visits to Alsace. From April 1933 to January 1934 he was at Lambarene for the fourth time. He gave much time to the preparation of the Gifford Lectures, which he had promised to deliver in 1934 and 1935. From February 1934 until February 1935 he was back in Europe. He gave a series of lectures at Manchester College, Oxford, on "Religion in Modern Civilization," which he repeated at London University College. The Gifford Lectures at Edinburgh were on the great thinkers of India, China, Greece, and Persia. The lecture on the Indian thinkers grew later into a book, which was published under the title of Indian Thought and Its Development.

On February 26, 1935, he reached Africa for a stay of six months, during which he prepared a second series of Gifford Lectures. Then for a year and a half he was in Europe, from September 1935 to February 1937. He gave his lectures, and was busy with many organ recitals. Just at this time he was asked by Columbia Records in London to make a series of recordings, which he finally completed on the fine organ of St. Aurelia's, Strassburg, in October 1936. Louis–Edouard Schaeffer has written an interesting newspaper story of the making of these records on the wonderful Silbermann organ there.[1]

"The organ stops. In the frame of the door that leads from the interior of the church into the sacristy Albert Schweitzer appears. I have surprised him in the midst of his work, in shirt sleeves. He has even taken off his vest here in the late autumn in the cold church. I see again the imposing head that reminds one of Nietzsche, the

[1] Neueste Nachrichten, Strassburg, November 11, 1936.

powerful form with the broad shoulders which seems to me today even heavier and more crammed with energy than ever. We know of the lofty spirit that drives this man to ever new undertakings. We know especially about the iron, almost mysterious will that disciplines and steels body and soul in an astonishing vital effort. The task he has been mastering for some days now in St. Aurelia is in accordance with his character—nothing less than filling thirty records with Bach and César Franck. He is completely absorbed in his work. The theologian, the preacher, comparative religion, the significance of the Apostle Paul and his mission, the burial and resurrection of Christ, the doctor and surgeon, the jungle hospital—all this has passed into the background. It is now the master of the organ who speaks, the interpreter of Bach.

"Before the organ over the church pews hangs the microphone; it carries the tones of the organ to the receiving apparatus in the sacristy. Here the wax disk turns, and here the needle scratches the organ tones in the surface of what looks like a thick, deep yellow honey cake. 'You are arriving just at one of the most difficult places,' said Albert Schweitzer to me, as he took me up to the choir loft with him. About half of the piece he is about to play is exclusively in the pedals. He supports himself on the organ bench with both hands, and plays with assurance and energy the difficult foot pedals once or twice through. Then he telephones the sacristy that he is ready. The man in charge of the reception there puts on a new disk and lowers the needle. Now a muffled bell beside the console gives the signal, and then beside the organ, exactly as in the theatre, a red light goes on. The organ begins. Once more Schweitzer props himself up with his hands on the organ bench; and while I watch the amazing touch of his feet on the pedals, I am struck by the elegant, close-fitting low shoes which I have never seen on Schweitzer at other times. He puts them on only for his organ playing, and on his concert trips carries them with him in a linen bag to the organ lofts.

"Another muffled signal comes from the sacristy; the transcription is finished. Schweitzer does not seem completely satisfied, and we go down to listen to it. He notes a couple of minor changes he wants to make, then goes up to the organ for a second rendition, which finally satisfies him.

"After a short pause for rest Albert Schweitzer begins a Bach Adagio. How smoothly the notes of the Silbermann organ flow! When one hears the warm, swelling basses the instrument seems to be mysteriously enraptured in technical purity and freed from the bonds of mechanics. To the 'elegant slowness' of the Adagio, as he himself expresses it, Schweitzer lends the last measure of maturity, and gives each sound wave its full resonance, soft splendor, and resounding luminosity. Because of this the transcription is a couple of minutes too long. What I felt only vaguely and without any total impression while I was beside the organ becomes a certainty when we go down in the sacristy to hear the record. The tender and spacious motifs of the Adagio, its magic lustre and restrained fire, flow happily into the soul. 'How beautifully the basses sound!' 'Yes,' nods the doctor, 'it turns out well.'

"At a long bench in the sacristy sits a music critic from London. With the music before him he follows the transcription. He points to one place and asks, 'Why do you play a trill just here?' 'Look,' exclaims Schweitzer eagerly, 'here is a trill, and here is one; therefore there must also be one here. Bach was too indolent to draw it in. You must remember that Bach wrote everything just for himself. When Bach played the Adagio he put in a couple of trills right at this place.'

"Meanwhile it has grown late, and the church has become very cold. The organ builder Härpfer from Boulay is testing the organ. It is as temperamental as a woman, and the organ builder says, while he tries the reeds: 'What do you want to do? The colder it gets in the church now, the more easily it gets out of tune.' 'Then we will quickly make two more records,' Schweitzer decides, and rises from his reclining chair near the organ.

"At half past nine in the morning he is already practising again. While they are making arrangements for the first transcription, and an organist from Berne is having a look at the pedals and stops, he tells me how it happens that he is making records in St. Aurelia. He has already played Bach for 'His Master's Voice,' but the trials made at that time in the London concert hall, Queen's Hall, did not turn out to his satisfaction—the organ was too harsh. For the Columbia Records he sought in London for an appropriate instrument, and played next on the organ of Tower All-Hallows, the All Saints Church in the Tower. Finally he suggested the possibility of transferring the transcribing to the St. Aurelia Church in Strassburg. The experts from Columbia found conditions ideal in this church, located in an out-of-the-way corner behind the Weissturmstrasse. In a medium-sized room with excellent acoustics the beauties of the organ are kept. The organ itself does not have to be a mighty instrument, fitted out with all the technical novelties—it is sufficient that it has all the stops. The Silbermann organ in St. Aurelia is specially fitted for Schweitzer's interpretation of Bach. Shortly before the war, and a year after the organ at St. Thomas, it was restored by the Lorraine organ builder Frédéric Härpfer. In the course of the conversation Schweitzer asserted repeatedly that he considered Härpfer the most noteworthy artist among the organ builders of our time.

"Schweitzer's work is filled with unusual harmony. Is it not an evidence of an even deeper and special accord to give Bach's work anew to the world on an organ that comes from the middle of the eighteenth century, originating in the time of Bach and erected by Johann Andreas Silbermann, a Strassburg organ builder whom Bach so greatly prized and revered?"

For two weeks of incessant toil Schweitzer played in St. Aurelia, for the wax records, some of the great organ works of Bach's later years and in addition some of the works of César Franck. The three records then placed on the market are unfortunately no longer available.

In 1935 the city of Leipzig invited Schweitzer to speak at the great Bach festival there; but Schweitzer politely refused. He did not set foot in Germany all the time that Hitler was in power

In February 1937 he was back again in Africa for his sixth sojourn there. He hoped this time to be able to finish his Philosophy of Civilization, on which he had been working steadily since 1923; but the pressure of work at the hospital made it impossible. He had accumulated a large amount of material, and had planned to publish two additional volumes to complete the two already issued. In the end, however, he resolved to complete his Philosophy in a single volume, and to publish in a separate work the chapters on the Chinese thinkers, in whom he had become profoundly interested.

In 1938 he published a little volume of anecdotes about the natives of Africa called From My African Notebook. In February 1939 he arrived in Europe once again; but this time, his stay was to be of the briefest. On the way back from Africa he had become convinced that war was imminent; and if it were to come he knew that his place was at his hospital. Suddenly he changed all his plans, and went back to Africa on the return trip of the steamer that had taken him to Europe, arriving March 3. Then came the terrible war years; the activities of the hospital seriously curtailed for lack of funds and supplies, yet still maintained by the sacrificial devotion of the little staff, who wore themselves out without respite or relief. Even after the war was over Dr. Schweitzer was not able to return to Europe, for the hospital had to be reorganized and new doctors and nurses recruited and trained.

Finally, in October 1948, Dr. Schweitzer was back again in Europe after an absence of almost twelve years—broken only by the few days in Europe in February 1939—back again with his loved organs, with his circle of close friends, in the great world where his life and thought had become increasingly known and respected. There was no rest for him in Europe; requests for lectures, recitals, and other services came streaming in to the "house that Goethe built" in every mail. Friends and admirers came to call on him; groups of people from schools and churches made pilgrimages to his door. Most of the requests for lectures and recitals had to be declined; the burden had become too heavy for one man to carry.

Twice he declined the cabled invitation to give the principal speech at the Goethe Bicentennial Convocation and Music Festival at Aspen, Colorado, but when Schweitzer realized what the fee offered might do for his hospital, he accepted, "for the sake of his lepers." And so in the summer of 1949 Albert Schweitzer found himself for the first time in America, for a few brief and crowded weeks. He delivered the address at Aspen—at some risk to his health because of the unexpectedly high altitude—received an honorary LL.D. from the University of Chicago, visited organs and friends and pharmaceutical houses in Cleveland, New York, and Boston, and then sailed back to Europe for a few feverish weeks of preparation for his return to Africa. More than ever his previous return to Europe and his visit to America had been a triumphal journey, crowded with recognition by the communities with which he had been associated—Gunsbach, Kaysersberg, Mulhouse, Strassburg. The French Government bestowed on him the Legion of Honor. In America he was hailed as one of the truly great men of the world.

But all this failed to divert him in the slightest from his course of duty. He made a hurried journey to Sweden and Denmark. Unable to write letters in the shaky third class carriage, he memorized something from César Franck, his fingers playing on his knees, his feet tapping the floor. In October of 1949 he was once more on his way back to Africa for more months of arduous work on the equator. These months proved to be among the hardest he had ever known; sometimes he felt like a drowning man, gasping for breath. For again the hospital was understaffed, and much of the work he usually turned over to others he again had to do himself. He even had to operate again, and at the age of seventy-five painstakingly learned new surgical stitches. The meeting of the International Bach Society occurred in April, but its president was unable to attend. He could not leave his hospital.

This difficult period of his life came to an end in May, 1951, and he spent the rest of the year in Europe. There followed another sojourn in Africa before he returned to Gunsbach in 1952.

That summer he made eight new records for Columbia, this time in the church at Gunsbach, which was so dear to his soul. He had first tried other organs, but this small instrument in the church of his boyhood seemed to him the best of them all, at least for his purpose. It was his own organ. Every pipe in it, every stop in it was familiar to him.

Most of the records he made at this time were filled with the music of his beloved Bach, but César Franck, and Mendelssohn, and Widor were there also.

When he had finished, the music was all played back to him through a loud-speaker from the sound-recording truck outside. And Albert Schweitzer sat in the pews and for the first time in his life heard himself play up there in the organ loft.

On October 30, 1953, the Nobel Peace Prize was awarded to Schweitzer in absentia. Schweitzer himself was in Africa building a new village for his lepers.

XI

The Musician at Eighty-Four

SOONER or later many of the world's distinguished musicians find their way to the little village of Gunsbach, which will be remembered in history only because it was the European home of Albert Schweitzer. On one memorable day, Mr. Valentyn Schoonderbeck, professor of organ at the Lyceum of Music in Amsterdam; Mr. Bangert, director of the Conservatory of Copenhagen and Domkantor at the great Roskilde Cathedral where the Danish kings are buried; and Doctor Antonia Brico, orchestra director from Denver on her way to Finland to give a series of concerts, were all there; and on special invitation the Hutt Double Quartet had come from Colmar. The founder and leader of this quartet had been Professor Edouard Hutt, a close friend of Doctor Schweitzer's and a very competent musician, and Doctor Schweitzer had invited the men of the double quartet to visit him in appreciation of a concert they had given in the Evangelical Stadtkirche of Colmar for the benefit of his hospital work.

After pleasant fellowship at the house they all went to the village church. Doctor Schweitzer wished them to see and hear the organ, of which he was very proud. The organ had been repaired and renovated in 1928 according to the specifications he had drawn up. In the course of the Second World War the tower of the church had been blown down, and dirt, plaster, and water had got into the organ, so that in 1949 it had to be thoroughly overhauled, cleaned, and tuned by the firm of Härpfer from Boulay in the Moselle—again under the constant supervision of Doctor Schweitzer. Now it was in excellent condition, and the Doctor's guests must hear it.

Doctor Schweitzer sat at the organ in the high balcony at the rear

of the church. One by one he played for them the various stops—
first the flue stops, then the mixtures—which he humorously called
the vitamins of the organ—and finally the pedals. Then he said:
"Now I want to show you what is possible with such an organ,"
and he played from memory Bach's Toccata in D minor, the chorale
prelude to "Herzlich tut mich verlangen" [With all my heart I long],
and a part of the lovely 6th Organ Sonata by Mendelssohn.

Then he slid off the organ bench, bowed, and said, "Now it is
your turn." He walked over to the steep stairs in the corner of the
balcony and descended to the floor of the church, where he went
forward and took his place in an empty pew alone. The Hutt Double
Quartet sang Bortnianski's Doxology. Professor Bangert played one
of the variations which Johann Pachelbel wrote on Schob's chorale
"Werde munter mein Gemüte" [Be gay, my spirit], and a Prelude
and Fugue in D by Dietrich Buxtehude. The Double Quartet sang
again. Finally Professor Schoonderbeck threw open the chorale book
and improvised beautifully on "Was Gott tut, das ist wohlgetan"
[What God does is well done], and ended with Bach's "Wie wohl
ist mir, O Freund der Seelen" [How well it is with me, O Friend of
souls].

The next morning Schweitzer was busy again in his study, and the
villagers passing on the street could see his graying head bowed
over his writing table, his lively eyes intent upon his work, his
fingers grasping the old-fashioned fluted glass fountain pen with
which he writes laboriously. "What a head!" said one. "What knowledge!" said another. "He has done wonderful things!" said a third.
"He sits at the window there, writing, writing, writing, until far into
the night," said a fourth with awe.

Every day offerings were laid on the window sill, as tributes of love
and respect: mirabelles or radishes, apples or grapes. Doctor Schweitzer smiled, and remembered the old seigneurs of the Middle Ages,
whose retainers descended from their high, strong castle at the mouth
of the valley and levied tribute on all who passed by.

It was always like this when he returned to Europe, in 1954, in
1955, in 1957. He was happy to get back from Africa, back to Gunsbach, back to the loved routine of his Alsatian home. To play the
piano with pedal attachment across the hall while the maid cleaned
his room and made his bed after breakfast; to greet the visitors who
came in endless numbers to this house by the side of the road as to a

sacred shrine; to make an excursion to Strassburg on the business of the hospital; perhaps to play the organ in the Evangelical church at Munster; perhaps to advise about organ construction with the organist at Turckheim; perhaps to play for the Catholic mass at Colmar, where the beauty of his music would find at the other end of the church an echo in the exquisite loveliness of Schöngauer's "Madonna of the Rose Bush."

He seldom preached now in the Gunsbach church, but he often played the organ for the simple services there; sometimes he sat down in a playful mood to improvise the lilting measures of a waltz at the piano upstairs in his home; sometimes he walked through the village streets with his old felt hat pulled down, his small black bow tie (the only one he has) tied around the white wing collar (a size too large), his hands clasped behind his back, stooped a bit, but still vigorous, with no outward sign of the fatigue that is his constant companion; in the evening sometimes he strolled along the road towards Munster to sit quietly for a little while on the bench he had erected there beside the highway.

This was his usual routine in Gunsbach. But the work in Africa was paramount. He had not been able to return to Europe in 1950 for the 200th anniversary commemoration of the death of Bach. He was eagerly expected, but he could not come.

Most tragic of all was his absence when his wife died. Taken seriously ill in Africa, she had returned to her daughter's home in Zürich. Shortly afterwards she passed away, in May 1957.

One great satisfaction, however, has filled these latest years. This was the long delayed publication of the complete organ works of Bach, on which he had been working for more than half a century. At the end he was greatly helped by the distinguished organist at the First Congregational Church in Los Angeles, Edouard Nies-Berger, and Schirmer in New York issued the eight volumes. This is the crowning musical achievement of Schweitzer's life.

Today at eighty-four he continues his work in Africa—scorning the idea of retirement, making of each day a ministry of mercy as he works in his hospital, and of each night a ministry of music as he sits at his loved piano.

The last of the many times I heard him play at Gunsbach I shall always remember. It was evening when we found our way to the little

darkened church, Doctor *Schweitzer* with his organ shoes in their
little white bag. Doctor *Schweitzer* took his place on the organ bench,
and I sat down beside him. He turned on the light above the console,
selected the registration he wished, and began to play, with not a
note of music before him. First it was the great, monumental works
of Bach, as only he can play them, with stately, expressive dignity.
Then it was César Franck, pater seraphicus; then Mendelssohn, so
important in the evolution of modern organ music. Schweitzer gave
himself to the music, oblivious to everything around him, his head
bowed over the manuals, molding the music, endowing it with the
transforming magic of his own superb execution. It was like the evenings when he used to play at St. Thomas and St. Aurelia in Strassburg.

After a while I slipped down from the organ loft and picked my
way silently down the center aisle of the church to one of the front
pews. From this place Doctor Schweitzer was invisible—as he would
wish to be: it was not for the organist to intrude; the radiance of the
music was most beautiful if the window through which it streamed
was invisible.

The little church was full of memories even for me; how full it must
have been for him! There in the high pulpit his father had preached.
There on the other side from the pulpit his mother had had her
place among the women. He and his brother and sisters had sat with
the other children in the front pews, where he could see through the
chancel screen the angels of the Catholic altar. Up where he now
sat he had begun as a small boy of nine to play the organ. And now
he was there again, alone with his music and his memories, his heart
singing forth its paeans of praise and prayer, in this little village
church as in a great cathedral.

It is thus that I want to remember him. There were those who
remembered Bach in just that way.

Appendix

THE QUESTIONNAIRE ON ORGAN CONSTRUCTION [1]

1. From a purely artistic standpoint what is the best action from the key to the wind chest: mechanical (tracker), the Barcker lever (Cavaillé–Coll), or pneumatics? Is the size of the organ determinative in the choice of the action? What do you think of the opinion that little organs up to fifteen stops should still be built mechanically? What pipe pneumatic system do you consider the best? What electric system has in your experience proved to be the best? Over how many years does your experience extend?

2. What do you think of the slider wind chest and the ventil wind chest in their influence on the forming of the tone? Have you had experience with the favorable tone-producing qualities of the slider wind chest on well-maintained old organs?

3. What is your judgment of the arrangements in the organs built during the past thirty years?

Please sketch on the accompanying sheet No. 1 the model arrangement of an organ of ten registers, of fifteen registers, of thirty registers, of forty-five registers, of sixty registers.

In these arrangements count only the original, speaking stops. What do you think of the use of borrowed registers, of unifying?

4. What do you think of the tone and the expression of the modern organ? What is to be praised in modern intonation, what to

---

[1] Die allgemeine Umfrage bei Orgelspielern und Orgelbauern in deutschen und romanischen Ländern," in III. Kongress der Internationalen Musikgesellschaft, Wien, 25. bis 29. Mai 1909. ("The general questionnaire sent to organ-players and organ-builders in German and Romance Countries," in the III Congress of the International Society of Music, Vienna, May 25–29, 1909.) Vienna: Artaria & Co., Leipzig: Breitkopf & Härtel, 1909; pp. 581–583.

254   MUSIC IN THE LIFE OF ALBERT SCHWEITZER

be criticized? With what wind pressure should foundation stops be
intoned? What is the best wind pressure for the mixtures? What for
the reeds? With what pressure should organs which can be supplied
with only one wind pressure be intoned? With 70, 80, 90, 100, or 110
water mm. [2.76, 3.15, 3.55, 3.94, or 4.33 inches]? What is your
opinion of differentiations in wind pressure in middle-sized and
larger organs? What comments would you make regarding the commonly chosen dimensions and mouths?

5. What dimensions do you consider the best for manuals and
pedals? Are you for little or big keys, for keyboards near one another
or rather far apart? Do you prefer the straight or the curved pedals?
How should the pedal lie under the console? What range of notes
should it have?

6. Do you consider it wise to have the dimensions of the console
prescribed by the authorities?

7. What do you consider to be the simplest and at the same time
the most advantageous arrangement for the normal console? Are you
in favor of fixed combinations, synthetic stops, cylinder crescendo,
or blind combinations? What do you think of the various blind combinations being offered today even on middle-sized organs?

Should the couplers and registration helps be arranged as draw-
stops (the German way) or as pedals (the French way)? Are you
acquainted with organs where these are arranged both as drawstops
or as pedals, either independent of each other or connected with
each other, so that the pedal draws the stop at the same time or
releases it, and vice versa? Are you familiar with devices which add a
new registration to the drawn registration without retiring the drawn
registration? What do you think of the practical value of such stops?
How would you arrange super- and suboctave couplers?

Please sketch on the accompanying sheet No. 2 what is in your
opinion the simplest and most practical console arrangement for two
manuals and for three.

8. What do you think of the tone, the position and the outward
appearance of the organs in concert halls which you know?

9. Are you in sympathy with the architectural design of the organs
now being supplied? What do you think of the usual plans in respect
to the architectural appearance? Do you not believe that the rück-

positiv that projects from the choir loft of the church and hangs down below it should be favored more than previously for its architectural appearance and its tone effect?

10. What do you think of present organ prices, on the basis of the arrangements of the organs known to you? Do you believe that truly durable and artistic work can be had at such prices?

11. What do you think of echo organs?

12. Other remarks, experiences, or suggestions.

❦

THE ORGAN THAT EUROPE WANTS [1]

IT is fitting that our gratitude should first of all be here expressed to the Committee of the Third Congress of the International Music Society, gratitude it richly deserves. Through the initiative of Professor Guido Adler of Vienna, *Lektor* Bagster of the same place,[2] and Mr. Thomas Casson of London, the means for printing and circulating the questionnaire on organ building, the results of which will be reported here, were provided; and through the creation of a section of the Congress on organ construction the opportunity has been given to organ builders and organ players to discuss on an interconfessional and international basis the problems with which all friends of church music and organ playing are concerned. This is the first time this has happened.

It was high time that it happened. In recent speeches and remarks about organ building it has been difficult to distinguish between personal opinion and generally current conviction, for the two have usually been inextricably intermingled. Moreover, the publications about organ building have frequently been mistrusted, because they seemed to conceal a recommendation of this or that house—a mistrust often unfair, yet sometimes just.

[1] *"Die Reform unseres Orgelbaues auf Grund einer allgemeinen Umfrage bei Orgelspielern und Orgelbauern in deutschen und romanishen Ländern,"* in *III. Kongress der Internationalen Musikgesellschaft,* Wien, 25. bis 29. Mai 1909. Vienna: Artaria & Co.; Leipzig: Breitkopf & Härtel, 1909; pp. 581–607.

[2] A *Lektor* was a foreign teacher of his mother tongue appointed for a time by German universities. C. R. J.

The time had come, therefore, for a large amount of material to be assembled, from which general tendencies and general convictions could be clearly deduced. To this end the questionnaire about organ construction, with its twelve groups of questions, was sent out. The result has exceeded our expectations. The survey given here is based upon approximately 150 questionnaires answered in detail, most of them from Germany, Austria, France, Italy, Switzerland, and the Netherlands. Many of the answers were large treatises worthy of being printed. How much labor is represented by this material may be judged from the fact that the study of each answer took an average of six to ten hours, because it had to be examined from many sides. I trust that those who have thought with us, worked with us, and now speak to us from a distance may be aware of our appreciation.

In our analysis of the returns no names will be mentioned—difficult though it is for me to be unable to recognize personally those whose opinions are reported. The reason for this is that all personal factors should be minimized, to remove all grounds for suspicion that this or that individual, this or that firm, is being favored. The answers will be given in the order of the questions on the sheet that was sent out.

The Connection between Keys and Chest

The answers to the question about the connection between keys and chest were anticipated. The French and the representatives of the Romance countries favor mechanics and the Barcker lever; the Germans, Austrians and Swiss favor pneumatics. In this connection it should be said that German organists who are acquainted with the Barcker pneumatic lever favor it almost without exception, and that some French organists for practical reasons favor pipe pneumatics.

It is interesting to see that the artistic advantages of mechanics and the disadvantages of pipe pneumatics are recognized even in the camp of the supporters of pipe pneumatics. In about two-thirds of the answers from the German experts and organ players this stereotyped phrase occurs again and again: "The artistic ideal for clear and plastic playing and for elastic precision is mechanics." And in more than half these answers the opinion is sympathetically upheld that organs up to fifteen stops should once more be built with mechanical action.

Thus is expressed a critical appraisal of pipe pneumatics, which has taken shape only within the past ten years. Until that time pneumatics had been preferred to the tracker because of its alleged absolute precision; this prejudice accounted for its rapid victory.

More precisely, the critics of pipe pneumatics mention its slowness for distances over twenty meters, as well as the fingering difficulties it causes within the boundaries where it functions well. The expression "dead precision" often occurs. "Even the better pneumatic systems are always somewhat disconcerting to me when I play," writes a competent artist. "I retard, I hurry, as though at every moment I had to struggle with the instrument to make it obey my rhythmic intention." Another expresses his feeling in these words: "With many pneumatic organs the expression is extremely precise. A pressure of the keys—and the tone is already there. And yet when I play a composition in a quick tempo I feel betrayed and sold out; I drag, I hasten, I play incorrectly, and it is as if I were kneading dough. Experience has taught me that the pneumatics itself is not to blame, but rather the spring pressure under the keys, in contrast to the pull of the tracker."

In the face of such universal observations by the artists, it signifies little that many organ builders are astounded that any objections at all should be raised against pneumatics; and that one of them disinters the ancient anecdote about a player who complained that he could not play Bach well on a pneumatic organ and received the well-merited answer that he should learn.

It is significant, however, that in the circle of the critics the conviction is almost universal that none of these complaints could have prevented the victory of the pneumatic system in those countries where it has prevailed. "The future is no longer with mechanics," is the word on all sides; even the supporters of the Barcker lever admit that it will hardly conquer those countries in which it is not already domesticated.

The following advantages are attributed to pneumatics:

1. simplicity of the arrangements;
2. cheapness;

3. noiselessness in good systems;
4. independence of temperature;
5. its advantages in the arrangement of playing helps.

It is the last fact that brings even Romance organ builders into the camp of the pneumatics.

The general judgment is then as follows: on the whole the victory is conceded to pneumatics, but its artistic improvement is desired. Those who study the nature of playing severely criticize the false assumption, so widespread among organ builders and organ players, that that organ speaks precisely whose keys release the sound at the slightest touch. That is a deception. Our pneumatic systems work badly because, in order to simulate precision, no free play is provided; without such free play no artistic playing is possible; artistry demands that before the tone comes the finger should feel the key.

As a second disadvantage, the excessive lightness of pressure the finger has to exert upon the key is generally recognized.

As a third, the kind of springs used are objected to; the simple down-pressure of a spring will always be unpleasant to the finger; it does not suffice to give the feeling of elastic resistance, which in the mechanical action controls the rising and falling of the keys, so that the result is a clearly integrated playing.

In the fourth place, it is argued that when one has to supply the pipes also with the wind from the pneumatic system, the pressure in the pipes in small and middle-sized organs must be greater than usual.

The solution, then, is the improvement of the pneumatic system; and not by any means the pipe pneumatics only, but the pneumatics of the keys as well. The triumph of the "primitive key" is clear. The proper fall and the proper free play of the key must be provided; and an elastic manner of playing suitable to the finger must be sought. One task is here indicated.

Among the solutions which lead to the ideal, that one only will be named here which provides a mechanical leverage in the console, which then in turn operates the pipe pneumatics. This opinion would be supported by a good many of those who answered, even among the Germans. They want, in place of the spring, a "weighted lever for the finger," which would also be a kind of mechanical transmission.

This union of mechanics and pipe pneumatics would perhaps have the additional advantage that one could employ pneumatics without hindrance for distances of more than twenty meters by lengthening the mechanical action accordingly.

More than once the thought was expressed that in small and middle-sized organs the connection between the keys and the chest should be mechanical while the controlling devices should be pneumatic.

The chest which utilizes the outgoing wind is generally considered the best system; though the utilization of the incoming wind has also its intelligent defenders.

The enthusiasm for electricity is not great. Isolated voices are indeed heard from those who think that even the smallest organs should be electric; but in general the attitude towards electricity is cool and somewhat skeptical. "How far can we depend upon it?" is the recurrent, stereotyped question. The French are almost without exception opposed to it. Among the others are those who recognize electricity as a necessity to overcome distances that are beyond the capacity of pneumatics, though even here some champions of electricity think the Barcker mechanism the best. Concerning the advantages and the durability of a particular system the judgments are often diametrically opposed, and this often in relation to the same instruments. One hails the electrical action in question as precise, another is not pleased with it; one praises it as very durable, another says of the same instrument that he has continual trouble with it.

Whether the wholly electric or the electro-pneumatic system is preferable cannot be decided from the answers.

The Germans who answered believe that the future belongs to the electric systems that have proved their worth in very big organs. On the other hand, the same circles must admit that the keys, as they are now constructed on electric organs, are almost beyond imagining unsatisfactory and primitive for playing.

The Chest

In the answers to the second question, concerning the slider wind chest and the ventil wind chest, one is as much surprised as in the answers to the first question about mechanical and pneumatic actions. The majority defend the artistic advantages of the slider wind chest for promptness of speech and tone formation. The effect of the slider wind chest on the reeds is especially emphasized; the statement is often made that the total effect of an organ is appreciably better with the slider wind chest than with the ventil wind chest. A competent German organist states "that with the slider wind chest one can get a delicate and sustained tone without any hissing aspiration," which is not characteristic of the ventil wind chest; another goes so far as to make the ventil wind chest responsible for the concertina-like tone of the modern organ. In several answers one reads of the impression that the tone production of the Silbermann organs makes on attentive observers. It is interesting to note that even German and Swiss organ builders, who work with ventil wind chests, recognize the advantages of the slider wind chest. What is adduced against the slider wind chest often goes back to the fact that the writers have in mind the poor slider wind chests of the old village organs, and are not aware of the existence of good old slider wind chests and improved modern wind chests, as the French build them. Otherwise they would not state that a slider wind chest can never furnish sufficient wind for a considerable number of stops.

Justly, however, the remark is made in various quarters that the modern defenders of the slider wind chest credit it with more merit than it deserves; and that an objective judgment of its effect upon tone formation can be formed only on the basis of an experiment in which one hears the same pipes in the same room first on the slider wind chest and then on the ventil wind chest, since it can never be determined otherwise whether the tonal advantages are really to be attributed to the slider wind chest. It is therefore highly significant that one organist who answers, and who is at the same time an accomplished organ builder, has with great care carried out this experiment. He used for the same pipes first the slider wind chest, then the ventil wind chest, then the diaphragm chest; and pronounced in favor of the slider wind chest, which he could identify by its sound even blindfolded and therefore not knowing which wind chest was to be used.

Various things are mentioned to explain the favorable effect of the slider wind chest. One of its defenders remarks, "The thinning of the air in the slider wind chest channels, along with the lessened wind pressure, is the cause of the prompt, elastic, and beautiful expression of the Silbermann and French instruments." Others think that the direct admission of the wind is responsible; still others believe that the slider wind chest has a certain capacity for vibration and resonance which the other chests lack.

In spite of the artistic recognition the slider wind chest receives, it appears from the questionnaire that people in countries where it is not current will never go back to it. "From the artistic standpoint I am for the slider wind chest, from the practical standpoint I am for the ventil wind chest, or the diaphragm chest"—dozens of times this opinion appears in the answers. Most organ builders are no longer equipped for the construction of slider wind chests; they are more expensive to build, and to be good demand very careful construction; moreover, the ventil wind chest offers advantages for a cheap and convenient arrangement of the controlling mechanism that the slider wind chest does not have.

Therefore the solution here also appears to be this: to keep the modern, but in such a way that the artistic advantages of the old may as far as possible be united with it. Let the ventil and pneumatic wind chests be built in any manner desired; but arranged in such a way that they permit to the greatest degree possible the direct admission of the wind to the pipes. This is the way pointed out by several German builders. One remarks that if the pipes are not placed too closely together any chest will finally give good results.

The Disposition of Registers

The judgment in general is pretty uniform concerning the arrangement. It is asserted that the arrangements of the past thirty years are no longer suitable to the nature of the organ, but that for some years past a noticeable improvement has been evident. On all sides more mixed stops are demanded; fewer thick, eight-foot pipes should be built, and sixteen-foot stops in the manuals should be used more sparingly. An organ richer in lovely overtones is once more desired. At the same time there is a demand for the enrichment of the manuals with good reeds. Several times the remark is made that more four-foot stops than formerly must be built for the proper blending of the eight-foot foundation stops with the mixtures. These principles should be applied not simply to the big and middle-sized organs but also to the smaller ones. Even for organs of ten stops a mixture and a reed should be provided. By and large we have then a reversion to the old ideal of the organ; it has been realised that an organ equipped only with foundation stops is incomplete.

Concerning the distribution of the stops on the manuals, two somewhat confused conceptions arise together. For some, the second and third manuals are simply miniatures of the great organ; for others, each manual should present a distinct individuality, in which the numerical gradation of the organs has no importance whatever. In general, however, the enrichment of the other organs is advocated. In this respect northern Germany is most backward.

Of the greatest value are the arrangements sent in; for here each man could draw up his plan without any reference to its cost, and solely to express his dominant ideal. The French prefer the reeds at the expense of the mixtures and foundation stops; the arrangements of organ builders from the south of France are typical in this respect. The Italians lay great stress upon the mixtures, the *ripieni*, and thus greatly if not completely neglect the reeds; the Germans permit the reeds and mixtures to disappear almost entirely—even when their expressed principles might have led us to expect something else. In the arrangements of the pedal the Germans call for an excessive number of sixteen-foot and eight-foot foundation stops, while in contrast the French and English pedals are poorly equipped with them.

In principle it is generally agreed that the smallest organs—even those with fewer than ten stops—should have two manuals; though some voices call for at least ten stops in each manual. The three-manual organ usually begins with thirty registers. One cannot clearly discern from the answers whether four or five manuals are generally considered useful for the bigger organs. Outstanding organists are of the opinion that three manuals—all three representing distinct tone personalities—suffice for as many as seventy stops, and that four or five manuals are often misused.

The Swell

Concerning the swell box many voices are heard expressing the old opinion that a little organ, and particularly a church organ, does not need a swell box; one of the answers characterizes the introduction of a swell box in little organs as "a nuisance." But in general the principle still prevails that every organ should have a well-constructed and well-furnished swell box. Different opinions are still to be found as to whether, of three organs, two belong in the swell box. Prominent musicians in general think one swell box organ sufficient, especially when the organ is placed in a church auditorium; some organ builders point to the danger of marring the tone by too much wood inside an organ. The question whether an entire instrument should be encased in the swell box is not at the moment being seriously discussed; the question arises mainly for very little organs, and for big organs in concert halls.

The divergence of opinion about principles of arrangement is naturally most noticeable in connection with small organs. The sketches sent in for ten, fifteen, and twenty stops are farthest apart. In the German arrangements the second organ becomes far less important than the first; whereas the French usually furnish it more completely, and always provide either a reed or a reed and a mixture. In German organs the two-foot stops, the reeds, and the mixtures are first placed in the great organ, and the second organ is provided with such stops only as the number of stops increases.

The French and British arrangements for three-manual organs are concerned with the completeness of the first and third organs, and let the second remain by comparison imperfect, so that it often numbers only half the stops of the third organ; they do this because of their conviction that the second organ is supplemented by coupling the third to it. In the German, Austrian, and Swiss plans the organs shade off in the order of first, second and third, so that neither of the two supplementary organs is complete, and the third, the swell-box organ, is often greatly stunted. The principle ever gaining more headway in Germany, that the full instrument should be clearly affected by the swell box of the coupled third or second organ, is practically negated by these arrangements.

The Octave Couplers

With reference to the octave coupling, most of those who answer are of the opinion that this is not to be dispensed with, particularly in small and middle-sized organs; but only that superoctave coupler is designated as artistically defensible which really brings in an upper octave. It is interesting to note that the earlier octave coupling, which was generally bad, and which brought in the upper octaves of the first organ, is severely attacked because of its crude effect; and in the same way the pedal superoctave coupler, which brings in the upper octaves of the pedal, is rejected as inartistic and of little use. The opinion is often expressed that the sub- and superoctave couplers should be limited to the supplementary organs, where they are less conspicuous. It is desired then to play the upper and lower octaves of the supplementary organs from the great organ. One organ builder proposes that the octave coupling should be so arranged that it would work the same when one plays on the supplementary organ itself as when one couples the great organ to that particular secondary organ; furthermore, the superoctave coupling of the third organ, or of the second and third organs, would be activated also by the coupling of the pedal to the particular organ or organs, whereby the bass would get an excellent touch, and attain a wonderful clarity. Organists who have tried such octave coupling have spoken appreciatively of its effect, and have recognised its great importance, particularly for the smaller church organs. We must not fail to say that many artists entirely reject octave coupling.

Borrowing

With reference to borrowing, the following distinctions, according to the answers which have come in, are to be made. Borrowing in the usual sense means that to supplement one organ arrangements are made to add to it one or more stops of another, or that the pedal should be enriched in the same way by stops from the manuals. To be distinguished from this is the combination of stops by which the series of octaves in one register is used in other pitches for the production of new registers, by which at times a three- and fourfold use of the same series of pipes is provided.

The principle of composition stops is defended in different ways. Its enthusiastic supporters see in it the revolutionizing of all organ building, and want to see it used on all organs, great and small. Others see in it only an emergency device to give a greater number of stops to small organs and to organs installed in small rooms. In general there is no great enthusiasm for composition stops. The opinion persists that this road is a deviation from true art, and results in sham organs, in which the distinctive character of a single stop cannot appear because the same rank of pipes must serve in different registers.

Borrowing by which the stop as a whole may still be played from another keyboard is, by and large, neither approved nor tolerated as an aid in small organs. It is believed that borrowing can be used in small organs to solve the pedal problem. But again and again we are made aware that the toleration of borrowing must be kept within the narrowest limits, because in the end it would result in the falsification of the entire organ. It is desired that in the arrangements the borrowed stops should not be counted twice, but only once; in order to prevent the unfair competition formerly carried on in this domain.

That borrowing which has as its purpose to make every stop usable from every manual is something very different. It would completely destroy the arrangement of an organ. The organist disposes of so many stops, which every time he divides among the different keyboards at his discretion and in accordance with his need. This ideal, called the "free keyboard," is vehemently defended by some organ players. Others do not go so far, and want only to play certain solo stops from each keyboard.

The Organ Tone

In the judging of the tone of the modern organ there is a unanimity of praise and blame which appears nowhere else. The praise—to take the good first of all—is for the voicing of the single stops, which is much more characteristically formed than on the old organ. The blame is directed at the *ensemble*; this criticism is particularly pronounced among the German and Austrian experts. There is hardly one among them who does not complain about the *forte* and the full modern organ. Always the same expressions are used: too strong; too dull; too flat; too blustery; too plethoric; too coarse. One of the Romance organists very well says, "Most organ builders confuse noise with fullness of tone." It is important that the organ builders themselves express this opinion.

The unpleasant cloudiness in the *ensemble* of the stops is explained by different circumstances, one emphasizing one thing and one another. Very often the domination of the shrill strings is held responsible; also the sharpness and the bad composition of the mixtures are blamed for the lack of rich and beautiful overtones. "Our mixtures have no brilliancy and no silver tones," writes a well-known organist. The poor quality of our diapasons is also pointed out. It is easy to convince oneself of this by pulling out together the diapason eight, the octave four, and the octave two, and listening to the result.

If, accordingly, the general judgment is that we have lost the true brilliancy of the organ to the orchestral effects, it must still be remarked that not everyone complains in the same manner of this change. From the answers we may conclude that today there are two conceptions of the organ, not one: the first, which abhors the orchestral in itself; and the second, which sees therein an evolution towards another type of organ. The alternative is church organ or concert organ.

Some organists express themselves in favor of the separation. One writes: "I do not hesitate to state that a complete separation of the church organ and the concert organ must and will come, so that the two instruments will hardly resemble each other any longer." Others desire to see the separation, but not in such an extreme form. Most, however, condemn the distinction, and find fault with any organ when the domination of characteristic stops, intoned without reference to the total sound effect, becomes too marked. They admit only one ideal for the organ: an instrument which contains indeed characteristic modern stops, but so shaded as not to injure the fullness and tone beauty of the entire instrument. It is generally admitted that it is for us to effect a reconciliation between the old organ and the modern one. One organist proposes that the great organ and the pedal should be kept with the old soft tone color, but that the other manuals should be modernized.

Wind Pressure and Dimensions

General unanimity rules, moreover, in the opinion that the unpleasant total sound effect is indeed partly a result of modern arrangements, but that wind pressure and scales are in incomparably greater measure responsible for it. Too strong wind pressure, too narrow scales, too high mouth: these comments recur again and again, so that the comparative reading of answers in this section becomes extremely monotonous.

These complaints are not unjustified. It appears from the statements of the organists that the average wind pressure that produces the tone equals about 100 mm. [3.94 inches] water column, whereas Silbermann worked with 65 and 70 mm. [2.56 and 2.76 inches]. The narrow scales and the high mouths are only the consequence of the high pressure, since the construction of the pipes must be adapted to the wind pressure. Thus we have come to the narrow, high-mouthed pipes, which are the cause of the harsh, unbearable tone in the upper register; the old measurements, with the exception of the diapasons, are considerably broader, and all have lower mouths. Abnormal wind pressure, abnormal pipes—this is what ails our art of organ building. It is a comfort to note that at last it is being generally recognized.

How did we come to get this wind pressure? Because we wanted strong-toned organs, and because we were looking for precision in the form of an unnaturally prompt speech in the pipes. "The inspector," one organ builder writes, "sat down at the organ, and the moment he stretched his finger over the key the tone had to be there already." In order to satisfy such demands, nothing remained but to overpower the pipes and to tear the tone from them with a high wind pressure, instead of permitting it to produce the tone naturally; which always takes a small fraction of time, whether we are dealing with a pipe blown by a human mouth, or with one that stands on a chest. "It is the high wind pressure that is responsible for the unnatural, unarticulated, thundering entrance of the tone," writes one well-known musician, "and the hissing noises that accompany it are also attributable to it."

A second temptation to high wind pressure came from the use of pneumatics for the pipes. In small organs, particularly when one has to think of economy, the most important thing is to get along with one and the same wind pressure, and to make the pipes function with the same pressure as the pneumatics. It happens, therefore, that many small and middle-sized organs have a wind pressure of up to 110 mm. [4.33 inches].

The generally expressed verdict is: back to the lower pressure, to the broader scales, to the lower mouths. With reference to the scales, many informed persons think that not only the scales themselves are false, but also the interval at which the scales are halved.

A normal pressure of 80–85 mm. [3.15–3.35 inches] for the foundation stops and of 70–75 mm. [2.76–2.96 inches] for the mixed stops is suggested. For the reeds the most favorable pressure proposed is 100–120 mm. [4.33–4.73 inches]; many, however, would go as high as 150 mm. [5.91 inches] for single reeds. A few Italian organ builders work today with the lowest wind pressure. One of them gives for the foundation stops 45–50 mm. [1.77–1.97 inches] and for the solo stops and the reeds 60–80 mm. [2.36–3.15 inches].

A reasonable difference in wind pressure is in general favored, because it is also of course the most natural thing for each kind of pipe to receive its most favorable wind. But the additional cost of these differences in bellows, wind channels, and chests always cause some discouragement. It is a cause of rejoicing to find the conviction that it is a crime to voice small organs with high wind pressure. A medium wind pressure of 80–85 mm. [3.15–3.35 inches] is suggested, with which, when only one pressure is available, foundation stops, mixtures, and reeds sound well; yet one will commonly usually use in organs with pneumatic action the pressure of the pipe pneumatics for the reeds. It is interesting to see that those acquainted with reed stops propose that in the larger organs should be installed not only modern reeds with high wind pressure, but also those which sound with only 85–90 mm. [3.35–3.55 inches] and give the soft tone of the old trumpets. Especially favored are the soft English trumpets.

In general, the principle is upheld that the wider and bigger the pipes, the more moderate the pressure. In this connection, it seems remarkable that in spite of this many answers propose that the pedal should receive a stronger wind than the manuals. On the other hand, some want for the foundation stops of the pedal not more than 80 mm. [3.15 inches], and report that with this they have got specially clear and full pedals.

A French organ builder employs a special differentiation in wind pressure by dividing his wind chests into three parts, so that the lower register of the stop gets a great deal of wind at moderate pressure, the middle register a moderate amount of wind at a higher pressure, and the upper register very little wind at a high pressure. The results of this differentiation are very good, especially for beautiful expression; but the expense is correspondingly high.

The answers often bring out that the wind pressure must be adapted to the size of the room, so that to achieve an adequate tone we may have a high pressure for big rooms. Others are of the opinion that the size of the room has nothing to do with the pressure to be applied to the foundation stops and mixtures, but that we get a much more beautiful effect if somewhat larger scales are used for big rooms and a richer supply of wind is provided.

From the answers this fact in any case emerges, that when we are concerned with wind pressure and scales we are in the center of the problem, and that the time is past when we may leave the decision in these matters to the organ builders; yet it is also evident that a number of experts are wholly uninformed about this subject. There are a few who think that the experts do not need to concern themselves with wind pressure and dimensions.

Concerning the question of scales, the complaint is made in various quarters that many organ builders no longer make their own pipes but get them from the factories, and therefore accept the scales and mouths which happen to be in vogue at the time, instead of making their own artistic experiments and copying old and tested scales. In the end, the question of scales is not a problem in higher mathematics and physics, as it sometimes might seem, but a problem of simple artistic experimentation and imitation.

"To bring scales, wind pressure, and tone into harmony," therein lies, in the opinion of one of those answering, the task which confronts organ builders if they wish once again to create tuneful and beautiful instruments.

The Pedal

On the question of the pedal the opinions are very diverse, above all concerning the range. England, France, Switzerland, and the south German provinces are generally in favor of having the same pedal board for every organ, small or great, with thirty notes, extending to C-f^1, and a few even want it to go to C-g^1. The North will be satisfied with a pedal for middle-sized and smaller organs of twenty-seven keys reaching to C-d^1, and wants a pedal to C-f ^{1} only for big instruments. It has been often remarked that this difference does not make sense, since modern compositions all presuppose a pedal extending to f^1, and are not to be played exclusively on big organs. The higher costs for a pedal with thirty keys are so slight that opposition from this point of view is not understandable.

The range is much more conditioned by the presupposed dimensions of the pedals. "How can anyone expect me to compass a pedal of C-f^1?" an angry Northern organist asks. We can understand his irritation if we remember that he accepts as correct the old royal Prussian measurements of 1876, which are so great that acrobatics were required to reach the f^1. On these pedals 112 cm. [3 feet, 8 inches] were necessary for C-d^1. The new Prussian arrangement of 1904 has 104 cm. [3 feet, 5 inches] for the same range of keys; the Mecheln dimension—shown on Catholic Day ^{1} at Mecheln in 1864 —provides 97½ cm. [3 feet, 2 inches] for twenty-seven keys; the modern French pedals are still narrower.

Those who go farther into this question of pedal dimensions express themselves in favor of the Mecheln measurements. From the North, however, rises the anxious cry that the pedals might be too narrow and the keys too small. That the pedals of Bach's time were even narrower and smaller than the Mecheln pedals, and that nevertheless he had no objection to them but played tolerably well on them even by modern standards, seems not to have come to the mind of many an excellent respondent to the questionnaire.

---

^{1} The German Catholic Day was first observed in 1848. Since 1880 it has been an annual observance. C. R. J.

The solution of the problem of scales is closely tied to the decision concerning another alternative: the straight or the concave pedal. If the concave pedal is accepted in principle, then the large proportions no longer play as significant a rôle, since the foot can easily cover an even longer span because of the concavity. The answers inform us that even in those countries where this pedal is not well known the opinion in favor of it has greatly advanced in recent times. Even those who are not acquainted with such a pedal in practice say candidly that it commends itself to natural reflection. Therefore a majority have come to favor the concave pedal, which only a few years ago was not thought of.

As for the position of the pedal in relation to the manual, most people still hold fast to the dogma that c must lie under c^1; the ardent advocates of the pedal of thirty keys remark, however, that the abandonment of this principle can be justified, and that it is indeed feasible to let the middle of the manual be over the middle of the pedal, since otherwise the upper half of the pedal keyboard would be wider than the lower.

In relation to moving the pedal farther under the manuals, voices are heard to the effect that a somewhat deeper position—something like that which the French use—would be an advantage for comfortable playing.

The Manuals

In the answers to the question of the manual dimensions, it is emphasized without exception that the manuals should be brought as close together as possible, so that changing from one manual to another may be expedited to the highest degree. It is well known that Bach expressed himself in favor of this principle. But very few draw from this demand the consequence that we must then build somewhat shorter keys, as we did forty years ago.

Concerning the range of the keyboard and the breadth of the keys, some demand a close imitation of the dimensions of the modern concert piano; others point to the fact that *legato* playing on the organ, with its sustained notes and finger substitutions, would be greatly facilitated if the keys were shortened, and in this they refer to the measurements of the old keyboard. At any rate, there is more conviction here than in the demand that we should accept the keyboard dimensions of the concert piano. It is axiomatic that the dimensions of a keyboard should be adapted to the necessities of the kind of playing practised on it. The pretext that familiarity with the dimensions of the piano keyboard would constitute hindrance for playing on a somewhat narrower organ keyboard is contradicted by wide experience, and would collapse of itself at the slightest trial.

The Striving for Unity

Complete unity in the measurements of the console have not been achieved, then, even though the proper lines for a future unity are much more clearly revealed than we might have expected. What is the opinion about letting the authorities regulate the dimensions of the console? Affirmative and negative answers clash rudely and in equal numbers. There is nowhere, however, much faith in the possibility of achieving unity in this way. Often a middle way is sought. It is to be desired that the experts should first come to an agreement, and then that what is recognized to be good may of itself in time be everywhere realized; therefore only one thing needs to be desired of the authorities, namely, that they should place no difficulties in the way of what the wide circle of experts recommends as simple and practical, but should permit it to find acceptance alongside the arrangements existing at the time.

What many have to say concerning the extent of the unity to be sought after is well worth taking to heart. They believe that we should not exaggerate the notion of unity, and seek to create circumstances shaped for the benefit of the traveling musician, to the extent that these shall everywhere find the same measurements and arrangements to relieve them of the necessity of familiarizing themselves with strange instruments. The striving for unity has nothing to do with such demands; it desires only that whatever is generally recognized to be practical should everywhere prevail. That a genuine artist should quickly find himself at home on any organ constructed with a certain amount of intelligence, even though it has other keyboards and pedals than the one to which he is accustomed—this must be considered as axiomatic.

The result of the answers, then, is that the authorities in countries

and districts where official specifications exist should modify these
in the interests of a desired unity to such an extent that an opportunity is given to experiment with that which elsewhere is recognized
to be practical, and if it really proves to be so, to let it prevail.

The Playing Aids

In classifying the answers to the question about the arrangement
of the console, we have to distinguish between what is wanted in
the way of playing aids and what their arrangement should be.

A simplification of the console is everywhere desired. It is found
that the middle-sized and smaller organs are particularly overburdened
with all possible draw-knobs and pistons, sometimes quite useless,
which are often in striking contrast to the number and quality of
the stops.

The synthetic stops, on which a few years ago we used to place
so much emphasis, have fallen completely into discredit.

The same fate has befallen the fixed composition stops. "It is not
the organ builder, but I, that determine the registration," says one
energetic gentleman; others are less drastic in their words, though
just as decisive.

The register crescendo is attacked by many as the work of the
devil, by others regarded as a necessary evil; by most, however, it is
considered a useful aid, when it is properly placed and intelligently
used. It is thought to have special advantages in the accompanying of
cantatas, passions, and oratorios, when the steps in the changing
tone color and tone strength are concealed by the singing voices and
the orchestra.

The blind combinations are generally approved, and make the
fixed ones wholly superfluous. Even the French and the Italians
recognize the worth of this device. In German lands, on the contrary, an opinion is expressed in favor of a pedal to bring in the
mixtures and reeds, especially in the larger organs.

The situation is therefore much clearer than one might have expected. As constituent helps in the organ of the future, only blind
combinations and crescendo register are envisaged; in large organs
something should be considered in the way of pedals to bring in the

mixtures and reeds. Everything else is more or less superfluous trimming.

There are different opinions about the number of general blind combinations. Some would get along with one, or on larger organs with two; others want from four to six. This latter demand is to be explained by the fact that the draw-stop which brings in the blind combination is usually so arranged that it works on all the manuals and the pedal at the same time, so that several blind combinations are of course necessary for repeated changes in tone.

Most of those who answer consider this kind of arrangement so necessary that they do not take into consideration how much more useful a blind combination would be if it were so arranged that it could be restricted to each single manual or to the pedal, and then at will, by the use of another draw-stop, all the keyboards could be brought in together. Only a minority consider the advantages of this arrangement, by which each manual and the pedal would have its own blind combination stop, and at the same time another stop would be provided to place the whole organ on a blind combination.

The question whether from the artistic standpoint those playing aids are most advantageous which add new stops to a drawn registration or retire them, without cancelling the drawn registration, is generally recognized in principle as most important, in so far as it makes a change in tone color possible without an interruption, as is usually desired in the masterpieces; since these much oftener have in view the modification of the tone color and the return to the first registration than the continuing change of the tone colors.

It should be mentioned that only very few among the organ builders have seen the significance of this question; a considerable number of them reply that they cannot imagine the usefulness of such an arrangement. It is clear from this how unwise it is to turn over the arrangement of the console to those who often have room in their thinking only for technical considerations and none for artistic ones.

Concerning the kind of playing helps, two proposals, which have been tested practically and artistically, are made. One is that we should have two sets of blind combinations: one that cancels the drawn registration, another that adds the stops prepared to the drawn stops. The second proposal anticipates the double use of the same set of blind combinations; by a previously drawn stop, which either fixes the hand registration or makes it unstable, a device operates which either adds the prepared registration to the existing registration, when one introduces the blind combination, or detaches it from it—depending on whether one has given a fixed or fluid character to the drawn registration by the draw-stop.

As to the arrangement of the register crescendo, the observation is made that it has value when it is connected with a stop or tablet movement which permits it to work so that it either annuls or supplements the drawn registration and the blind combination.

It is desired, moreover, that the sequence in which the stops are introduced should not be determined by the organ builder alone but by the artist in coöperation with him, so that the crescendo would be beautifully and effectively planned.

Among the artists themselves, however, there is no unanimity about the arrangement of the register crescendo. Some think of it as exhausting itself upon a single keyboard, whereby, however, the possibility of an unbroken crescendo is given up. For the others the ideal lies in an unbroken crescendo on the whole organ; they want to bring in the stops on the coupled manuals, without regard to their progression on the single keyboard, so as to produce the most beautiful total crescendo of which the organ is capable. Both arrangements can be defended; the second is more commendable because it usually is concerned with the total crescendo through the use of the register crescendo.

Worthy of much consideration is a proposal which brings into the foreground these opposing principles. It is that over the draw-knobs other knobs should be placed with which the player can determine each time at his own discretion the crescendo that he wants to realize with the register crescendo, not only in the sequence of stops but also in the use of the couplers. If this can be carried out—and our organ builders assure us that it is technically possible—then with one stroke the register swell has become something very different from what it was, and offers an artistic help of the first rank.

The tendency that comes to light in the desired playing aids may be expressed in two sentences. The first is: away from the principle of rigid, unchangeable combinations, even for the register crescendo.

The second aims at such an arrangement of the blind combinations and register *crescendo* that they can either keep or replace the drawn registration. A supplementary demand is that the blind combinations have draw-stops for each separate organ, and at the same time a stop that brings them all into play together. If this is accomplished, then we are freed from the motley organ which has been built for the past thirty years, in which there is a clash of the most diverse principles.

The Arrangement of the Playing Aids

As to the arrangement of the playing aids desired, the answers show sharply divergent opinions. The group influenced by the French desire pedals for the feet, the Germans want draw-stops for the hands. With conviction the defenders of the first theory assert that one usually has a foot free in playing, never a hand; with the same conviction the others maintain that the feet already have too much trouble with the playing pedals to be further bothered with couplers and combinations. If one goes to the bottom of the answers, one notices that we are really dealing with two different artistic ideals. In accordance with one, the player wishes to manipulate the couplers and combinations himself; in accordance with the other, he turns this responsibility over to one or two helpers. The second is plainly favored by German musicians in their answers, and is set down as the rule for concert playing. Thereby we should arrive again at the distinction between the concert organ and the church organ, between concert playing and playing for divine worship, and therefore any general conception of the organ and of organ playing would be impossible.

But the way is open for an agreement: in that even many musicians with German tendencies are outspoken for the practical worth of pedals, consider the technical demands which the utilization of them raises no longer as insuperable as it seemed a short time ago, and have come to value an independence from assistants in playing. On the other side, the players with French ideals have had to admit that the ideal of self-sufficiency is not always possible when one has to do with a rather complicated registration, so that draw-stops which make possible the assistance of others are in any case an advantage.

Thus the majority envisage the outcome of this conflict in a double arrangement of playing helps, and want the most important resources made available both as pedals and as draw-stops, so connected that what has been introduced or cut off by the foot may be at the same time introduced or cut off by the hand, and vice versa.

No technical difficulties stand in the way of satisfying this demand; and the costs involved are very moderate for the advantages secured, particularly when the organ builders are prepared for it. The support won for the idea of the double availability of the playing helps—a fairly recent idea—is surprisingly large. About four-fifths of the answers are in favor of it.

As for further details of console construction, it is to be noticed that the recently customary method of arranging a playing help in such a way that it offered two adjacent draw-stops—one for the introduction and the other for the release—has more and more been given up, because this method needlessly doubles the number of stops. It is desired that the same stop should serve for the introduction or the release, as one pushes it in or lets it return to its original position.

There is no agreement yet about the movement of the pedals. Some want the same movement for bringing in and cutting off the stop, following the English model. To introduce the stop one presses the pedal, which rises again of itself; when one presses it a second time the stop is cut off. The French principle is that the pedal when pressed down automatically catches at the side; to release it one needs only to detach it from this catch by a slight pressure, whereupon it comes quickly up again. This has the advantage that one can always see whether a coupler or a combination is on, and that one can release several depressed pedals at one time by gliding the foot lightly over them and letting them rise again. It is to be supposed that this method will triumph. The direction of the hooking should be always towards the outside in the movement of the foot; the pedals lying at the right should hook to the right, those lying at the left should hook to the left.

Deserving of every consideration is the advice in a number of answers that the pistons should not be placed in the middle under the manuals, where they are hidden by the hands and sleeves of the player, not only from his controlling eye but also from his assistant, but in disregard of symmetry should be shoved over to the left, where they are more accessible to the eye of both the assistant and the player: to the player because he much oftener has his left hand free—thanks to the pedal, or can make it free at need—than his right. The use of the thumb to press the pistons while the fingers play quietly on is not to be thought of, no matter how often it is proposed.

The Arrangement of the Stops

The remaining opinions concerning the console have to do with either self-evident or unimportant things. Concerning the distribution of the stops beside or above the manuals, no single idea emerges; in this thing only everyone is agreed, that we must put an end to the absence of planning. Foundation stops, mixtures, and reeds must no longer be all mixed together like cabbages and rape. The French like to arrange foundation stops at the left of the keyboard and the mixtures and reeds at the right. This arrangement has its advantages; the disadvantages are that one never has an organ as a whole before him, and that this distribution is often very difficult to effect. The Germans want to keep all the stops of a single organ together; this is very clear in many respects, but it has still the disadvantage that one has to find the reeds and mixtures under the foundation stops. A compromise proposal suggests that the stops be arranged in the German fashion by organs at the side of the manuals, but that the mixtures and reeds be placed at the outer edge, whereby the control of the draw-stops is greatly facilitated.

The preference for register knobs or tilting tablets remains undecided. German organists have become accustomed to the tablet; but already voices are lifted there again to praise the beauty, the solidity, and the other advantages of the simple register draw-knob.

Questions of Detail

There is a good deal of wrangling in the German camp as to whether the register crescendo should be installed as a cylinder pushed by the foot, or as a balanced pedal. There are mutual recriminations. The stubborn defenders of the cylinder in the north greatly outnumber the defenders of the balanced pedal. The latter object principally to the jolting movement which is unavoidable in the use of the cylinder.

It should of course be taken for granted that the apertures for the balanced pedal are generous, that the balance has the proper breadth, that the balancing movement is even and comfortable for the foot, and that it can be stopped in any position. How seldom this may be taken for granted in actual construction is evident from the answers; almost all the players complain, particularly—as one of them expresses it—because the balanced pedal seems to be better adapted to the foot of a little ballet dancer than to the masculine boot. Complaints are also voiced that many organ builders reverse the motion, so that the *descrescendo* is produced by pressing down the pedal and the *crescendo* follows when it is brought back.

Thus may be summed up the most important results of the questionnaire concerning playing helps and console arrangements. The interesting point is that even here the proposed solutions show one and the same tendency, the "simplication of the console."

The Concert Organ

The answers to the question, "What do you think of our concert organ?" has turned out to be really classic. Almost without exception the organists answer, "Not much," underlining both words; and the organ builders declare that it would not be becoming to them to pass judgment on the work of their colleagues. We have to do here mainly with the answers from German lands, since in the Romance countries there are very few organs in concert halls. The Romance organists express themselves, however, as little edified by German concert organs.

It is the unanimous judgment that the architects are primarily responsible for the undeniably artistic failure in the construction of concert organs. They are to blame for the fact that these organs have been set in holes where they cannot be played effectively; and where, in addition, distance makes almost impossible any good collaboration by organ and chorus and orchestra.

It is also emphasized that these organs sound bad because they all speak with too high a wind pressure. The mistakes in modern mensuration and intonation come out in the dry acoustics of these halls—dry in comparison with the acoustics of vaulted stone churches —two and three times more conspicuously than in the auditoriums consecrated to the service of God. Therefore these instruments have about them something harsh and shrill, which is the general complaint. As for the problem the concert organ has set for modern acoustical art, it is crystal clear that the latter is not equal to such problems because it does not even recognize them.

The Question of Appearance

The appearance of the modern concert organ is also criticized. The words "miserable, devoid of taste," and their synonyms are heaped upon it in an almost alarming manner. A number of respondents go into a rage over the fact that these organs lose all external similarity to the ecclesiastical instrument by the concealment of their pipes. On the other hand, a few justify from an artistic point of view this fault, due to a lack of money. They seek to prove that the appearance of pipes is not appropriate for a hall, and that the exterior of the organ in these rooms should be a painted surface, which hides the pipe work. A few would like to see the sight of pipes banished even from the church, and one proposes for the front of the organ pictures from Bible history.

The opinion is unanimous that the design and the construction cannot please because there is too much emphasis on economy. Furthermore, the haste with which the work must proceed in view of the short time allowed for delivery makes genuine and excellent wood carving impossible. Therefore modern organs cannot compare in appearance with the old.

Several organ builders remind us of the dangers to the sound which arise from such a crowded case. For smaller instruments the simple English arrangement of external pipes with no wood at all is often to be recommended for esthetic and practical reasons.

The Rückpositiv

The rückpositiv projecting out into the church has both friends and enemies. The enemies find it ugly and do not think much of the acoustical effect. Further, they would have us remember that such a projection prevents the proper disposition of the choir, and hides from the organist the view of the church. The defenders are in an impressive majority. They not only mention the architectural significance derived from interrupting the bare balcony rail we now see before the organ, but they speak also of an interesting acoustical effect. In the disposition of a choir before the organ they emphasize the fact that the *rückpositiv* can be set so low that we need not be concerned about its concealing anything. A number of those who answer want to have the *positiv* just for the sake of the singing, because only in this way is it possible to bring the pipe stops so close to the singers and the orchestra that we can properly speak of an accompaniment. Whoever has heard the Bach Passions accompanied by organs with the *rückpositivs*, which form with singers and orchestra a compact mass, knows how to prize them as they deserve. The organ builders as a body are against the *rückpositiv* because it is difficult to set up and costly to construct. When they assert, however, that the small size of the case will permit them to install only three or four stops, we may be permitted to reply that it should be easy to build a projecting structure for as many as ten. Of course, for the *rückpositiv* there may be considered only rather narrow eight-foot stops, a disproportionately large number of four-foot stops, and delicate mixtures.

Prices

In answer to the tenth question, about prices, organ builders and organists alike agree that prices are far too low for good and artistic work. A single organ builder had the effrontery to say that they were sufficient, but had nothing to say about the quality of the work. Most of those who answer are of the opinion that even the usual factory wares cannot in the long run be delivered at these prices. Among the experts there are groups who have not yet taken this question seriously enough; otherwise it would not be conceivable that a number should declare themselves incompetent to speak on this point—though it is easy to get informed—and that others think this something that concerns only the organ builders. But those who hold such views are a diminishing minority compared to those who appreciate the seriousness of the situation.

That the artistic ability of the organ builder is in question needs no proof. But prices are too low, as trustworthy organ builders assert, even for stereotyped factory work. The question raised on many sides, "What will some day become of the organs built under such circumstances?" is alarming in its significance. It is often said that we are approaching a period of repairs and renovations—a period that will startlingly prove that the cheap organ is in the end more expensive. Nothing can be said for the durability of the organs now being built. In many ways the era of repairs and renovations has already begun.

The little firms most clearly see the critical situation into which organ construction has been brought by the conscienceless, mutual underbidding of the organ builders, by the false economy and the shortsightedness of buyers and organ inspectors. But even the bigger firms, which for a while thought lower prices would cause the downfall of the medium-sized and smaller organ builders and leave them untouched, are beginning to be worried lest they themselves be involved. One of the foremost German organ builders writes, as characteristic of the shocking situation, that recently he lost an order for a 5000-mark organ because another underbid him by 400 marks, though he himself had set the lowest price possible, and sacrificed all profit. It is also characteristic of the situation that the representative of a still larger firm remarks that it is able to continue only through its large sales and through the most farreaching utilization of machine work; and also because the organ maker has invested in the business only his own money. Thereby, however, he is admitting that organ building has ceased to be artistic handwork. In the complete use of machine work lies a great danger: the machine can never produce anything but the same work—always the same; it is the negation of that individualism in the little things that is the essence of artistic work. Most desolating is the remark of an organist who has also worked as an organ builder and can appraise the situation exactly. "If the cheaper zinc did not more and more take the place of tin, there would be hardly any profit left in the business."

And if it is asked why our organs are so badly toned, one familiar with the situation knows it is because the man who tones it is so poorly paid and has to work so rapidly that an artistic tone is not to be expected.

The Echo Organ

In the answers to the question of the justification for the echo organ, yes and no, conditional and unconditional, arise incoherently. Many reject it unconditionally as an inartistic plaything. "Angel song which drips down from a hole in the roof of the church," one calls it; another characterizes it as "the greatest of all wonders for old women, but an agony for musically sensitive ears." One group thinks it has some value as an appurtenance for the concert organ; as a concession to those who want such sensations—but protests immediately against its all too frequent misuse.

Others go farther, and consider the echo organ indispensable for concert use but not to be tolerated in the churches. A further group, which we may call the extreme right wing, thinks that the echo organ is particularly appropriate for the church. One member of this group asks, "Is it not exactly in accordance with the supernatural, to which we have to give expression in the service of worship and in the playing of the organ, that we should have sounds which float down upon us as if from the heights of heaven?"

On the technical side of the question, it is remarked that an echo organ can never be in tune with the main organ, because it is placed in another, higher part of the room, and accordingly has another temperature. Because of the distance it is impossible for it to work in harmony with the second and third organ, even with the use of electricity.

In numbers the judgments divide as follows: two-thirds of the respondents deny any justification at all for the echo organ; a quarter would permit its use, with certain precautions, in concert organs; the remainder assert that it has real justification either in the church or the concert hall.

It is interesting to note that in regions where good swell organs are built, only flat "no's" are given the echo organ question. Usually it is added that everything really musical which one tries to secure with an echo organ can be had with a beautiful, elevated, and well-furnished swell box.

Special Remarks

The twelfth question asked the respondents to make remarks, to share experiences, and to make suggestions they considered important; and the most valuable of these remarks are mentioned here, beginning with the technical matters.

That organist who is also an accomplished organ builder, and who has already been quoted several times, tells how, in pursuing and amplifying the ideas of the well-known Abt Vogler, one can get, in rooms which will not permit the installation of an open sixteen-foot pipe, the same effect by having a covered eight-foot pipe of quintadena quality speak with an open eight-foot one.

An organ expert pleads for the manufacture once more of beautiful metal gedackts and flutes; and urges us to replace the sixteen-foot violone, which speaks with difficulty and makes the whole pedal lazy, with a broad-scaled sixteen-foot contrabass speaking under lower pressure, or with a salicet bass, which would give the bass in fact the same volume.

A number of times the thought was expressed that the organ builder should be considered once more with greater interest from the scientific side, and that a part of the work and strength that are now devoted to purely historical studies in the domain of musical science should be devoted to the old and new organ construction. A few good doctoral theses on organ construction would surely not be a bad idea.

Several organ builders and players speak for a good tremolo stop. Others call our attention to the fact that it would be a good thing to introduce some day a unified list of stop names, so that the same thing would not appear under so many different names—one of the evils of the culinary art.

Another suggestion was made that each organ should be provided with a thermometer, and an indicator to show at what temperature the instrument, and particularly the reeds, were tuned.

A proposal aroused our sympathy that the few remaining beautiful organs from the eighteenth century should be adopted and classified as historic monuments, in order that they should not fall victims to the vandalism of modern times like so many of their beautiful sisters, but should be intelligently and worthily restored so that they might outlive our modern instruments.

It has also been suggested that we form a collection of old and beautiful organ cases, and make them known, so that architects and organ builders can cultivate good taste by studying them.

We are warned by organists who love the old cases not to force new and enlarged organs into them. A number of other respondents who have seen this repeatedly happen take the opportunity to speak out passionately against the current widespread craze for enlargement. They do not think it fitting, that an instrument of forty stops should be installed in a room once comfortably filled by an instrument of twenty-five. The complaint is general that in the planning and ordering of organs too much attention is given to the number of stops and too little to their quality.

It should be remembered that many of the answers preach a crusade against architects who dare to assign the organ even in the churches to a completely inadequate and unsuitable position; and never take the trouble to inquire in authoritative quarters whether an organ can properly be placed in the room assigned to it.

The Problem of the Organ Inspector

Along with these technical questions the problem of the inspectors is often discussed. People point to the ignorance, the conceit of infallibility, and the instincts of a *pasha*, which not infrequently are found in government inspectors. It is asserted on all sides that one root of evil lies in the system of inspection as we now have it. The answers make clear that there are many intelligent and excellent inspectors. It would be a great mistake to generalize too much from the outspoken complaints, even though they come from many sides.

The evil lies not so much in the persons as in the institution. For a reform two roads are suggested. On one side, a different training of inspectors is desired. They should work for a year as practical organ builders and then pass an examination; their number should be decreased, and they should be better paid, in order that they may devote themselves entirely to their duties.

Others see the principal evil, not so much in the inadequate professional training of the inspectors, as in the fact that the incumbent rules without restraint in a particular area, making it impossible for any opinion but his own to be heard, and therefore putting on all the organs in that area the stamp of any erroneous ideas he may have. There is a known case of an inspector who considered the pedal C-f^1 superfluous, and never would permit the construction of a complete pedal, even when the organ builder added the three notes at his own expense. There is no need to emphasize the disadvantage that accumulates when a whole generation is allowed to have only those arrangements that conform to a particular scheme.

Certain proposals, therefore, are directed against the sole authority of the official inspectors, so that any organist interested in organ construction might have opportunity to be active in that field, and upon the invitation of the congregations to serve them as an inspector. No one person alone should decide the plan and building of an organ, but a commission of several should be appointed, so that every peculiarity in the plan of the organ and every personal prejudice in the choice of a builder may be avoided.

One comprehends the bearing of these remarks only when he reflects that in countries and regions where the institution of official inspectors exists it is often impossible for experts to secure any currency for their ideas or to render any service. If in the past decades there has been little constructive criticism on the art of organ building, one major reason is that many useful resources, both younger and older, have been paralyzed. It is to be noticed that not even in the Germany of the eighteenth century was there any privileged system of inspection; instead, the congregations called experts of their own choice. And it should also be mentioned that in countries which have no official inspectors organ building is in no worse condition than in the others; on the contrary, it has been advantaged by the freedom it has enjoyed, for this freedom has directly benefited the art. How far the authority of the official inspectors goes in many districts is evident in the demand made by one inspector that even private organ building should come under his jurisdiction. In this way organ building would fall entirely under official control.

The natural consequence of requisitioning a group of experts for the building of an organ would be that the office of inspector would cease to be an appointment for life, and would become an honor, with very modest compensation for travel and time. It is taken for granted that such a reform would take place only with full consideration for the present incumbents of the official posts, which they should be permitted to occupy for life.

Into the same category fall the remarks which characterize as unsuitable the custom of calling in the inspector only at the beginning and at the end of the installation of an organ. Usually he has the estimate to approve and the complete work to examine, but is wholly eliminated from the construction. "The organ examinations," remarks an inspector, "have only a conditional value, if the expert is brought in only when everything is finished. At that time he has usually nothing more to do than to inspect the damage." The proper thing would be for him to supervise the installation and the intonation. What might result from this, those who have been permitted to take part in the construction of an organ under these circumstances can testify.

If, however, such work were expected from the inspectors, it is clear that where previously one sufficed at least six or ten would then be necessary. It is pointed out at the same time that the inspector would get technical experience in organ building by this method. What he really needs to know he would learn on the spot by questions, observations, and common trials and tests with the organ builder.

The Organist and the Organ Builder

A number of observations have already been made upon the relations between the artists and the organ builders. Our artists, it is said on all sides, have nothing to do with the organ builders, or the builders with them; from this comes the often astonishing technical ignorance of the organists and their lack of intelligence in what they demand artistically of the builders; so that both are to blame for the stagnation in modern organ building. Improvement can come only when, by a gradual reform in the ways mentioned above, the construction of each organ becomes for the builder and several organists an opportunity for fruitful discussion and intensive collaboration.

The Economic Situation of the Organ Builder

A last group of remarks has to do with the economic situation of the organ builder and improvement in his standing. It is emphasized above everything else that the maintenance of the middle-sized and smaller organ builders is indispensable for the art. Of course there must be big concerns; they are required for the international market, and are created for it. But the smaller and middle-sized builders are equipped to produce worthy instruments for the church, and to watch over them with loving care. The big organ firm cannot fulfil these tasks as can the local master of organ building resident in a particular region. The big builder makes his own way; but to intercede for the support of the master of organ building, in the old excellent sense of the word, and with the idealism that surrounds it— this is the task of the church and of art, to both of which he belongs.

It is not only the low price that endangers the middle-sized and smaller builders; other things enter the situation. First mentioned is the short time allowed for delivery. Hardly has an organ been ordered when it is expected that it will be finished. One instance is known in which the builder was requested to install an instrument of over forty speaking stops in the space of three months. The reports on these questions are hair-raising. The smaller and middle-sized builders must divide the work among themselves. If one of them has to postpone delivery for a year he may not get the contract. The big firm can take a chance on a much shorter period. This almost childish conduct on the part of the buyer is to blame for much suffering among the masters of organ building, and often puts their very lives in jeopardy. One year they may have to let a number of good orders go by, because they are more than completely occupied; the next year they may have hardly anything to do. With a little understanding and a little coöperation on the part of the buyer both sides would be served.

The sense of almost all the answers is that the master of organ building must be so placed that he can serve his art without worry about his living, and with the assurance of a modest income; without having to wear himself out in a price war, and without having to submit himself unconditionally to the whims of an expert. If things go on as they are, in twenty to forty years organ building in most countries will be so ruined, artistically and economically, that it will have ceased to exist as an artistic handcraft.

But it is everywhere emphasised that only the capable ones should be maintained. When master joiners set themselves up as organ builders they ought to go quietly under; and when workers in the construction of organs make themselves independent without a penny of capital there is also nothing we need do to help them.

These, then, are the most important conclusions from the answers to the questionnaire. These answers have given all of us the impression of a clear conviction everywhere that ways and means must be found to help organ building out of the intolerable artistic and economic position in which at the moment it finds itself, and that, by and large, there is agreement in the minds of all earnest observers as to the means that must be taken. It is expected, however, that we who are here assembled should after mature consideration express these convictions clearly, and help to shape a common opinion which in time shall triumph over thoughtlessness. From this expectation we shall derive the fervor of our work and its joy.

Index

Ach, ich sehe, jetzt da ich zur Hochzeit gehe (Ah, I see, now that I go to the wedding), Bach, 120 n.
Ach, lieben Christen seid getrost (O dear Christians, be comforted), Bach, 120 n.
Adler, Guido, 201, 255
Adlung, 109
Adolinanongo, 199
Africa, 61, 64, 137, 184, 188-94, 197 ff., 226, 228 f., 243, 246 f., 250, 252
Agricola, 72
Albert Schweitzer Jubilee Book, A. A. Roback, ed., 180 n., 196 n., 228 n.
Albert Schweitzer: Life and Message, Magnus Ratter, xv
Albinoni, 107 f., 115
"Allgemeine Umfrage bei Orgelspielern und Orgelbauern in deutschen und romanischen Ländern, Die" (The general questionnaire sent to organ players and organ builders in German and Romance countries), Schweitzer, 253 n.
All Saints Church, London, 246
Alsace-Lorraine, 9, 13, 33
Amsterdam, 249
Altenburg, 113
Altmann, Doctor, 40
Altmann-Kuntz, Mrs., 33
Altnikol, 76 f.
Amelia, Princess of Prussia, 113
America, 12, 248
A minor Fugue, Bach, 162
Andende, 190
Arnstadt, 71
Aspen, 247
Ast, Miss, 33
Atlantic City, 225
Augustus III, 90
Austria, 11, 202, 256

Bach, Anna Magdalena (Wülken), 74 ff., 78
Bach, Bernhard, 96
Bach Biography, Philipp Spitta, 73
Bach, David, 76

Bach, Elias, 77, 89
Bach, Family of, 70-80
Bachgesellschaft (Bach Society), 116, 175, 179 f.
Bach, Gottfried Heinrich, 76
Bach, Johann Christian, 77
Bach, Johann Christoph, 70, 77 f., 91
Bach, Johann Sebastian, ix, xiv, 3, 7, 10-13, 21, 26 ff., 30 f., 33 f., 36 f., 39-42, 55, 57 ff., 63-136, 144, 150, 153 f., 160 f., 160 n., 163, 165 f., 168, 170-75, 171 n., 179, 183 f., 186 ff., 191 f., 194 ff., 198, 211 f., 217 f., 224, 227-32, 234 ff., 238 f., 241, 244 ff., 250 ff., 257, 271, 281
Bach, Juliane Friederike, 77
Bach, Karl Philipp Emmanuel, 64, 72, 74, 76 f., 111, 113, 115 f.
Bach, Ludwig, 96
Bach, Maria Barbara, 71
Bach's Organ Works, 217
Bach, Regine Suzanna, 79
Bach, Wilhelm Friedemann, 73, 75-78, 96, 98 f., 110, 115, 118
Bagster, Lektor, 255
Bangert, 206, 249 f.
Barcelona, 180, 194
Barcker, 154, 158, 253, 256 f.
Basel, 125
Baumgart, Hans, 236
Bavaria, 61
Bayreuth, 16 ff., 27, 56-61, 66, 125, 136
Beatitudes, César Franck, 55
Beckmann, 176
Beethoven, Ludwig van, 13, 17, 21, 47, 55, 57, 78 f., 111, 122, 125, 133
Bellermann, 26, 97
Bergen, 233
Berkowski, 236
Berlin, 10, 30, 41, 100, 112, 118, 170 n., 188, 201, 239
Berlioz, 57, 130, 133
Berne, 245
Birkright, 39
Birnbaum, 103 ff.